DEAN

First published in Great Britain in 2019 by Dean,
an imprint of Egmont UK Limited
The Yellow Building, 1 Nicholas Road, London W11 4AN
www.egmont.co.uk

Written and designed by Cloud King Creative
Edited by Jane Riordan

Copyright © Egmont UK Limited 2019

ISBN 978 1 4052 9723 3
70455/001
Printed in Italy

ONLINE SAFETY FOR YOUNGER FANS

Spending time online is great fun! Here are a few simple rules to help younger
fans stay safe and keep the internet a great place to spend time.
For more advice and guidance, please see page 64 of this book.

- Never give out your real name – don't use it as your username.
- Never give out any of your personal details.
- Never tell anybody which school you go to or how old you are.
- Never tell anybody your password, except a parent or guardian.
- Be aware that you must be 13 or over to create an account on many sites. Always check
the site policy and ask a parent or guardian for permission before registering.
- Always tell a parent or guardian if something is worrying you.

Stay safe online. Any website addresses listed in this book are correct at the
time of going to print. However, Egmont is not responsible for content hosted by
third parties. Please be aware that online content can be subject to change and
websites can contain content that is unsuitable for children. We advise that
all children are supervised when using the internet.

Egmont takes its responsibility to the planet and its inhabitants very seriously.
We aim to use papers from well-managed forests run by responsible suppliers.

EVERYTHING
FORTNITE

CONTENTS

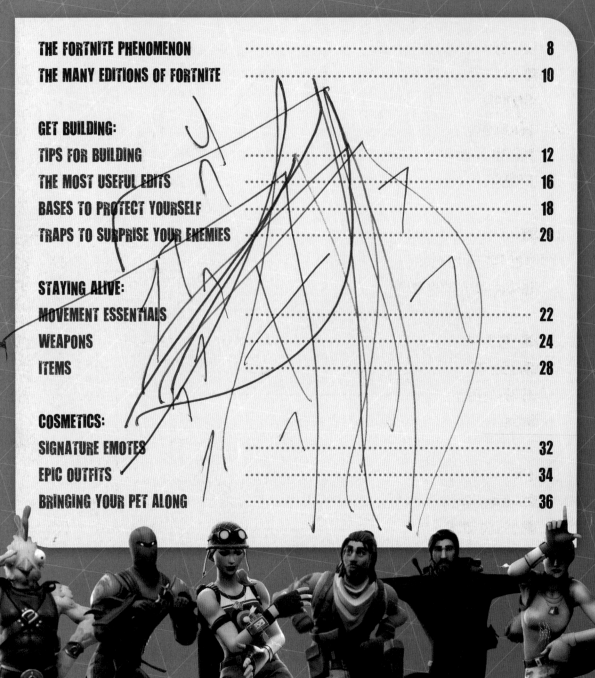

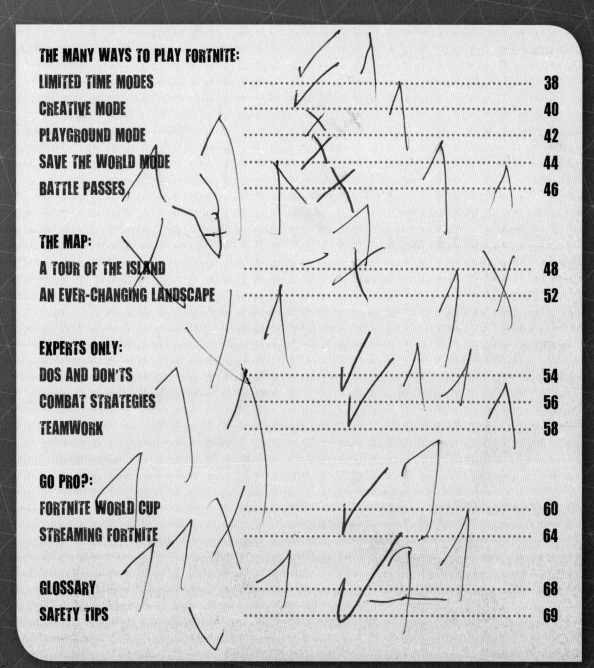

THE FORTNITE PHENOMENON

HELLO AND WELCOME ...

... to this totally unofficial, completely essential guide to everything *Fortnite*, the game that's taken over the entire world. It's a phenomenon the likes of which has never before been seen in gaming. You can't escape it!

Don't let the **rabbit outfit** fool ya!

Hang out for a little while just about anywhere in the world and you'll see people performing *Fortnite* emote dances. Halloween has been infiltrated by people in officially licensed *Fortnite* costumes wielding Rainbow Smash Pickaxes. *Fortnite* events and conventions attract tens of thousands of devotees.

Fortnite is best known for its ultra-popular Battle Royale mode, which has captured a staggering 250 million players. In 2018, it earned Epic Games over £2 billion in revenue!

SO YEAH, IT'S KIND OF A **BIG THING**

It's easy to see why *Fortnite* has become so big. It's an intense and infinitely replayable game in the Battle Royale genre.

If it's the gameplay that brings people in to the world of *Fortnite*, it's the customisation that keeps them playing. There are hundreds of cosmetic options that allow players to create their own truly unique characters and show them off to the world. They won't give you an edge in fighting, but people love the hundreds of outfits, gliders and, of course, dances.

THERE CAN ONLY BE ONE WINNER

Each match sees 100 real-life players dropping into an island from a flying Battle Bus. They enter the match completely weaponless, forced to scrounge for weapons and build their own defences by mining their surroundings.

Fortnite is also constantly evolving over each successive season, with the island itself transforming and offering new challenges and ways to play. Massive events are witnessed by millions of people who jump in to find out all the new features it will provide.

There's no better time to play *Fortnite* and we're going to tell you everything you need in order to beat the competition. Good luck and we'll see you down on the island!

The 100% UNOFFICIAL EVERYTHING FORTNITE TEAM

THE MANY EDITIONS OF FORTNITE

Fortunately Epic Games has made *Fortnite* available for almost every gaming platform, letting you play no matter what console you have.

COMPUTER

Not much beats a great computer set-up for gaming. These can display the fastest and best looking versions of the game, depending on your system specs.

- *PC: Windows 7/8/10 64-bit*
- *Apple Mac: macOS Sierra and above*

CONSOLES

While the game is available on all three of the major consoles right now, the Nintendo Switch has a bit of an edge due to its portability. Of course, you can't just take it anywhere and play – you'll need a strong Wi-Fi connection in order to play the game at all, since it's entirely online!

- *Xbox One*
- *Xbox One X*
- *PlayStation 4*
- *PlayStation 4 Pro*
- *Nintendo Switch*

YOU CAN PLAY FORTNITE ANYWHERE!

MOBILE

This may be the quickest way to jump into a match, but the touch-screen controls can make it hard to win! *Fortnite* simply plays better with a mouse and keyboard or a controller. However, with mobile devices, you can play on the move!

- *iPhone: iOS 11*
- *iPad mini 4/Air 2 and above*
- *Android*

CROSS-PLAY

Fortnite offers cross-play (cross-platform play), which means that you can play against people on other gaming systems!

To do this you'll need to add your friends to your Epic Games account – you won't be able to see your Xbox friends on PS4 if you don't.

TIPS FOR BUILDING

In *Fortnite* the person who builds the best is often the winner. If you don't know how to create cover or gain higher ground, you're a sitting duck. Check out these tips and rack up your Victory Royales!

GET BUILDING

CHECK YOUR SETTINGS

Here's one easy way to ensure that you're set up for success. Go to the Settings menu and make sure that 'Turbo Building' and 'Auto Material Change' are switched on.

Turbo Building allows you to just hold the build button to continuously place structures. This can be confusing for newcomers to the game but if you want to build as fast as you can, you could use this help.

Auto Material Change makes sure that you're always building from available materials. You won't have to switch to stone after running out of wood, as the game will do it automatically for you.

DON'T FEAR WOOD

Lots of noobs think that they always need to use metal while building, as it's far stronger than stone or wood. Wrong! Wood has many uses, most of all because wood structures build up to full strength much more quickly than the others. Wood is also much easier to find and harvest, so if your structure is destroyed you can easily rebuild it from your stockpile. If you need a quick wall or a ramp, using wood will enable you to get what you need, fast ... even if it has half the hit points of metal.

TURBO BUILD

PRACTISE, PRACTISE, PRACTISE

You can't learn how to build if you don't practise. As with anything in life, that's the only way to get better!

But it's hard to practise in the regular game, where your structures can easily be seen by enemies that will try to take you out.

One tip is to try and land far from everyone else for a few matches to get a feel of

things, but you can also just enter the Playground mode and take all the time you need to figure things out. See how the pieces fit together and form structures and shoot at them to figure out how many hits they can take before they are destroyed.

It's only once you know how to build that you can really compete in *Fortnite*!

GET BUILDING

HARVEST THE WORLD

Your harvesting tool is the best way to build your resource stockpile, but there are some ways to make sure you get resources even faster. When you're swinging your pickaxe at an object, you'll see a circle appear. Aim at the circle and it will do twice as much damage to the object, harvesting them much faster.

Another trick is to just constantly harvest! When you're running around a building, keep swinging away with your pickaxe at any object you come across including the walls and floor - just be careful not to take the floor out from under yourself! This won't give you as many resources as if you devote time to harvesting objects, but the resources it provides can come in handy during crucial moments later on in the match.

THE ART OF THE EDIT

EDITING YOUR CREATIONS

When you build a structure, you don't have to leave it as is. You can edit your creations to your own vision, changing all sorts of features. You can add doors to walls or change the pyramid roof into a ramp, allowing you to build two ramps at once. While figuring out how to build in Playground mode, go back to your structures and try to change them to see what's possible!

You can only edit structures that you or a teammate created, so don't even attempt it against enemy structures.

Once you're close to a structure you can edit, you'll see the word 'Edit' on your UI. If you hit the button you'll see the edit blueprint for the structure, which can be manipulated by moving the cursor over it. You can also rotate the build this way! Saving it will quickly change the structure to this edited version.

ANCHOR YOUR BASE!

Don't forget that a structure has to be attached to the map in order to be structurally sound. Your ramp will be completely destroyed if someone takes out the bottom piece, so it needs to be well built. Don't build tall structures without making sure there's a large base, or players can just come along, take it out, and you'll fall to your death.

THE MOST USEFUL EDITS

These are the main edits you'll need to learn to do on the fly. The faster you can edit your buildings, the better you'll be when faced with a fast-building foe.

WALLS

- Doors – remove the middle and bottom middle pieces to craft a door that lets you escape from a closed structure.

- Windows – open up the middle of a wall, or the middle left and middle right pieces in order to shoot enemies from cover. Great for a sniper tower!

- Arches – edit arches by removing the bottom row. They are good for sneaking out of a structure or opening up a path for your team to move through.

- Wedges – allows you to move through walls, or quickly sneak up on an unsuspecting enemy who thinks the wall is solid.

RAMPS

- Half ramps – sometimes needed when you've closed yourself in! This small ramp is half the width of a regular one, so it doesn't offer as much protection.

FLOORS

- Corner edits – take the corner out of a floor and you can easily drop down to a lower level.

ROOFS

- Corner cover – take one corner out of a roof piece and you'll be given a tall triangular piece you can use for cover!

- Ramps – many people don't know this, but if you take out the top or bottom two squares of a roof you can make another ramp!

RAMP UP YOUR BUILDING!

GET BUILDING

BASES TO PROTECT YOURSELF

If someone starts shooting at you, start building! Building walls can protect you from sniper fire if you don't know where an enemy is. Quickly edited doors can provide you with exits to allow you to come out on another side and surprise an enemy.

You'll need to know these especially for the end of a match, as the circle will likely get so small that it will all come down to building and cover.

THE 1x1

This is the mainstay of *Fortnite*. It can both cover you and help you get the high ground, so it's an essential build to master.

The faster you can build this, the better. Start out by placing a flat base if you're not on solid ground, and then quickly building walls around you by spinning while holding down the build button. Then jump and place a ramp directly underneath yourself! Move to the top of that ramp and start it all up again, building walls and ramps until you have a 1x1 tower reaching far into the sky.

FALLING WITH STYLE

Once you're up there you might need to quickly come down. The easiest way to do that is to jump, but if you built a tall tower you'll eliminate yourself. Slow your fall by building ramps and floors as you descend, keeping close to the tower to do so.

RAMP IT UP

To get up above other players quickly, use ramps!

The problem with just building ramps is that it leaves you open to attack. The trick is to build a ramp, run up it and build a wall just behind the ramp. This will protect your ramp from attacks and allow you to build bigger and bigger ramps.

Floors will also add protection to your ramps. When you get even more experienced, you can do it with wider ramps and bring your whole squad up to fire down on the enemy.

TAKE THE HIGHER GROUND!

TAKE COVER!

COVERING FIRE!

Someone have you outgunned? Need to make a quick escape? Use the pyramids. If you have high cover you can build a wall out by alternating floor pieces and pyramids. The floors will protect the pyramids and by moving up and down over them you'll hopefully avoid any gunfire.

TRAPS TO SURPRISE YOUR ENEMIES

Traps aren't as easily found as weapons, but they can be invaluable to take out any opponents nearby. They are most often used in the Save the World mode, but are brutal in Battle Royale and can get you instant kills. Other trap pieces can even be used to aid your team.

SPIKE TRAPS

These cause 150 damage to any unlucky fools who walk over or near them. Put them in places that your enemies won't notice, such as behind doorways and on ceilings of indoor areas. If you want to be really sneaky, drop some great loot right near it to attract greedy players.

WHEN YOU FIND THEM, USE THEM!

QUICK QUIZ:

How many registered players did *Fortnite* have as of March 2019?

- [ ] 1 Million
- [ ] 10 Million
- [ ] 250 Million
- [ ] 500 Million
- [ ] 1 Billion

Answer: 250 Million. That's not active players (people playing on the regular), but it's still astonishing.

COZY CAMPFIRE

This is one for your friends. Stay and warm yourself up, healing up to 50 health. It takes a while, but it can make all the difference.

LAUNCH PADS

These traps are basically big trampolines that let you fly into the sky. Once you bounce high into the air you can deploy your glider, allowing you to cover a lot of distance and travel away from the Storm.

MOVEMENT ESSENTIALS

If you want to win, you've got to stay alive and the only way to do that is to know how to move. Practise moving and shooting while waiting for a match to start and get ready – as soon as you land, your movement skills will be the only thing keeping you alive.

CAMPERS NEVER WIN

It may be tempting to find a good quiet spot at the start of a match and just camp out, but you're never going to win that way. Unless you're super lucky and pick the perfect spot, the Storm will move you on at some point. If you stay in one spot you won't be able to find all the loot you'll need to compete at the end of the match. You really don't want to face someone with full shields and Legendary weapons when you have nothing but a harvesting tool.

KEEP MOVING!

CAN'T STOP, WON'T STOP!

When you're in the open, never stay still. Keep moving and don't move in straight lines! Zig-zag while running, duck into any cover and no one will be able to snipe you. The key is to never be predictable.

BE SNEAKY

On the flipside, when you're near cover – use it! Crouch to make sure enemies don't hear you clomping around and use bushes, trees and buildings to make sure you stay out of sight.

ENGAGE YOUR ENEMY

It may be tempting to stop moving in order to aim at your enemy, but you need to learn how to move and aim at the same time.

IF THEY GO LOW, YOU GO HIGH

Always go for the high ground during a fight. The tops of mountains, hills and buildings will allow you to see enemies before they even know you're there and get a drop on them – literally. Let your opponents have to build ramps up to you while you stay put and take them out at a distance.

SLIPSTREAMS AND AIR VENTS

A new addition for Season 9, these offer new ways to get around the map. Slipstreams can be jumped into for a quick boost around the world. Just be warned that you're defenceless while you're in them and anyone near a slipstream can easily hear your whoosh of noise as you fly by.

GOTTA GO FAST

Vehicles can offer additional protection, but they also make a ton of noise and will give away your position. They're best used when you really need to get somewhere in a hurry, such as when the Storm is incoming. Use them to zoom across the map and then run to cover when you get to where you're going, because you'll have likely attracted the wrong kind of attention.

BALLERS

These are useful as you're protected from gunfire and fall damage. They have a boost that allows you to smash up enemy structures, and you can use their grappling hook to latch onto enemy vehicles to stop them!

DRIFTBOARD

These snowboards offer absolutely no protection, but they're fast and allow you to shoot and use items while you move. One shot will knock you right off the board, so try not to get hit.

QUADCRASHER

This fits two people and gives you a bit of protection. It builds up boost as you drive and can be used to smash through almost everything.

PIRATE CANNON

You can use this to fire cannonballs that deal a ton of damage (50-100), or launch yourself! They can work as decent hiding spots since you can jump in the barrel!

WEAPONS

Weapons in *Fortnite* are a bit fluid. They can disappear from the game into the 'vault', or reappear without notice. Patches can change how useful they are on a weekly basis. There are no guarantees in the game, but these weapons are the tried and tested ones that pros around the world use. Learn how to use them and climb up that leaderboard!

LEGENDARY ASSAULT RIFLE

Known to fans as the SCAR, this is the most essential *Fortnite* weapon. It does a ton of damage, offers great aim and reloads quickly. It doesn't matter if you're a noob or a pro, anyone can use this. If you see one, grab it.

DRUM GUN

This was brought back from the vault and then promptly nerfed because it was so OP. It is still one of the most popular weapons in the game, mostly because of its speed. It's basically an assault rifle that shoots at submachine gun speed. Rat-a-tat-a-tat!

SUPPRESSED PISTOL

Sure, this little weapon won't do much damage, but if you want to be sneaky there's nothing better. If you catch someone unaware, fire a few shots and move to another position to fire some more. Your opponent will get hit and have no idea what's happening!

COMBAT SHOTGUN

The loss of the Heavy Shotgun to the vault was huge, but this made up for it. It holds 10 shells and shoots with great accuracy. Plus, it fires super fast, making it a real beast in the right person's hands.

ROCKET LAUNCHER

These do a good job of shooting rockets that make people go BOOM! They're dangerous if you don't know what you're doing, as you can easily blow yourself up too. If you aim well, no one is safe. Not even building structures will stop you – just blow those up too!

HEAVY SNIPER RIFLE

One shot, one kill. You better hit that target though, cause this rifle takes forever to reload. When you spot an enemy across the map just be sure to take 'bullet drop' into account and aim a little above them, then you'll have another kill under your belt. As simple as that.

PROXIMITY GRENADE LAUNCHER

The Grenade Launcher is a powerful weapon but it's hard to aim, as grenades bounce all over the place. Enter the Proximity Grenade Launcher. This does the same, but as soon as it's near an opponent it explodes. It's foolproof!

BURST SMG

Why shoot just one bullet at a time when you can fire off four-round bursts? This SMG has heavy recoil that can make aiming tricky, but if you manage to land every shot, you can take an enemy out in a single shot. Just stock up on bullets.

MINIGUN

This weapon will chew through anything you aim it at. It doesn't need to reload as long as you have ammo, but it will overheat after six seconds, so be sure to ease up on the trigger. The one major drawback is that it takes a moment to spin up and start firing. Once it does though, your enemies will wish they had better camouflage.

SUPPRESSED SNIPER RIFLE

Sure, this doesn't do nearly as much damage as the Heavy Sniper Rifle, but it does allow you to hide your position. It's also much more accurate and has less bullet drop! Grab some cover and fire on your enemies with ease, knowing they will never figure out where you are.

FLINT-KNOCK PISTOL

This pistol uses heavy ammo, as you'll see when you fire it. This pistol is so powerful it will not only knock back whoever you hit, it will send you flying too! It's terrible for long-range battles, but use it as a close-range shotgun and you'll be set. Just don't expect to get off more than one shot.

REVOLVER

The Revolver may be a bit slow and it takes forever to reload, but get off a close-range headshot with the Revolver and you can achieve an insta-kill. This little weapon does a ton of damage and offers some great aim, making it good for close- to medium-range encounters. Just don't expect to reload during a battle.

INFANTRY RIFLE

This is a super-accurate weapon that gives you a 2x headshot multiplier, but you'll have to pull the trigger for each and every shot. It doesn't hold many rounds and is basically useless to anyone who can't aim. But if you're a decent shot, this can be one of the most effective weapons around.

VAULTED ITEMS

GONE, BUT NOT FORGOTTEN ...

These were taken from us too soon, but as the Drum Gun showed, you never know when these will reappear!

- Heavy Shotgun
- Boom Bow
- X-4 Stormwing Plane

ITEMS

As with weapons, items come and go as Epic Games pleases. What's vaulted today may be unvaulted tomorrow. They keep introducing great new ones that you'll love, though!

STORM FLIP

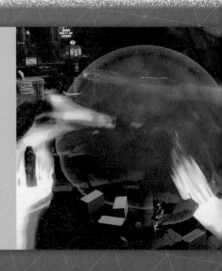

Finally, you can control the Storm. In a safe zone? Throw this item and it will spread out a mini-Storm that damages anyone caught within. Find yourself caught in the Storm? Just throw this item and it will create a mini safe zone to protect! You're no longer subject to the Storm's whims – you are the Storm.

CHUG SPLASH

The latest and greatest way to recharge your shields. You don't have to drink the Chug Splash, you just have to throw it at someone and it will give them 20 shield points instantly. Sure it's only 20 points, but it will affect everyone within the splash radius, so you can cover your whole squad if you get them together! Playing solo? Throw it at your feet and shield yourself!

GRENADES

These items were vaulted, but they're back ... for the time being. They're common so you'll find them everywhere. All the better to blow everything up. Your enemy won't be able to out-build you if you keep throwing these!

BOOGIE BOMB

Rather annoy your foes than blow them up? The Boogie Bomb is a dance party packed into a grenade. Anyone caught in the blast radius of this bomb is forced to dance for five seconds, leaving them completely open to attacks. You have to be very careful that you don't end up in the radius of the bomb yourself, or you'll find yourself in an impromptu dance-off.

STINK BOMB

These bombs don't just smell, as the gas they shoot out is so bad it does damage to your enemies. Keep an eye out for the tell-tale yellow gas and keep your nose clear. They can easily catch someone by surprise if used correctly, like anywhere indoors. If you're feeling especially evil you can build up walls around an enemy and trap them in with your stink bomb.

GLIDERS

Fall damage is the worst. There's no way to feel dumber than falling to your death. If you have a few gliders on you, you can avoid that. This lets you reuse the glider you used when jumping from the Battle Bus anytime you fall a distance. They are essential if you try to outbuild opponents and keep the high ground!

BUSH

If you prefer suppressed weapons and sniper rifles, you need the best cover you can find. Why not dress up as a bush? This won't completely fool enemies, but if you're just scanning the horizon for players you likely will pass right by any stationary bushes. Just try to keep still and be the best bush you can be.

TREASURE CHESTS

It may seem obvious, but those treasure chests you see sparkling all over the map? You can open them to find items. Surprising, we know! While you can find weapons and gear littered on the ground everywhere, treasure chests are the best way to find valuable items. When you open them the items will come flying out, so be ready – someone can swoop in and grab your loot if you're not ready!

While you should always be looking out for treasure chests, you should also be listening out for them as well. Treasure chests emit a high-pitched sound that's obvious when you hear it, so if you do, stop and look around. Sometimes they're hidden behind walls, so break them down!

TREASURE CHEST TRAP!

There's only one good reason not to open a treasure chest and that's if you have a spike trap handy. Place it right next to the chest and chances are that the next person to come across it won't check for danger – they'll go right for the chest and get eliminated!

VENDING MACHINES

Vending machines were added in Update 3.4 and offer yet another way to arm yourself. They are rarer than treasure chests, and come in different rarities, just like weapons. Each one has three items that it cycles through. When you use the vending machine you'll get whatever loot is currently featured, so wait a bit and you can see all the options. Vending machines used to require you to trade in materials for the weapon but Update 8.10 made them free, so there's no reason not to grab a weapon when you spot one!

SUPPLY BOX DROPS

If you ever see a blue flare glowing on the ground and a little blue box on the map screen, that's an indication that a supply box is incoming. These boxes are randomly dropped in the eye of the Storm and fall very, very slowly with a parachute. They hold incredible loot and always have at least one Legendary item inside. The problem is that every other player will be trying to claim it for themselves! To help things you can shoot the parachute to make it drop down to the ground quickly, letting you scoop up the loot and run away before anyone else arrives.

R.I.P. - TREASURE MAPS

Season 8 had a heavy pirate theme, so it was no surprise that there was buried treasure involved. You were able to find rare Treasure Maps that led you to guaranteed loot, which you couldn't see except for an 'X' marked on the ground. Holding open the map made an arrow appear that showed where you should head and while it was sometimes out of the way from where you wanted to go, it was almost always worth it! Use your pickaxe to dig at the ground and you'd uncover a chest with legendary weapons, Chug Jugs and ammo. Maybe they will unvault sometime in the future!

QUICK QUIZ:

Which pop star teamed up with Ninja, breaking Twitch viewership records?

- [ ] Taylor Swift
- [ ] Drake
- [ ] Lil Nas X
- [ ] Joe Jonas
- [ ] Lizzo

Answer: Drake
Drake played Duos with Ninja in March 2018 and the world took notice. It's regarded as the moment when people started taking the game as a serious force!

SIGNATURE EMOTES

Emotes are what give *Fortnite* its personality. It's one thing to completely pwn an enemy and another to do the floss over their heaps of loot. There are dozens of different emotes you can purchase in the game using V-Bucks, or earn using a Battle Pass, but here are some of our faves.

ORANGE JUSTICE

The most ridiculous dance ever is still one of the best emotes you can buy. You can't mess with a classic, so this is a good one to have on hand for any situation.

INFINITE DAB

Why just dab once when you can dab FOREVER? Pick this up for an ultimate, never-ending dance. Just be careful not to hurt yourself with all those dabs.

TAKE THE L

For people who don't mind clowning around. Use this emote to force your opponents to take the loss and totally humiliate them in the process.

CLUCK STRUT

Speaking of humiliation, show ultimate disrespect to an opponent by doing the chicken dance. Tuck those arms in and get clucking to show people what you really think of them.

CRACKDOWN

Turn yourself into a stop-motion character with this dance. Want to convince people they're lagging? Use this emote near them and the jerky motion will confuse them into thinking their connection is broken.

BEST MATES

This emote is hilarious enough on its own, but it increases in hilarity the more players are doing the dangly arm dance at the same time. Get your whole squad to do it at the same time and you'll be unstoppable (and ridiculous).

BUNNY HOP

It's cute, it's humiliating for opponents - it's the best of both worlds! Pretend you're a little bunny, tuck those elbows in and hop. It's as easy a dance as you can perform and it's hilarious to see evil outfits getting their cute on.

FLOSS

Sure, everyone and their mother is doing the floss now ... sometimes literally. It has totally invaded the world and is in danger of being completely overused. But it's still a great dance.

TIME TO BUST A MOVE!

FLOSS BOSS

33

EPIC OUTFITS

There's no shame in being a no-skin – using a free default outfit that comes with the game – but there are so many different looks you can rock in *Fortnite*. Every new season brings new outfits to buy and wear forever, but once the season's gone, so is your best chance to get them. Outfits rotate in the shop every day, so if you want a specific one, make sure to keep an eye out. These are our favourites throughout *Fortnite*'s history so far.

LOVE RANGER

While he can't fly, the Love Ranger can still make you fall in love with his great look. He looks so much like a statue that players have used him to trick people into thinking that he's part of the background.

PEELY

A most a-peel-ing outfit. Peely truly changed the game, offering a look far different to those *Fortnite* had before. He's almost become the unofficial mascot! Peely is even a reactive outfit that ripens with time, meaning that the longer you survive, the more delicious you'll get.

RAVAGE

There are few outfits that are scarier to see come swooping down on you than Ravage. It comes bundled with Dark Wings back bling, so that you can truly look like you're a flying raven of the night and put fear in the hearts of all that see you. Make sure that your foes sleep nevermore.

DEADFIRE

While he looks like a normal cowboy at first glance, Deadfire gains supernatural powers the more people he takes out. At 10 eliminations he becomes this fiery wraith creature. All the better to show the world how dangerous you are.

BUNKER JONESY

Poor Jonesy got stuck underground for years and years and came out in the future looking like this. How did he survive that long? Well ... he was trapped with Peely and stuck there long enough that his giant banana friend become really ripe and delicious and, well ... *gulp*. Anyway, be careful not to trip on that beard!

GINGER GUNNER

Gingerbread is supposed to be a sweet treat for the holidays, which is why it's surprising that this outfit inspires so much terror. Perhaps it's the blank look in her eyes and constant leering smile as she takes you out. Happy holidays?

DJ YONDER

Forget that marshmello guy – the best DJs wear llama masks. DJ Yonder wants to share his talent with the world, but not enough people share his love of music. Stock up on Boogie Bombs and force people to dance to your music before blasting them.

DUSK

You might want to make sure you're dropping in at night before picking Dusk. Her red eyes and pale skin show that she might not enjoy too much sunlight. Enemies seeing her better learn to protect their necks.

DANTE

Show you're not afraid of death with this perfect Day of the Dead-inspired outfit. He uses a guitar called the Six String Striker as a pickaxe, and his outfit even glows in the dark!

GHOUL TROOPER

Who doesn't love zombies? This is the rarest outfit in the entire game, since it was made available in Season 1 and hasn't shown up again ... yet. We're waiting for it to rise from the grave.

BRINGING YOUR PET ALONG

Why wear a backpack when you can bring your best friend for the ride? Sure, a battlefield doesn't seem like the best place for your furry pals, but they don't seem to mind. Pets launched in Season 6 and they continue to add new ones to carry. Here are our fave companions so far.

KYO

Maybe you flinch at the idea of bringing a real-life pet into the crosshairs of a *Fortnite* match, in which case you might think Kyo is a better alternative. This little robot is so expressive that it might not be the case, though! Kyo screams an electronic scream during your jump and excitedly looks over your shoulder in a vehicle. It won't take you much to fall in love with this cutie.

HAMIREZ

Just because she's hanging out on your back doesn't mean she's going to be lazy. Hamirez brought along her wheel to keep things running and show you how it's done. She even has a water bottle, because you know how important it is to hydrate.

MERRY MUNCHKIN

This little guy was only unlocked during the 14 Days of *Fortnite* event during Season 7. He screams when he's scared, gets angry in combat and will dab whenever you get a kill. Plus if you ever get hungry ... well, he'll always be there for you.

SCALES

Maybe you'd rather be riding the dragon than the other way around, but this little fella's gotta start somewhere. His black colour is the rarest, but pink and blue look just as great. Just remember to shout "Dracarys" when you spot an enemy.

CAMO

This little chameleon always looks like he's up to something, but he won't hide his feelings. He'll jump up and clap for joy when you're winning and change colours to match the rarity of whatever item you pick up. It's just too bad this cute guy can't teach you any hiding tricks.

DODGER

This artful fox comes with her own goggles ready to wear, as she's no stranger to battle. A camo outfit for Dodger shows a war-torn version wearing a helmet and dirt, presumably from being in a ... fox hole?

THE MANY WAYS TO PLAY FORTNITE

Sure, *Fortnite* took the world by Storm thanks to its 100-player Battle Royale mode, but did you know that there are a lot of ways to play the game? Epic is constantly adding new modes to change up the experience and you can also still jump into the original Save the World mode!

LIMITED TIME MODES

Limited Time Modes are just that – modes that are here for a little while before they're gone. Occasionally the most popular ones are brought back but if you see one you like, play it while you can!

FOOD FIGHT

This battle of the fast food restaurants, sees players getting split into two teams to defend the honour of their chosen establishment – Dur Burger or Pizza Pit. When the match starts there is an impassable wall between the two teams that gives everyone a few minutes to build up a fort. You win by destroying the opposing team's mascot, so build decent defences and divide your team into attackers and defenders!

50 vs 50

This mode kicked off the very first LTM. Rather than playing solo or in little squads, here we have two massive armies fighting each other. This mode was so popular it came back a few times, each with a few different twists. Others changed up the gameplay even more, such as Soaring 50s, which lets you redeploy your glider whenever you're higher than 10m off the ground.

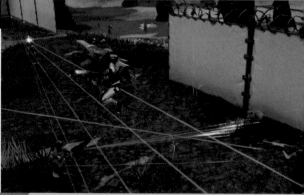

AIR ROYALE

This mode turns *Fortnite* into a dogfight simulator! It's a duos battle that allows you to pilot X-4 Stormwings, in order to shoot down enemy teams. Each plane only has three lives and if you hit the ground, you lose one. This time, the Storm actually closes in from the sky, making the fights increasingly lower-altitude and dangerous as the battles go on.

FLOOR IS LAVA

You played this as a little kid, when you'd leap around the furniture in your home trying not to touch the floor. It's the same principle in *Fortnite*. This time the entire island is slowly being filled with lava, leaving players scrambling for high ground to avoid becoming toasty. Hope you have decent building skills!

SNIPER SHOOTOUT

Some people love this one, some people hate it. Whatever the case, everyone agrees it changes the game up completely. The only weapons available are sniper rifles, so everyone plays it sneaky, trying to hide and take out enemies from across the map. This can be frustrating when you get taken out with a single shot out of nowhere, but it forces you to learn how to play with sniper rifles!

SOLID GOLD

G-O-L-D – it's gold. Every single chest holds a gold weapon in this mode, meaning that you can't blame someone's win on the fact that you had a lousy common weapon any more. No, this mode features nothing but the finest. It even gives you more material from farming! Stay gold.

HIGH EXPLOSIVES SQUADS

Are you sad that explosive weapons are hard to find in Battle Royale? Pick this LTM, since every single weapon you find will be explosive! Rockets and grenades will be flying non-stop, making for an exhilarating experience. Seek cover, if you can. Just beware that this mode makes building pretty much impossible, since everything will be destroyed almost as soon as you put it up.

BLITZ!

This mode is perfect for anyone looking for a quick match because it limits rounds to 15 minutes! When you start this mode, get ready right away because the Storm starts moving right at the start of the match and the wait between circles is decreased. You are going to have to move in order to survive this! Fortunately, they've upped the amount of loot you can find to give you a fighting chance.

CREATIVE MODE

Ever wished you could make your own *Fortnite* map? Creative mode lets you do just that. You can transform a smaller version of an island into whatever you like! Each player has their own private island that they can do what they like with in this sandbox mode.

AR PHONE

Enter Creative and you'll notice the AR Phone sitting in your inventory. This tool allows you to manipulate any objects on the map and is as powerful as it sounds. Choose this phone and you'll be able to grab anything you want and rotate, move and tweak it until it's exactly where you want. You can even use this to duplicate objects easily! Learn how to use the AR Phone if you really want to master Creative mode.

FLY AWAY

It's easy to forget, but you're not limited to walking in Creative mode. Don't forget that you can fly at will in this mode just by jumping twice! Hit it twice more to land. There are even some vaulted items available here!

EXCLUSIVE!

One cool thing about Creative mode that Battle Royale devotees might not know is that there are some awesome goodies here that can't be found anywhere else. Creative mode allows you to place things like electric fences, ice sheets, and even pinball bumpers.

ATTACK THE BLOCK

Head to the island called The Block and you can find a flat 25x25 area to build on. There's nothing there, so your creation is only limited by your imagination. But here's the fun part. Create something amazing, take a screenshot of it and tag it on social media with #FortniteBlockParty. Epic Games checks the tag all the time and if they like what they see, your creation might become part of The Block on the Battle Royale map!

PREFABS

Sometimes you can't be bothered to make entire structures from the ground up, wall by wall and floor by floor. Thankfully Creative offers a huge list of varied prefab buildings that you can choose from and just place wherever you want! They come in all sorts of varieties, everything from barns to basketball courts to temples. This can save you a ton of time and is also great for first-timers who are trying to figure their way around the mode!

SHARING IS CARING

While your island is private, there's nothing like sharing your creation with the community. When you make a map you get a 12-digit island code called a *Fortnite* Creative code, which allows other people to jump right into your island. This also allows you to easily experience some of the incredible creations that have been crafted already! People have recreated some of their favourite maps from other games.

Other people have made mazes and puzzles to test your brains, deathruns that encourage you to try to finish a map without dying, and even mini-golf courses!

GET READY, CAUSE THIS AIN'T FUNNY

It sounds silly, but one of the best uses for Creative mode is to learn how to build! You have an infinite amount of building materials here and can practise building to your heart's content.

Trust us, you'd rather learn how to switch to build mode and craft useful bases here than when you're getting shot at. No one gets to the end of a *Fortnite* match without knowing how to build your way out of trouble, so get used to it here in a stress-free environment of your own!

PLAYGROUND MODE

Think of this as a co-op mode. Playground lets up to four players drop into a private island and gives you four hours to do whatever you want. What can you do here? Turns out – a whole lot of things!

HONE YOUR SKILLS

Creative is a great place to practise building, but Playground is a great place to practise combat. Battle your friends without worry, as you'll respawn right after! There are more chances for building and getting great weapons too, as resources gather at 10x speed and there are many more chests and ammo boxes dotted around the landscape. You'll even be able to find 100 llama pinatas to destroy! Find all the weapons you can and learn how to use them here, against your (former?) friends.

EXPLORE

Since *Fortnite*'s map is ever-changing from season to season, sometimes you just want to walk around and see what's new. Playground mode offers a way to do that without the pressure of 99 other players trying to kill you at every moment. There is a lot to see and you won't be able to appreciate it at all when the bullets start flying. Use Playground mode to take your friends on a walking tour of the island!

IT'S THE NAME OF THE GAME

One favourite thing to do in Playground mode is to just play! Create your own custom games with your own rules and winning conditions. How about 2v2 football games in the stadium? Trying to see how fast you can build to the top of a mountain? The limit is truly your imagination, as long as the other players are game to try new things.

CUSTOMISER

Updates to Playground mode allowed for custom game options, letting you tweak the very rules of the game itself. You can change health to just 1 HP for one-shot matches, or change the time of day to fight at night. Try hiding player names and map locations for a more realistic battle! You can even tweak the gravity and pretend you're floating on the moon while you make massive leaps around the map.

BUILD YOUR MASTERPIECE

Work together with your friends and you'll be able to craft gigantic structures much faster than you would have by yourself. See if you can recreate famous landmarks or video game levels, or just build your very own deathmatch arena and fight it out!

BE IN THE MOVIES

Some folks even use Playground mode in order to make short films. Play director and have your friends act in your very own story, which you can later edit into a film. You can build 'sets', choose which costumes to wear and have one player work as the camera. Actors can even react to events using different emotes! Can you recreate your favourite film scenes?

SAVE THE WORLD MODE

Did you forget that *Fortnite* launched with this mode? And that it was in early access for years? Save The World was the original vision for *Fortnite*, a co-op game that saw you fighting off hordes of 'Husks' (listen, we all know that they're zombies) with up to three friends. It's easy to forget this today, since everyone knows *Fortnite* for the free Battle Royale mode. But this paid mode is still worth trying out!

SINGLE-PLAYER!

If you find Battle Royale too hectic, you can take a break here with an actual storyline! It's full of hilarious characters and an explanation of just what this whole Storm thing is. You can build your very own custom base and outfit it with all kinds of traps to protect it, like spikes that rise from the ground, cannons that shoot from walls and tyres that fall from the ceiling. Imagine it as a tower defence game! There's something about fending off hordes of Husks that's just ridiculously fun.

Hold

V-bucks

Valuable currency used to purchase goods from the store.

50

EVENTFUL

Epic has been good about adding tons of content to the mode to make it feel as if you're really building up your very own base of operations to fight against the Storm. They're constantly adding new cosmetics, weapons and Limited Time Events to make sure that every time you play there's something new to unlock. You'll save survivors that can beef up your home base, unlock new Heroes with crazy new abilities and send people on expeditions to get new supplies, all between completing missions.

MAKING IT RAIN (V-BUCKS)

While Save the World does cost money, it almost makes up for it in all the V-Bucks it throws your way. Lots of challenges and missions offer you the premium currency as a reward and before you know it you'll have hundreds to do what you want with. You can use them to buy new skins or weapons for Save the World, always knowing you'll get more V-Bucks soon as long as you keep playing. You can even use these in Battle Royale mode, which allows you to pick up Battle Passes or anything from the item shop that you want!

WAITING GAME

Whilst you currently have to pay to play, Epic Games have previously said that the Save the World mode would be free starting in 2018. That hasn't happened yet but it doesn't mean it isn't a possibility for the future so it might pay to wait.

DAILY GRIND

One legitimate problem with this mode is that you'll play similar missions over and over again. Fortunately there are challenges that give you different things to try every day, but still – you're mostly going to be doing the same missions. To advance in the game you'll either be protecting a specific location, or killing enemies, or building something. It can get repetitive solo, so make sure to bring friends along.

THE LIMITED CROSSOVER APPEAL

While you can use V-Bucks in both modes, you have to remember that the things you buy in Save the World don't transfer over to Battle Royale. Also note that if you spend money on Heroes in Save the World, as cool as your new outfit may be, it will only be available in this mode. Same goes for weapons and materials – you can stockpile them all you want, but you'll only use them against Husks. The reverse is true as well – those awesome emotes you unlock in Battle Royale can only be used there.

BATTLE PASSES

Battle Passes changed *Fortnite's* Battle Royale mode completely. It was inspired by *DOTA 2's* season pass tickets, and its success has seen it used in many other games, especially in free-to-play titles. If you really get into *Fortnite*, a Battle Pass will provide you with hundreds of hours of things to do. Not only does it offer exciting challenges to attempt, it also offers exclusive rewards that you can only get while the pass is available!

SEASON LEVELS?
BATTLE PASS TIERS?

The sheer amount of stuff going on can be overwhelming at first. Every Season starts you at Level 1. Your Season Level can be increased by getting XP in matches, usually by eliminating opponents, surviving for a long time, or placing high in a game.

Battle Pass Tiers are a completely separate progression and increased by accumulating Battle Stars. Every 10 Stars gets you another level and each level usually unlocks a new reward. You earn Battle Stars by completing challenges, although levelling up your Season Level gets you Stars as well.

It's a bit confusing at first, but the gist of this is – the more you play, the more you'll level up.

WHAT DO YOU GET?

You can purchase a Battle Pass for 950 V-Bucks (just under £8), which usually nets you a few rewards instantly. There are exclusive outfits, emotes, wraps, pickaxes, pets, gliders, music – everything! You can raise your Battle Pass Tier to Level 100, offering over 100 rewards to unlock, at least one per level. They would cost thousands of V-Bucks if purchased separately. It's all cosmetic stuff, though, so nothing you earn here will give you an advantage over anyone.

SEASON 9 BATTLE PASS

WHAT'S INSIDE?

When you buy the Battle Pass, you'll instantly receive two exclusive outfits - Sentinel and the progressive Rox! You can also earn exclusive rewards including emotes, outfits, wraps, pets, pickaxes, loading screens and new surprises. You'll receive a reward each time you level up. 100 tiers total for over 100 rewards.

There are also new challenges every week! These challenges unlock even more Battle Pass rewards.

△ HELP   ○ BACK

TO PAY, OR NOT TO PAY?

One thing to consider before picking up a Battle Pass is how much time you'll have to play *Fortnite* for the next three months. The only way to get up to Level 100 and unlock everything it has to offer is to play almost every single day, completing all the daily and weekly challenges. If you do, the pass literally pays for itself - you'll earn enough V-Bucks over the course of the pass to pay for next season's as well.

FORTBYTES

One recent addition to Battle Passes are Fortbytes. These little computer chips were added in Season 9 and offered new collectables to find throughout the entire season. There are 100 Fortbytes to find and they provide you with a cryptic message showing you how to get them. Find them all and you'll unveil an image that reveals a secret about the season's story, as well as giving you all kinds of rewards on the way! Some Fortbytes require you to use specific emotes in certain locations, while some just require you to level up your Battle Pass or get a set amount of XP. They give you a whole new way to play the game and we anticipate every upcoming season to continue offering something similar.

YOU CAN RIDE FOR FREE

Even if you choose not to buy the Battle Pass for a specific season, you can get in on the fun with the Free Pass. You can still level up, but it will be trickier. The Battle Pass gives you additional challenges that net you more Battle Stars, which lets you raise your Tier much more quickly. But even if you don't choose to pay you can earn exclusive rewards and take part in the events!

A TOUR OF THE ISLAND

Fortnite's map looks very different from when it started. Let's take a look at the new and changed areas of the map!

NEO TILTED TOWERS

The Titled Towers has been through a lot. The city has been destroyed by everything from comets to giant purple alien space cubes! Now it's become the futuristic Neo Tilted Towers and is home to Slipstreams that completely change up how the game is played. Plus, it has an awesome neon look.

JUNK JUNCTION

DIRECTINGPETE'S BLOC

HAUNTED HILLS

PLEASANT PARK

LOOT L

SNOBBY SHORES

NEO TILTED

SHIFTY SHAFTS

POLAR PEAK

USTY FLIGHTS

HAPPY HAMLET

MONSTER TRACKS

The reason that the robot was built was to fight a massive monster! It first appeared from under the ice in Polar Peak as a large, terrifying eye, scaring any players that went near. The beast soon broke out of the ice and destroyed a few locations on the way to the water, leaving massive footprints all over the ground.

PRESSURE PLANT

The volcano has exploded and in its place are a bunch of buildings for the Pressure Plant, which is presumably powering all the new futuristic areas of the map. All of that power was used to construct a massive robot, which was slowly built over many weeks before finally emerging!

MEGA MALL

This area replaced Retail Row and also features a slipstream tunnel circling it and air vents that allow you to jump around quickly. It's very much a full-functioning mall too and has everything you could ever want – toy stores, arcades, restaurants, etc. Shop for some gear while you're there.

HOT SPOTS

When you jump into a match you'll see a random location on the map highlighted in gold text. This is a Hot Spot and you might want to head there. These locations have little drones floating around carrying loot, which you can shoot down for high-value weapons. Of course, everyone else might be trying to do the same, so they can be dangerous areas!

A TOUR OF THE ISLAND PART 2

Sometimes you just want to visit interesting places. If you stop and look around the *Fortnite* map, you'll find all kinds of amazing things. While there are pros and cons for every location in *Fortnite*, these are some of the unique places that you can find.

THE BLOCK

Epic Games keeps this area updated with creations that players have crafted in *Fortnite* Creative. Players with more than 1000 social media subscribers can tag Epic Games and have their own place picked to become a part of The Block in Battle Royale. You never know what you're going to find, so check it regularly.

HAUNTED HILLS

If you're looking for a scary time, head to the Hills. The Haunted Hills are littered with everything you need, like a crumbling church and lots of tombs that contain loot. Plus, there's a looming haunted castle on the top of the hill. Pick an appropriately spooky outfit and hang out here. When enemies come near, pop out and give them a scare they won't forget.

FROZEN LAKE

An unnamed location in the former Greasy Grove. Once a nice suburban area until things went bad. The restaurant closed, there was a flood and then it froze, leaving the neighbourhood under a block of ice. That was fun though, as you could use it as an ice skating rink, or destroy the roofs of houses to see everything frozen inside!

JUNK JUNCTION

DIRECTIN...S BLOCK

HAUNTED H...

PLEASANT PARK

LOOT L...

SNOBBY SHORES

NEO TILTED

SHIFTY SHAFTS

POLAR PEAK

FROSTY FLIGHTS

HAPPY HAMLET

SUNNY STEPS

It's hard not to love this area, which is populated with Aztec temples. It's full of gorgeous architecture and tons of treasure chests, making it one of our favourite spots. Just be careful when you visit though – it's notoriously difficult to find out where your enemies are when you hear them stomping around here. They could be hiding anywhere!

DESERT RACE TRACK

There are a few race tracks on the map, but this is probably the best one. Someone left Quadcrashers here for anyone looking to put down their guns and pick up some wheels. The course has plenty of twists and turns, and it's fun to zoom around it. Wait on the starting line until you see a countdown and you'll be ready to ride!

Map labels: SUN..., AZY LAGOON, PRESSURE PLANT, LONELY LODGE, DUSTY DIVOT, MEGA MALL, TY SPRINGS, PARADISE PALMS, FATAL FIELDS, KY LANDING

AN EVER-CHANGING LANDSCAPE

Nothing stays the same in *Fortnite*. Almost every single area has changed in some way and each season offers new, sometimes drastic, changes to the map. Here are some of the craziest events that have happened!

DAY OF THE METEOR

In Season 3 players were shocked to see a Meteor streak through the sky. On day one of Season 4, the Meteor landed, crashing into Dusty Depot and turning it into Dusty Divot. It littered the area with space rocks, allowing players to float around when used. This was the moment when people realised Epic Games wasn't playing around – things could change at any moment!

PREPARING FOR LAUNCH

Near the end of Season 4, another big event occurred. A countdown timer appeared on screens throughout the map, but no one knew what it meant. In the last few hours, a siren began blaring from the villain's lair that had sprung up. When the countdown reached zero, the rocket being built in Snobby Shores took off and tore a rift in the sky.

It was such a remarkable thing that players put aside their weapons to watch it together, crafting huge ramps to get a look at the sight. One player decided to take out the bottom of one of those massive ramps at that exact moment to drop everyone and get the most kills ever!

CAUSING A RIFT

Right after the rocket launch, rifts started to crack apart the sky. Rift-To-Go items appeared too, allowing you to control your very own portable rift that can be deployed whenever you want. They're great for getting out of a tight spot, but it causes so much noise that everyone will look up and see where you're heading.

MARSHMELLOS, ANYONE?

Finally, a real reason to use those dance emotes! DJ and producer Marshmello hosted a virtual concert that became the largest event in *Fortnite* history so far. According to Epic Games, a staggering 10.7 million people attended the concert and that doesn't even include the many more who watched it later on. A reactive Marshmello outfit allowed players to dress up as him soon after.

KEVIN THE CUBE

One day a giant purple cube appeared in Paradise Palms out of nowhere. Touching it revealed that it was bouncy and gliding on top of it would send you shooting off into the sky. Then, it started to move.

For some reason the community decided to name it 'Kevin' and they tracked its movements. It went towards Loot Lake, burning purple runes into the ground. It melted into the water, turning it purple. Then, it spun around

and shot out white light, exploding and transporting nearby players into a weird area out of time and space where everyone was floating around glass butterflies! Returning home, players found that Leaky Lake had replaced the area. Weird.

ERUPTION

You just don't add a volcano to a game for nothing. Once it erupted, rocks flew across the map. One hit Polar Peak mountain, cracking it and unleashing a giant monster. Retail Row's parking lot was destroyed. Tilted Towers was almost completely obliterated, leaving one building behind!

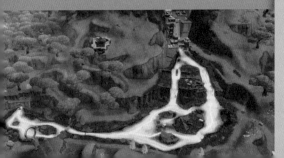

DOs AND DON'Ts

THE MAP

DO start to learn the locations as well as you can. It's better to have a handful of locations you're super familiar with, than to just know a little bit about a larger number. That way you'll know where treasure chests and vehicles are likely to spawn and what areas are the most dangerous and to be avoided.

DON'T just jump somewhere without a plan. Take the time to learn the ropes and you'll be a better player for it. Follow others in your squad until you get the hang of things, and then lead the way yourself!

LANDING

DO make sure to look at the map before you jump. If you want a quick, fast game, head for a gold Hot Spot, where there are Legendary items and lots of players. If you want to stock up on loot somewhere quieter, pick a spot far from the path of the Battle Bus.

DON'T drop blind. Lots of players just jump the instant they're able to and the mass of people landing in the same location makes for confusion and lots of quick eliminations. If you're skilled you might make it out alive from the pack, but chances are you'll just be sent right back to the lobby for nothing.

BUILDING

DO build towers whenever possible near the endgame. The better you are at building, the longer you'll survive in the game.

DON'T forget that fall damage can kill you quicker than an enemy's bullets. Make sure your ramps and structures have a good base underneath them that can't be easily taken out, or keep gliders in your inventory for a quick and sneaky exit.

THE STORM

DO keep an eye on the clock. There's nothing worse than getting caught up in looting and not realising you have to travel across the entire map to safety on foot!

DON'T freak out if you're caught in the Storm. Even later in the game it won't instantly kill you. If you have healing items you'll be able to keep moving inside it if needed!

WEAPONS

DO swap out weapons for rarer versions. If you have a blue (Rare) weapon and spot a gold (Legendary) version, swap it out.

DON'T forget to reload your weapons. Keep a mix of weapons that use different types of ammo too – make sure you have enough!

LOOTING

DO grab whatever you can at the start of a match. Know what is where so you can quickly switch between them when needed.

DON'T keep things you don't need. Use shield items as soon as possible to make room for more weapons. Try to keep the strongest shield and health items on hand though.

WHEN YOU SPOT AN ENEMY

DO prepare your attack. Is there a way to corner your foe? Can you use a Stink Bomb or Storm Flip to get them to head right towards you, all the easier to take them out? Fight with intelligence, folks!

DON'T instantly attack without thought! If it's a squad you'll have given your position away. If they're too far away, they can just escape from you! If you get the drop on someone you have an advantage – don't give that away!

VEHICLES

DO jump on a vehicle when you need to move quickly. Use the boost feature whenever possible and you'll even be able to travel quickly up and over mountains!

DON'T forget that everyone nearby will be able to hear and see you coming. Vehicles make a lot of noise, so sometimes crouching around and moving quietly is the way to go, especially as the eye of the Storm gets smaller and smaller.

WHEN ATTACKED

DO put up walls between you and enemies. The sooner you have cover, the faster you can fire back.

DON'T stand still and look around, trying to figure out where the fire is coming from. A motionless target is an easy target. Keep moving!

GAMEPLAY

DO take breaks. While *Fortnite* has daily challenges, you don't need to play non-stop! Playing for hours and hours can leave you fatigued and sloppy and sometimes you'll just need to give your eyes, fingers and brain a rest in order to be competitive once again.

DON'T give up. The more you play, the better you'll get. When you first start you'll feel like it's hopeless, because there are so many good players out there. Just remember that even the pros started out just like you!

COMBAT STRATEGIES

Fortnite is all about survival. Hiding can get you far, but you'll need to know how to fight in order to stay alive ...

PEACE AND QUIET?

Many players love landing in quieter areas of the map, away from the Hot Spot and Battle Bus path. This allows you to loot in peace and prepare for the fight to come. The disadvantage is the loot you find might not be as great as the others, but by doing this you can let others whittle numbers down while you just focus on looting and breaking things into materials. When you're in the final rounds of the game, you'll be full of ammo and ready for everyone else!

BREAK UP A PARTY

If two players are fighting each other, you might be ready to get an easy elimination. Just wait for one to eliminate the other and then attack while they're picking up the downed player's loot. Chances are they're low on health and shields and not ready for your attack! Just make sure not to give away your position and have them both come after you.

MOVE OUT OF THE WAY!

If you stand still you're putting yourself in danger of a sniper, who might be watching you waiting for that exact moment to fire. Even when looting items off the ground, keep moving back and forth and make yourself a hard target!

ENGAGE, ESCAPE, ENRAGE

If you're sniping from across the map, move away right after you fire. If you keep firing from the same position you'll just give yourself away. Move to another place and fire again, then move somewhere else and fire from there. Your opponent will get furious and not know what's going on, leaving them open to mistakes. And *Fortnite* players who make mistakes are *Fortnite* players who hang out in the lobby.

MANAGE YOUR INVENTORY

Pro streamers make sure their inventory is in a specific order so they know what's there without even looking. The typical order is this, from left to right; weapons, from close to long-range; grenades and explosives; and healing items. If that doesn't work for you, figure out your own system. By assigning items to specific spots, you'll save yourself from flipping through the inventory trying to figure out what's what. Plus, dropping unneeded items can free up some space and also trap unsuspecting people who think they've come across free loot.

GO VERTICAL

At the end of a match, when the circle is tiny, it all comes down to vertical builds. If you manage to make a tower before everyone else, they'll all be trying to build up to you while you can just fire down on them. This is why we've stressed how important building is, so practise this as much as you can!

COMBAT TIPS

- Aim for the lowest point of the ground to land faster than opponents. Your glider deploys depending on how far you are from the ground, so if you aim for a lower altitude than the place you want to go, you'll be able to zoom down faster and get there first.

- Finding it hard to hit your targets? Try going into the settings menu and tweaking your aiming sensitivity. You might be better off with a lower sensitivity that offers better aim.

- Crouching improves accuracy, but don't use it if an enemy is firing at you. It makes you smaller, but it also makes you slower.

- Just hit the ground? Grab a weapon ASAP and then start smashing things up to get some materials. You'll need both for your first fight.

- In a battle? Hit that jump button and don't stop. Practise jumping while shooting, as it makes you harder to hit, even if it makes it harder to aim.

- Find shields? Hold onto a few good ones. You'll need them to recharge back up to 100 after your next encounter.

- Try not to use grenades and other explosives early on. They're best used later on in the game, when structures are everywhere.

- If you're in a bad fight, build your way out. Use walls to stop incoming fire while you scale buildings and mountains using ramps.

- Is an enemy sniping at you from the top of a tall base? Check the bottom to see how well it's connected. If it's only a couple of pieces, shoot them out and drop the whole thing! If they don't have a glider, you'll get an elimination.

- Players drop loot when they die. You can choose to either pick it up, or trap the area and lie in wait for anyone who comes scavenging.

TEAMWORK

Playing Duos or Squads? Recent updates to *Fortnite* have made teamwork even easier and more essential.

STICK TOGETHER

If you land far from your team, you're going to lose. Staying together with your squad is key to your survival! Unlike Solo mode, where it's clever to be on the move, in Squads you should be moving from base to base, and getting ready for an attack every time as you loot the new location. More people = more noise, so you're that much more obvious to enemies.

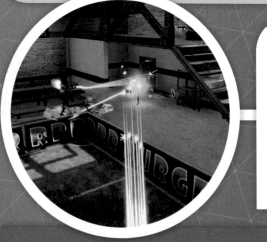

WORK TOGETHER

Fortnite doesn't have classes, but you can coordinate with your squad to pick different roles. Someone who picks up a sniper rifle can try and flank an enemy position while the rest of the squad fires from the front. When you're fighting an enemy squad, don't all choose different targets. If you concentrate your fire on one player, they'll go down that much quicker, leaving the rest of the squad weaker.

PINGING

The new ping system helps players work together better than ever. Pressing left on the D-pad or clicking the mouse wheel will put down a ping on your entire team's map. If you're highlighting a weapon or item it will tell your team what you've found. Double tap to put out an 'enemy seen' ping! These pings can help anyone too shy to speak over a headset and they're useful to explain just what you're seeing as quickly as possible. Use it whenever possible.

QUICK QUIZ:

Which four of the map's named locations have been around since Season 1?

Answer: Pleasant Park, Lonely Lodge, Salty Springs, Fatal Fields. All the rest are new, or have been destroyed or changed in some way thanks to the world's events!

SHARE AND SHARE ALIKE

Don't hog all the loot. If your squad is as well-armed as you are, you've got a better chance of survival. Don't forget that you can go into the inventory menu and drop items or ammo for your friends. Arm them with whatever you aren't using at the moment. If someone is a better shot with a certain weapon, grab it for them and pass it over when you're near!

RESPAWNING

The new Reboot Van means even when you're down, you're not out. If someone from your squad dies, they'll drop a Reboot Card that lasts for 90 seconds. Grab it to turn it into a Reboot Van and bring them back into the game! However, when someone is brought back, they'll be almost brand new. They'll have a common pistol and some ammo, but no shields or anything else. Drop some loot to bring them up to fighting speed.

Either way, you might have to be ready for a fight. The Reboot Van makes a ton of noise, letting every other nearby squad know that someone is coming back. It's a hard opportunity to pass up. If you're respawning a friend, try to hide behind the van if you can, as it's indestructible!

Make finding some loot for your newly-rebooted teammate a priority; a Common Pistol isn't going to get them very far, especially later on in the game. You'll also need to think about dropping them some materials and those, all-important, healing items.

GO PRO?

FORTNITE WORLD CUP

Feeling confident in your *Fortnite* skills? Maybe you're ready for the next level. The top professional *Fortnite* Players earn millions of pounds a year in prize money. It's not all fun and games, though – to get to this level you've got to work.

The *Fortnite* World Cup is one of the largest events in eSports history. The only other eSports competition to come close is *DOTA* 2's The International tournament. The World Cup features the finest players from the entire world, so getting to the top of the millions of *Fortnite* players is an achievement only a tiny fraction of players can hope to achieve.

WHO CAN COMPETE

The Online Opens stage is open to everyone, with some restrictions:

- You have to be older than 13 years old, and need parental or legal guardian consent if under 18.
- You can't have any violations and have to be on good terms with Epic Games.
- Your account level needs to be at least 15.
- You have to enable 2-Factor Authentication and link your account to an Epic ID if you compete in the Finals.

But if you can do all of that, then you're in!

QUALIFYING

It's not as easy as just signing up for the finals. There are multiple qualifying rounds first! Fortunately they're really easy to join, as they are online modes in the game. No travel required!

There are five separate regions depending on where you play the game: North America, Europe, Asia, Brazil, and Oceania. You'll start off competing only with players from your region, but once the dust has settled you'll be fighting the best players from the world. Take a look on pages 61-63 at the 2019 tournament to see how it works.

STAGE 1: ARENA MODE

Players had to earn as many points as they could to get to the top of Arena mode and qualify for the Open tournament.

STAGE 2: THE OPEN TOURNAMENTS

These took place every weekend, with any players who qualified that week in Arena mode playing. These tournaments gave players three hours to score as many points as they could, but only within 10 matches. This was the final chance for you to qualify for your region, because the top 3,000 players from each of the five regions were able to move to the next and last stage, the Open Finals.

STAGE 3: THE OPEN FINALS

These took place every Sunday as well. The top 3,000 Stage 2 winners from each region would compete in a similar tournament. They could play up to 10 matches in three hours and again the goal was to get as many points as possible in that time period. This was it ... the last chance.

THE SCORING SYSTEM

SOLO POINTS
Victory Royale: 10 points
2nd – 5th: 7 points
6th – 15th: 5 points
16th – 25th: 3 points

Each elimination: 1 point

DUO POINTS
Victory Royale: 10 points
2nd – 3rd: 7 points
4th – 7th: 5 points
8th – 12th: 3 points

Each elimination: 1 point

MOST KILLS

Pro players have managed to rack up nearly 50 kills in a match – that's half the competition! How many do you think you can get in a single match?

GET CREATIVE

Along with the regular World Cup competition, Epic announced a brand new competition and it's Creative. No, it's literally Creative mode. Every week they asked people to submit a video of their best Creative creations and tag it with the event specific hashtag on YouTube. They picked the top submissions, all of which headed to the *Fortnite* World Cup Creative Finals. The top 15 finalists won $5,000 along with their spot!

ATTENDING

Thinking about seeing the World Cup in person? The tickets sold out fast, but there was no better place for *Fortnite* devotees. Everyone who attended the *Fortnite* World Cup Finals received free V-Bucks and a Season 10 Battle Pass, making the price easier to swallow.

PRIZES

Fortnite smashed eSports prize records. In the 2019 World Cup there was a prize pool of $100 million, with the champion alone earning $3 million. Anyone in attendance was guaranteed $50,000 for attending. So yes, players take it very seriously. This is a full-time career for many players at this point!

GO PRO?

STREAMING FORTNITE

Sometimes the best way to figure out new techniques in *Fortnite* is to watch the pros play. Fortunately there are tons of pros out there streaming the game every single day! Streaming platforms showcase thousands of gamers' livestreams, allowing anyone with a screen to get a glimpse into their world.

WHO CAN STREAM

The major channels such as Twitch and YouTube don't allow anyone under the age of 13 to stream and anyone between 13 and 18 needs the supervision of a parent or legal guardian. These streaming platforms can be a great place, but they can sometimes be a scary and overwhelming place for minors.

PRODUCTION VALUE

The influencers that really get into streaming spend a lot of money on it, buying expensive gaming chairs, webcams and microphones. A more expensive production makes for a slicker stream and a slicker stream makes for more views. It shows us that the streamer truly cares about the content they're putting out and for some of them who make a living by streaming, it's a necessity.

UNIQUE COMPETITION

New streamers have to know who came before them. It's easy to analyse the top influencers and see how they became so popular and up-and-comers often try to mimic proven success stories. But copying streamers never got anyone to the top. Clever streamers play to their strengths and avoid their weaknesses, engaging with their audience and offering a stream that's uniquely theirs.

THE BIG NAMES

With so many streamers out there, it can be tricky to work out which ones you'll want to follow. These are just a few that we particularly like. They really know their stuff, without feeling the need to swear about it and you're sure to pick up loads of tips and tricks from them:

- Ali-A
- CouRage
- DanTDM
- Dakotaz
- Lachlan
- Ninja

CHAT AWAY

A silent streamer is a streamer without many subscribers. Streamers know that their personality is what keeps people watching, because everyone's watching for their reactions. It may seem strange that people are constantly discussing what they're experiencing, but that's the way they grow their audience, by talking and being relatable.

KNOWING YOUR ARSENAL

Streamers know they have to improve their skills if they want to be taken seriously. If they're shooting a shotgun at a far-off enemy or placing terrible builds when engaged by a player, people are going to close their stream. Streamers need to know the current state of *Fortnite* – what events have taken place, what weapon changes have happened, what's been vaulted. Their personality can only take them so far.

WATCH (LISTEN?) OUT FOR MUSIC

Experienced streamers know the easiest way to get a strike on your channel is by using music that isn't yours. Services like Twitch and YouTube take copyright strikes very seriously, so they make sure to only use music that you have the rights to. Fortunately there are services like the Twitch Music Library that help give them music to play! Channels that don't obey can be muted or even blocked, so people are careful that they don't get taken down because of some tunes.

KEEP THINGS POSITIVE

It's so easy to be negative online. People always seem to respond to negativity and it's easy to be an 'angry gamer' who's constantly yelling about games. It may get people views, but it just makes them seem little and is no way to live. Remember, we're all just playing video games. No one wants to be one of the people contributing to a toxic environment and such behaviour can get you banned as well. The positive streamers are the ones with the strongest communities.

GLOSSARY

1v1 – when you battle another player, one on one. You might have to set this up beforehand, or you can do it in Playground mode.

2FA – 2-Factor Authentication, better security for your account! Pro players definitely need to have this activated.

Aimbot – this is a cheating program that aims for you and can even track players through walls. Once in a while you'll run across someone using one of these, even though they're not allowed to. Use these if you enjoy the idea of getting banned from playing *Fortnite* forever!

Big Pot – slang for the 'Shield Potion'.

The Bubble – slang for the safe zone. The 'bubble' that protects you from the incoming Storm.

Build Battle – when you race another player to build a tower as fast as possible so that you can get the high ground. Master builders can even block the other player's progress to get to the top.

Camper – someone who stays in one spot, or 'camps'. It's a good way to stay alive for most of the match, but if other players find you, you're done.

Choke – when you completely bungle a match. You can choke if you're scrambling to change weapons when you get attacked and get eliminated.

Clutch – the opposite of choking. When you're clutch you have done amazing things, fighting off multiple attackers or hitting perfect shots.

GG – shorthand for 'Good Game'.

High Ground – you have the high ground when you're higher than other players. Getting it is crucial, because whoever has it usually wins.

Knocked – slang for 'knocked down'.

Mats – slang for 'materials'. Any of the resources you use to build structures.

Nerfed – if Epic Games nerfs a weapon, they make it less effective. It might be slower, or less powerful, or have a smaller magazine. This is usually done when a weapon is OP.

No Scope – eliminating someone with a weapon that has a scope (usually a sniper rifle), without using the scope. It's a tricky shot.

No Skin – a 'no skin', or 'default', is a player who has one of the original skins in the game. Some people look down on players without fancy cosmetics, but others use them to trick other players into thinking they're worse than they are.

Noob – someone new to the game, who doesn't know what they're doing yet.

OP – overpowered. If a weapon is OP it means that it's so much more powerful than anything else in the game and the balance of the game is broken. If you see everyone in the game using a specific weapon, chances are it's OP.

Ping – the ping system lets you mark locations and items for your squadmates.

Reboot Card – these drop from eliminated players in Squads mode and allow squadmates to bring them back.

Reboot Van – the van that allows you to bring back eliminated squadmates, as long as you have their Reboot Card.

Spawn Island – the little island you spawn on before a match. Everyone will spawn here while you wait for enough players to arrive and you can practise building and shooting for a few seconds with the objects scattered around.

Stream Sniper – someone who watches a Twitch streamer and tries to join their game, just so they can watch their stream and figure out where they are. This is cheating, of course.

Vaulted – vaulted items are removed from the game, until they are 'unvaulted'. Epic takes weapons and items away occasionally, only to return them in subsequent seasons.

SAFETY TIPS

12 ™
www.pegi.info

YOUNGER FANS' GUIDE

Spending time online is great fun. As *Fortnite* might be your first experience of digital socialising, here are a few simple rules to help you stay safe and keep the internet an awesome place to spend time:

- Never give out your real name – don't use it as your username.
- Never give out any of your personal details.
- Never tell anybody which school you go to or how old you are.
- Never tell anybody your password, except a parent or guardian.
- Before registering with *Fortnite*, ask a parent or guardian for permission.
- Take regular breaks, as well as playing with parents nearby, or in shared family rooms.
- Always tell a parent or guardian if something is worrying you.

PARENTS' GUIDE

ONLINE CHAT

In *Fortnite*, there is live, unmoderated voice and on-screen text chat between users. At the time of writing, turning off text chat isn't possible. You can, however, turn off voice chat:
- Open the Settings menu in the top right of the main *Fortnite* page, then the cog icon. Choose the Audio tab at the top of the screen. From there, you can adjust several audio features, including voice chat. Turn the setting from 'on' to 'off' by tapping the arrows.
- On consoles, you are also able to disable voice chat completely in the Parental Controls, or you can set it so your child can only chat with users who have previously been added as friends. It's important to stress to your child that they shouldn't add anyone as a friend they don't know in real life. To find these controls, see opposite about in-game purchases.

SOCIAL MEDIA SCAMS

There are many accounts on Facebook and Twitter that claim to give away free V-Bucks, which will be transferred to their account. Be sceptical – it's important to check the authenticity of these accounts and offers before giving away personal information.

SOUND

Fortnite is a game where sound is crucial. Players will often wear headphones, meaning parents won't be able to hear what is being said by strangers. Set up your console or computer to have sound coming from the TV as well as the headset so you can hear what other players are saying to your child.

REPORTING PLAYERS

If you see or hear a player being abusive, you can easily report them.
- Open the Settings menu in the main *Fortnite* page. Select the Feedback option, which allows you to report bugs, send comments or report players.
- After you've been eliminated from a game, you're also given an option to report a player by holding down the corresponding button at the bottom of the screen.

SCREEN TIME

Taking regular breaks is important. Set play sessions by using a timer. However, *Fortnite* games can last up to 20 minutes and if your child finishes playing in the middle of a round, they'll leave their teammates a person short and lose any points they've earned. So, it is advisable to give an advanced warning for stopping play.

IN-GAME PURCHASES

Fortnite does offer the ability to make in-game purchases such as new clothes, dances (emotes) and equipment, but they're not required to play the game. They also don't improve a player's performance.

To set up parental controls:
- For PlayStation 4, you can create special child accounts that can be linked to your adult account, which lets you set monthly spending limits. Log into your main PS4 account. Go to Settings > Parental Controls > Family Management. Choose Add Family Member > Create User, and then enter your child's name and date of birth. You can set up specific parental controls.

- For Xbox One, you can create a special passcode to verify purchases. Go to Settings > All Settings > Accounts > Sign-in. Then choose Change My Sign-In & Security Preferences, and scroll right to Customise. Scroll right again and select Ask For My Passkey To Make Purchases, and choose Passkey Required. Simply pick a PIN your child won't guess.

- For PC and Mac, go into the account settings of your child's Epic Games account. Once in there, make sure there aren't any card details or linked PayPal accounts. You can easily remove them if they are there.

- For iPhone and iPad, whenever you make a purchase, you'll always have to verify it with either a password, the Touch ID fingerprint scanner or Face ID. But some iPhones are set up so that you only have to enter a password every 15 minutes. To stop this, go to Settings > Your Name > iTunes & App Store. Underneath you'll see a Password Settings Section. Go to Purchases And In-App Purchases, and choose Always Require. If your child knows your iPhone password, you can set up a second PIN for purchases. Go to Settings > General > Restrictions, then press Enable Restrictions. Choose a new four-digit passcode for In-App Purchases.

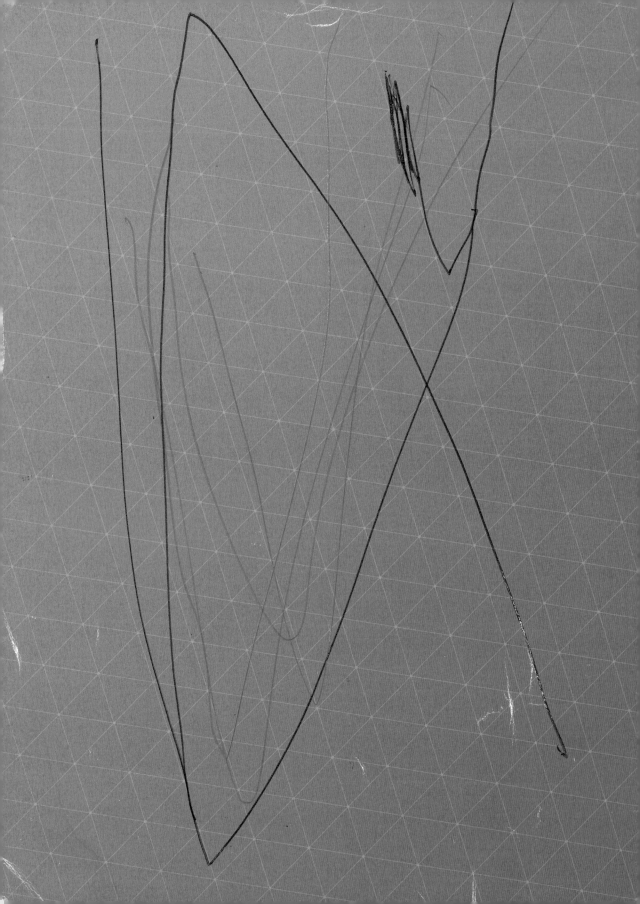

THE SIKHS

Faith, Philosophy & Folk

Text
Gurbachan Singh

Photographs
Sondeep Shankar

Silverdale Books

ੴ ਸਤਿਗੁਰ ਪ੍ਰਸਾਦਿ ॥

———— ✳ ————

Preface

The Sikh religion is amongst the youngest of faiths, having been founded just about five hundred years ago. Since the gurus all received divine inspiration for their writings, it is one of the revealed religions. While the faith includes some features existing both in Hinduism and Islam, it is not a fusion or synthesis of the two. Essentially, it is a separate faith and has evolved into a separate religion.

Again, though there are similarities with the Bhakti movement, the Sikh faith is not an integral part of the former. There are several differences between the two; Bhakti advocates renunciation, a Sikh's spiritual quest remains within *grahasti* (life of a householder). The focus of worship for Sikhs is the One Supreme, Formless, Eternal Lord and not any icons or human beings. Sikhs do not recognise any caste and believe in universal brotherhood. They are dedicated to *seva* (service) of all, as opposed to the seeking of emancipation or *moksha* of the individual. The Sikhs pray for *sarbat da bhala* (the good of all).

The translations of *Gurbani* wherever occurring in the text are my personal effort. I do not claim any literary merit but, to the extent possible, I have attempted to convey the essential meaning and spirit of the original.

Pictures of the gurus are included in this book. It must be kept in mind, however, that none is a true likeness for no pictures are believed to have been painted during their lifetimes. Each painting reproduced herein projects the artist's conception, the style of the school and the garb of the time.

In this modest endeavour, I have received valuable advice and suggestions from many friends, too numerous to mention individually. I thank them all. My wife and my son, Tejeshwar, a publisher of repute himself, have been my main inspiration and support. My gratitude and blessings for them.

Finally, my sincere thanks to Pramod Kapoor and Bela Butalia of Roli Books for their co-operation, assistance, understanding and, above all, their patience.

GURBACHAN SINGH

arrived at Eminabad he asked for shelter of a carpenter named Lalo. During this time a local official, Malik Bhago, organised a *Brahm Bhoj* (a feeding of Brahmins and holy men). He also invited Nanak who, having come to know of Bhago's reputation as a corrupt man, declined to participate. This incensed Bhago, who had him officially summoned. When he arrived, he was asked why he had spurned the invitation. Nanak sent for a piece of coarse bread from Lalo's dwelling which he held in one hand. In the other, he took savoury foods served at Bhago's feast. It is written that when Nanak closed both fists and squeezed, drops of milk oozed from the hand holding Lalo's bread while blood dripped from the other.

He there recited the following *shabad* in Raag Majh (name of a musical scale), included in the *Adi Granth* at page 141:

Hak paraya Nanka . . .
Usurped rights, O Nanak
Are as the flesh of swine for a Muslim,
And as the flesh of a cow for the Hindu.
Your Guru or Pir can guide you
Only if you remain honest.
Mere talk cannot lead you to heaven,
Righteous conduct alone can be your salvation.
Forbidden food, though smothered in
spices, remains forbidden.
O Nanak, that which is false, ever remains so.

* * *

When in Hardwar, a major pilgrimage centre on the river Ganga, Nanak saw a group of pilgrims standing knee-deep in the water. Escorted by a pandit chanting *mantras*, they were scooping water from the flowing river and throwing it towards the rising sun. He also waded in, stood alongside the group, and asked what they were doing. The pandit answered that the pilgrims were offering water to their deceased ancestors to assuage their thirst. Thereupon, the guru faced west and, in similar fashion, began to throw water. Asked what he was up to, he replied that he was watering his fields in Kartarpur. They all laughed and ridiculed him. How could the water reach his fields so far away? The guru expressed surprise and wondered how, if the water thrown by him could not reach his fields which were not too far away on this earth, it could reach souls no

longer on this earth and who, in any case, had no physical wants or needs!

* * *

Reaching Puri, the guru and his companions went to the Temple of Lord Jagannath. It was the time of *sandhya* (dusk) and *arati* (worship) was being performed with the customary ritual: *diyas* (oil lamps) on a salver were being waved before the idol, accompanied by burning of incense, blowing of conch shells, striking of brass plates, ringing of bells, chanting, and the waving of whisks. The guru and his companions stood on one side through the ceremony. At its conclusion, an irate pandit came over and upbraided them for not participating in the *arati*. Guru Nanak explained that the Lord of the Universe (Jagannath) is not to be found in wood sculpted by men. He then uttered his conception of *arati* in Raag Dhanasri included in the *Adi Granth* on page 663:

Gagan mein thal Ravi Chand deepak banay . . .
With the firmament
as salver, the sun and moon are lamps,
The stars of the galaxy are pearls
strewn before Thee;
Sandal groves of the Malai hills are
the incense
While the breezes sway as Thy whisk
and all the forests of the world
provide floral offerings.
What an *arati* it would be,
O Great Emancipator,
With endless music and song
ringing your praises!
You have thousands of eyes but no eye,
Thousands of forms yet no form,
Thousands of feet but no foot,
Without a nose while having thousands.
The same light is within everyone;
the light of God
Whose Glow illumines all.
Whatever pleases Thee, O Lord, is the *arati*.
My soul thirsts for the love of Thy Lotus Feet,
Bless Nanak, the *saring* (a bird), with
a drop of Thy Bounty
So that he may ever abide in Thy Name.

* * *

Facing page: Paath *in peace . . . A corridor in the Harimandir.*

On one occasion, the guru and his companions came to a village where they received a cold, even hostile, reception. As they left, Nanak blessed the village. 'May it thrive', he said. At the next village the reception was in complete contrast; warm and hospitable. Upon departure, Nanak said 'May this village become deserted.' Mardana was at a loss to understand this and questioned the Master on the incongruity. Nanak replied that it would be better if the ill-mannered villagers remained together so that they did not contaminate others

were enticed by him to take shelter. During the night, they were invariably robbed of everything, including their lives. Guru Nanak and his companions were also offered shelter for the night. After the evening meal, they commenced *kirtan* (singing of hymns), reciting the praises of the Almighty and of virtuous living. Sajjan waited in vain for his guests to go to sleep. Meanwhile, the words being uttered by Guru Nanak began to have an effect on him until he was overwhelmed by the power and profundity of what he heard. He broke into their room, fell at

Reading the scripture—a granthi *with* chavar *before the* Granth Sahib.

with their example of uncouth behaviour. In the second case, if the villagers scattered, they would spread the example of love, friendship and hospitality, thus benefiting others.

* * *

On the road again, one evening while approaching Multan, Nanak came across a dwelling offering free accommodation and food to wayfarers. It was owned and run by a man named Sajjan. Travellers who appeared affluent

the Master's feet and begged for guidance to salvation.

* * *

Babar, the founder of the Moghul empire, had made forays into northern India before he finally vanquished Ibrahim Lodhi in the Battle of Panipat. Evidently Nanak was witness to the violence and brutality perpetrated by the

Facing page: *Prayer in tranquility . . . tranquility in prayer. A corridor on the upper floor of the Harimandir.*

16

marauders at Eminabad. He vividly describes the occasion and complains to the Creator. The *shabad* (quoted partially) is at page 360 of the *Adi Granth*:

Khurasan khasmana kiya Hindustan daraya . . .
You patronised Khurasan but tolerated the terrorising of Hindustan.
Not taking the blame Himself, the Creator sent the Moghul against us.
Great havoc was wrought, so much lament; did Thou not have compassion?
O Creator, Thou art the same for all mankind.

And again on page 722:

Jaise mein avay Khasam ki Bani . . .
As I receive the Master's Word, so do I relay it, O Lalo;
He (Babar) has brought sinful hordes in the groom's party from Kabul and forcibly demands the bride.
Decency and morality have gone into hiding and falsehood prevails, O Lalo.
The days of the *kazis* and *brahmins* are past, Satan is now conducting the marriage service, O Lalo.

* * *

On arrival at Mecca, Guru Nanak went to the Ka'aba—the most sacred place of pilgrimage for Muslims. Fatigued after the journey, he lay down at the entrance and fell asleep. The keeper found him in the morning, sleeping with his feet towards the Ka'aba. He was awakened rudely and upbraided for daring to sleep with his feet pointing towards the House of God. Nanak apologised, said that he was a weary traveller, and asked the keeper to do him the favour of taking his feet and turning them in the direction where God did not dwell. To a startled keeper he explained that the entire universe is nothing but God's dwelling.

* * *

Twenty years or so Nanak travelled through unfamiliar terrain, climate and conditions. He met a great number and variety of people. He stayed with humble folk, or slept under the skies, met with the mighty and had discussions with learned men, priests, princes and ordinary people of all religions and persuasions. He visited temples, mosques, pilgrimage centres, festivals and fairs. Wherever he went, he spread his message of love, compassion, truth, righteous living and the Supreme Majesty of the One God. At many places he left a following but the people at every place he visited would long remember the experience.

By 1522 Nanak finally returned home; not to Talwandi but to Kartarpur, the town he had earlier founded on the northern bank of the river Ravi. He was then about fifty-three years old. He settled down there with his family, shed the mendicant's garb and resumed the dress and role of a *grahasti* (householder). Both his parent's died the same year and he attended to their last rites.

Bhai Gurdas (1551-1636), regarded as the first chronicler of the Sikh faith, describes in his *vars* (epic poems) the atmosphere and life in Kartarpur during the final phase of Guru Nanak's life. Resuming a householder's life, the Master continued his teaching. Seated on a cot, he expounded on the Divine Message, spreading understanding and dispelling the webs of ignorance and superstition. Discourses on right living, singing of *kirtan* (prayers), and extolling the Power and Virtues of the Almighty formed part of the daily activities, accompanied by recitations of the *Japuji* (prayer composed by him in praise of the Almighty) in the mornings and *sodar* and *arati* in the evenings.

He set up a community kitchen (the forerunner of the *langar*) subsequently institutionalised by Guru Amar Das, the third guru. Here foodstuffs were donated. Volunteers cooked and served meals to visitors coming to see Guru Nanak. Whosoever came was served without regard to religion or caste.

The Master began to collect a following. People from near and far, hearing of his life and preaching, came to Kartarpur to see him and hear him. They came to be known as Sikhs from the Sanskrit word *shishya*, meaning student or disciple.

In the village of Khadur, near Taran Taran, lived Lehna. Like his father, Bhai Pheru, before him, he was a *pujari* (one who leads the prayer ritual) at the village temple dedicated to Devi, the goddess Durga. Again, as did his father earlier, he conducted an annual pilgrimage of devotees from the village to Vaishno Devi. Setting out on one such journey, he heard about the guru at Kartarpur and took a detour. The

day he spent in the congregation made him decide that he need go no further. He parted company with his group and stayed back.

Avidly, he imbibed the atmosphere and teachings at the community in Kartarpur. Before long, he became an ardent devotee. He dedicated himself to the service of the community and of his guru and assiduously absorbed the teachings of the sermons. It is written that Guru Nanak put some of his followers, including both his sons, through some tests. Several incidents are described in the *janam*

The torch had been lit and passed on. It would be for his successors to carry and nurture it.

Evolution

Guru Angad moved to Khadur to continue the mission. Emulating his mentor, he preached the virtues of selfless service, piety and brotherhood. Personally, he led an austere life and a busy one. Several sources, including 'Balwand-Satay *di Var*' on page 966 of the *Adi Granth*, testify to the manner in which he was chosen successor

Implements used for cleansing the sarovar *(pool) laid before the* Granth Sahib *for ritual blessing.*

sakhis. Bhai Lehna unfailingly demonstrated his unflinching obedience, loyalty and devotion. The guru named him Angad to signify that he was an *ang* (limb) of his own body.

Bypassing all others, Guru Nanak named Angad his successor on 15 June 1539. His installation as guru took place on 7 September that year, about two weeks before Guru Nanak's demise. He made Angad more than his successor—he elevated him to be his equal. **Angad** became **Nanak II**.

by Guru Nanak. Sources also record his qualities of generosity, wisdom and humility. He was known for his practice of daily meditation and other austerities.

The routine he followed entailed rising well before dawn and, after a cold bath, meditating until daybreak. Thereafter, *kirtan* was recited in his presence. He then attended to the sick who had come to him for succour and assistance. Later in the mornings, he held well-attended discourses where he preached and expounded

A panel from the Harimandir.

The Sikh Gurus

GURU	Contemporary Rulers in Delhi	Birth	Death	Life Span	Installed Guru (at age)	Duration of Ministry
NANAK	Bahlol Lodhi 1450-89 Sikander Shah 1489-1517 Ibrahim Lodhi 1517-26 Babar 1526-30 Humayun 1530-40	15.4.1469	22.9.1539	70 yrs, 4 months	-	-
ANGAD	Humayun Sher Shah Suri 1540-55	31.3.1504	29.3.1552	47 yrs, 11 months	7.9.1539 (35)	12 yrs, 9 months
AMAR DAS	Sher Shah Suri Humayun 1555-56 Akbar 1556-1605	5.5.1479	1.9.1574	95 yrs, 3 months	1552 (73)	22 yrs, 5 months
RAM DAS	Akbar	24.9.1534	1.9.1581	46 yrs, 11 months	1.9.1574 (40)	7 yrs
ARJAN DEV	Akbar Jahangir 1605-1627	15.4.1563	30.5.1606	43	1.9.1581 (18)	25 yrs
HAR GOBIND	Jahangir Shah Jahan 1627-1658 (1666)	14.6.1595	3.3.1644	51	25.5.1606 (11)	38 yrs
HAR RAI	Shah Jahan Aurangzeb 1658-1707	26.2.1630	30.6.1661	31	8.3.1644 (14)	17 yrs, 5 months
HAR KRISHAN	Aurangzeb	7.7.1656	30.3.1664	8	7.10.1661 (5)	2 yrs, 5 months
TEG BAHADUR	Aurangzeb	1.4.1621	11.11.1675	54	20.3.1665 (44)	10 yrs, 7 months
GOBIND SINGH	Aurangzeb Bahadur Shah 1707-1712	22.12.1666	7.10. 1708	42 yrs, 9 months	11.11.1675 (9)	32 yrs, 10 months

Four panels from the Harimandir. *Guru Nanak (1469-1539) flanked by Mardana (right) and Bala.*

Guru Arjan (1563-1606), compiler of the Adi Granth *and builder of Amritsar.*

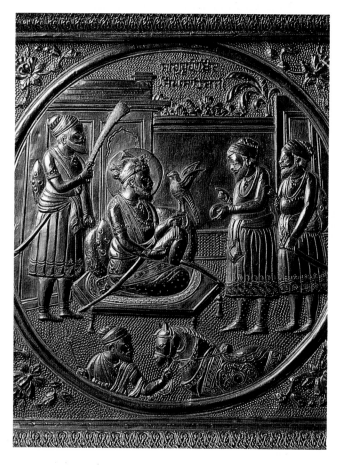

Guru Teg Bahadur (1621-75) counselling a group of pandits led by Kirpa Ram of Mattan at Chak Nanki.

Guru Gobind Singh (1666-1708), 'Vah vah Gobind Singh apay Gur chela'.

A panel from the Harimandir showing Guru Amar Das (1479-1574) and the baoli *(well) he got constructed in 1559 at Goindval.*

Genealogical Tables

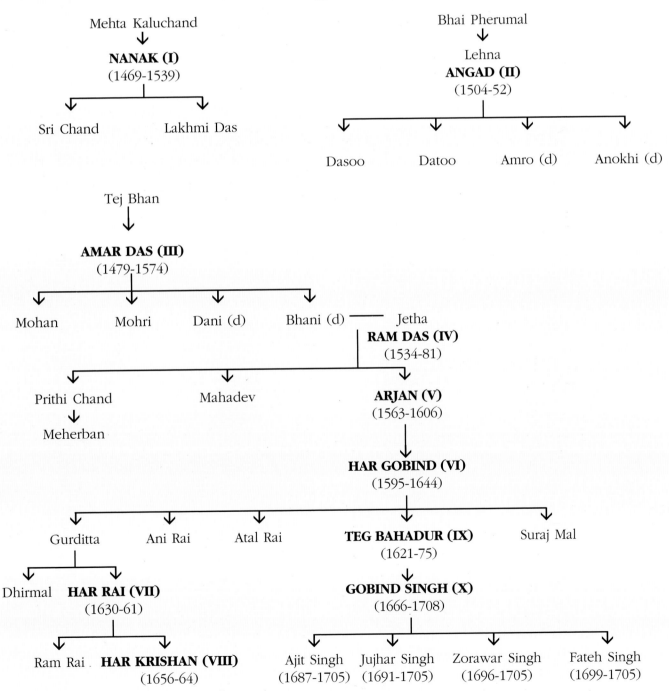

Mehta Kaluchand
↓
NANAK (I)
(1469-1539)

Sri Chand   Lakhmi Das

Bhai Pherumal
↓
Lehna
ANGAD (II)
(1504-52)

Dasoo   Datoo   Amro (d)   Anokhi (d)

Tej Bhan
↓

AMAR DAS (III)
(1479-1574)

Mohan   Mohri   Dani (d)   Bhani (d) —— Jetha
RAM DAS (IV)
(1534-81)

Prithi Chand   Mahadev   **ARJAN (V)**
↓   (1563-1606)
Meherban

HAR GOBIND (VI)
(1595-1644)

Gurditta   Ani Rai   Atal Rai   **TEG BAHADUR (IX)**   Suraj Mal
                                               (1621-75)
                                               ↓
Dhirmal   **HAR RAI (VII)**   **GOBIND SINGH (X)**
          (1630-61)   (1666-1708)

Ram Rai   **HAR KRISHAN (VIII)**   Ajit Singh   Jujhar Singh   Zorawar Singh   Fateh Singh
          (1656-64)   (1687-1705)   (1691-1705)   (1696-1705)   (1699-1705)

22

on Guru Nanak's *shabads*. The *langar* (kitchen) functioned daily, offering free food to whoever came—without any distinction or barrier. Frequently, he served the food while his wife looked after the cooking. His personal meals were simple; earned by making *munj* (the skin of a reed twisted to make string, widely used in rural Panjab for weaving the base of cots and stools).

Afternoons were invariably for the children, with whom he played and to whom he gave instruction—in reading, writing and the scriptures. Sometimes he witnessed wrestling bouts. In the evenings, again there was *kirtan* and sermons by the guru.

Kartarpur, which had been the centre for Sikhs, gave place to Khadur. Perhaps it was a conscious decision to move away from Kartarpur. The sons of the first guru lived there and might have created problems.

Guru Angad propagated the use of an alphabet, already in use for writing the language spoken by the people. It was derived from *Sharda* and *Takri*, two earlier scripts. He refined it and popularised its use. Some have suggested that Guru Angad invented the script. This, according to Bhai Kahan Singh, is not correct. He cites the *patti* (literally, wooden plaque on which school children learned to write) in Raag Asa composed by Guru Nanak. This is to be found in the *Adi Granth* at page 432, and includes all the letters in that alphabet and contains one which is unique in Panjabi speech. Because this lettering and vowel signs were used to record the sayings and compositions of the gurus, it came to be known as *'gurmukhi'*, that is, 'from the mouth of the Guru'. The language was Panjabi.

Bhai Bala had been Guru Nanak's playmate at Talwandi and later accompanied him on his travels. Guru Angad, being told of Bala, invited him to come to Khadur and narrate events from the first guru's life and travels. Hearing them, he instructed that they be recorded. This account of Guru Nanak's travels and teachings was inscribed in Gurmukhi characters as they were related in the guru's presence. The book is known as *Bhai Bale Vali Janam Sakhi*. Though it is now controversial—as a consequence, allegedly, of distortions introduced later—it still remains a source of information on the life and times of the first guru.

Guru Angad was an inspired poet who expressed his thoughts mostly in *slokas* (a verse form), of which sixty-three are included in the *Adi Granth*. However, his contribution to the evolution of the faith is more as a consolidator. For nearly thirteen years, he minded the flock, fostered the faith and expanded the circle of adherents.

One of those attracted to Khadur was Amar Das. He became a disciple in 1540 at the age of sixty-one. Over the subsequent twelve years, his devotion and service never faltered. Several instances of his dedication are recorded. Perhaps the most crucial one relates to the occasion when, on a stormy night, Amar Das, as was his routine, was carrying for his guru a container of water taken from the river Beas. He stumbled in the dark but saved the water from spilling. The noise disturbed a woman sleeping in a nearby hut. She rudely remarked that it must be Amru *nithavan* (homeless). When the incident was reported to the guru, he remarked that rather than 'homeless', his follower would be 'home for the homeless'. He added additional epithetic phrases for his disciple: 'honour of the unhonoured', 'strength of the weak', 'protector of the unprotected' and more.

In the course of time Guru Angad, in a manner reminiscent of his own case, chose Amar Das as his successor and asked Bhai Buddha to anoint him as the next guru. Guru Angad passed away on 29 March 1552 and **Amar Das** became **Nanak III** at the age of seventy-three.

Guru Amar Das moved his base to Goindval, a township which he had earlier helped to establish. This was located on the right bank of the river Beas on the main road then running from Lahore to Delhi. In due course it became the first ever place of pilgrimage for Sikhs. He married in 1502 and had two sons, Mohan and Mohri, and two daughters, Dani and Bhani. The third guru was called upon to husband a flock which by then was reasonably well organised

Previous page 23: Guru Ram Das, overseeing enlargement of the pond at Guru ka Chak, of which his son and successor, Arjan, wrote: Ditthe sabhay thhar nahin tudh jiha (p. 1362, Adi Granth). A panel in the Harimandir.
Facing page: Rotis (unleavened bread) being made for the langar . . . a daily activity.

and flourishing. He assumed the task with humility and dedication. He had chosen at a mature age to become a follower of Guru Angad and had imbibed lore about the founder of the faith. His own contribution would be significant.

As torch-bearer and shepherd, he took on his responsibilities with humble fervour. He continued to preach to the daily congregation while undertaking meaningful initiatives of far-reaching consequence. His sermons were in simple language and the similes and examples he gave were related to the daily experiences of

region and wished to see the guru, he was asked to first have a meal in the *langar*.

Guru Amar Das continued steps for reform in social practices. Modified ceremonials for birth, marriage and death were introduced at which *shabads* of the gurus replaced services in Sanskrit. While the people were happy since they could finally understand what was going on, the pandits were understandably angered as the demand for their services declined. The guru condemned and forbade the practice of *sati* (immolation of widows at their husband's pyre)

Nit Nem, *morning prayer in congregation.*

his audience. At the same time, he pursued social and political objectives designed to benefit the people at large and the nascent faith.

The *guru ka langar* became more renowned. In fact it was, to some degree, institutionalised. It was an effective method to foster and emphasize the equality and unity of human beings. Anyone wishing to have an audience of the guru was told: *'pehle pangat, pichhe sangat'*—first sit in a row (and eat), then the meeting. It is said that once, when the emperor Akbar was touring the

amongst his followers, discouraged *purdah* (veiling of women), advocated monogamy, inter-caste matrimony and widow remarriage—radical measures indeed in those times.

Bhani, his youngest child, was born in 1535. She was dear to her father and was devoted to him. She was married to Bhai Jetha, a devotee of the guru who had earlier come to Goindval.

Facing page: *A Sikh at prayer: '. . . a Sikh should, whenever possible, recite or hear* Gurbani'.

26

The fifth guru, Arjan (1563-1606), the first martyr of the Sikhs. Guler; circa 1820: Mohan Singh Collection.

The sixth guru, Har Gobind (1595-1644). Guler; circa 1820: Mohan Singh Collection.

The eighth guru, Har Krishan (1656-64). Guler; circa 1820: Mohan Singh Collection.

The ninth guru, Teg Bahadur (1621-75). Guler; circa 1820: Mohan Singh Collection.

She bore him three sons: Prithi Chand, Mahadev and Arjan.

Lore has it that one morning, when her father was about to sit on a *chowki* (a low stool) to commence his meditation, she noticed that one of its legs was broken. Unflinchingly, she placed the palm of her hand at the point to keep the seat stable for her father and stoically bore the pain. When he got up, he saw blood on the floor and the injury on her hand. Her father was greatly moved, blessed her and offered her a boon. It is said that she asked that future gurus should only be from her family. Though taken aback by this bold request, the guru, having given his word, had to consent. This single incident was to affect the future development of the faith.

In 1559, Guru Amar Das had a *baoli* (well) constructed at Goindval. It has eighty-four steps descending to the water level. Ancient Hindu scholars held that there are eight hundred and forty thousand forms of life through which a soul may have to transit before rebirth as a human, unless it attains *moksha* (liberation). This is part of the Hindu *karmic* belief. Many devout pilgrims to Goindval immerse themselves in the *baoli* eighty-four times, interspersing each dip with reciting the *Japuji* standing on each ascending step. Many Sikhs undertake this as a pious act, others do so in the belief that it will mitigate the severity of the future cycle of rebirth.

As a measure to organise an increasing following, which was also expanding geographically, the guru established twenty-two *manjis*—literally, beds—each of which he put in charge of a *masand* (an appointed representative), each a devout and pious Sikh. These representatives served to look after the local communities, to relay directives from the guru and to collect contributions.

He composed the most sublime and moving poetry, couched in simple language and easily understood metaphor. In 1554, just as he completed a panegyric to the Lord in Raag Ramkali (page 917, *Adi Granth*) consisting of forty verses, he was brought news of the birth of a grandson. He named the baby Anand, the same as the text. This composition is among the

more familiar *banis* in the *Adi Granth*. It has become *de rigueur* to recite this in an abbreviated version (the first five and the concluding verses) at all Sikh ceremonies. Altogether, 907 of his *shabads* are included in the *Adi Granth*. The twenty-two years he spent tending the faith represent a definitive phase of coalescing and building. Before his demise on 1 September 1574, he nominated his son-in-law, Bhai Jetha, as his successor.

Bhai Jetha was installed as **Guru Ram Das—Nanak IV**. The occasion is vividly described by Guru Amar Das's great grandson, Sunder, who was witness to the scene. The six verses are in Raag Ramkali, known as *Sud* (the call) at page 927 of the *Adi Granth*. Sunder records the guru's last words and actions: how he had become the successor to Nanak's mantle, how he had received the call of the Creator and welcomed it. Addressing those present as his family he explained the call of God; sent for his family members and admonished all not to mourn his passing, instead to recite *kirtan* and have *katha* (discourse); announced his successor—Ram Das Sodhi—and asked his son Mohri and others present to pay obeisance to him. Though extremely brief, this piece is an epic.

Guru Ram Das was forty when called upon to assume his elevated role. Much of his earlier life had, however, been spent in the service of the guru and of the faith he had adopted. He had been active in the *kar seva* (voluntary labour) when the *baoli* was being constructed and had undertaken other assignments for the guru as directed.

In 1574, he was assigned the task of developing a settlement which he named Guru ka Chak, at times referred to as Chak Guru. To the east there was a pond which he had enlarged. The work continued after his succession. The township was later renamed by his son, Arjan, as Ramdaspur and the pool as *amritsar*—the pool of nectar. The city is today known by that name, Amritsar.

In due course, the centre of his activities shifted from Goindval to the new township which, being on the main highway from Delhi to Lahore and further north, became an important trading centre. That a new settlement was founded by the Sikhs and a tank excavated indicates that they now had access to greater

Previous page 29: Guru Gobind Singh out hawking. Lahore with Jammu influence, circa 1900: Mohan Singh Collection.

resources. Also, that the following was increasing. The contributions for the construction were both in cash and kind. The labour was exclusively voluntary—*kar seva*—whether manual labour, or that of artisans, craftsmen or any other.

Guru Ram Das, like his predecessors, composed *bani*. The *Adi Granth* contains 638 of his *shabads*. Of these, four constitute the *lavan*, which are the central part of the Sikh wedding ceremony (the *Anand Karaj).*

He expanded the arena of activities of the House of Nanak, sent representatives further

rebellious, ambitious and jealous of his youngest brother. The second, Mahadev, had an ascetic nature and had become a virtual recluse. The youngest was closest to his parents and was innately pious and religious. He was consequently the natural choice as successor. Indeed, he seems to have been groomed by his father for the position. However, for the rest of his life he had to face the hostility and machinations of his eldest brother. To contend with these, he had the powerful support of two widely respected elders, Bhai Buddha and Bhai Gurdas. At the

Kar seva *in progress . . . never too young to begin.*

afield to spread the message and kept up the tempo of social reform while consolidating the measures already introduced. The relatively brief period of seven years that he was guru, while not eventful, were nevertheless significant in the evolution of the new faith.

Of his three sons, he chose the youngest, Arjan, as his successor. **Arjan** became **Nanak V** upon the demise of his father on 1 September 1581. Arjan was the youngest of the fourth guru's sons. The eldest, Prithi Chand, was

age of eighteen he had been until then the youngest to become guru. Four successors, including his son, would be even younger.

It is important to note that Arjan was the first guru to have been born in the new faith. Also, that he succeeded to the spiritual centre of his predecessor. The first guru had his base at Kartarpur, the second at Khadur, the third at Goindval and the fourth at Guru ka Chak (renamed Ramdaspur and finally Amritsar). Guru Arjan worked assiduously to consolidate and

No *puja* for me, nor *namaz*.
Only the One Formless will I worship.
We are neither Hindus nor Muslims,
We belong to the One, who is
both Allah and Ram.

We should see this as a sequential development of the basic teachings of Guru Nanak and their evolution during the stewardship of his successors up to then.

As the faith evolved and developed so also did opposition to it. Akbar's tolerance and liberal outlook had provided an umbrella for its growth. But this could not prevent covert jealousy and hostility which became overt soon after the emperor's death on 16 October 1605.

Unlike his father, the new emperor, Jahangir, was not an eclectic. In addition, he found cause to have a grievance against the guru. Prince Khusro, Jahangir's son who had rebelled, fled to the Panjab where, according to reports made by the guru's detractors, he received the guru's support and blessings. Those inimical to the Sikhs further encouraged Jahangir's animosity. Within a few months of his accession his ire found expression in action. To quote from his memoirs, *Tuzuk Jahangiri*: 'I fully knew of his heresies, and I ordered that he should be brought into my presence, that his property be confiscated, and that he should be put to death and torture.' The governor of Lahore, Murtaza Khan, was to implement the order. However, according to Sikh chronicles, Chandu Shah—a wealthy merchant and revenue official of the Moghul administration—importuned the governor to be entrusted with the task. Lore has it that Chandu had a personal animus against the guru; namely, a rejected marriage proposal for Chandu's daughter to be betrothed to the guru's young son Har Gobind.

Guru Arjan was subjected to the most horrendous tortures until his body succumbed on 13 May 1606—just seven months after Akbar's death. The Sikhs acquired their first

Facing page: A sevadar (attendant) clearing the surface of the pool of flotsam—flower petals, tree leaves, twigs, etc. which have fallen or been blown into the water.

Following pages 36-37: The Harimandir (foreground), the Darshani Deodi and causeway to the shrine, with the dome of the Akal Takht (far back).

martyr. A monotheistic, pacifist, non-belligerent philosophy was destined for a metamorphosis.

Har Gobind was installed guru on 25 May 1606, twelve days after his father's martyrdom, when he was not quite eleven years old. Baba Buddha, who had anointed the previous four gurus, placed the *tilak* (auspicious mark) on his forehead. *Masands* had brought a *seli* (a black cord worn over the headdress by some holy men) to be placed around his headgear.

He declined to let it be put on, declaring that the time for *selis* was over. It was now the age to carry weapons. Then he said that his *seli* would be the sword-belt and that, on his turban, he would wear an aigrette—the symbol of royalty. He asked for two swords to wear: one to symbolise *piri* (spiritual authority) and the other *miri* (temporal authority). He was evidently implementing his father's injunctions (as recorded in the *Sri Gur Pratap Suraj Granth*) to ascend to the *gaddi* (throne) fully armed and to have armed men attend on him. Moral and non-violent methods of protest against oppression, intolerance and injustice were set to be replaced by more active and sterner methods of resistance.

As a child, he had been placed under the tutelage of Bhai Gurdas for schooling in the religious texts and *dharma* (moral duty, as also religion), and of Baba Buddha for instruction in the martial arts. He absorbed both assiduously. He sired six children: Gurditta, Ani Rai, Suraj Mal, Atal Rai, Teg Bahadur and a daughter Viro.

Soon after becoming guru, he issued directives to his followers, asking for offerings of horses and weapons. Unlike his predecessors, he began to maintain a retinue of armed Sikhs. The more robust and hardy peasantry began to augment the ranks of the Sikhs, hitherto mainly drawn from the towns.

In 1608-09, at the site facing the main approach to the Harimandir, Har Gobind constructed the Akal Bunga (Abode of the Immortal). Since it became the principal *takht* (throne), it is also known as Akal Takht (Throne of the Immortal). It has become the primary seat of Sikh religious authority and the central point of political assembly. This is the location from where *hukumnamas* (recorded commands) are issued; the *Sarbat Khalsa* (the general assembly of the Khalsa) congregates; and *gurmattas*

(resolutions adopted in the presence of the *Granth Sahib*) are adopted.

Reports of the changed style of the sixth guru came as a surprise to the emperor. He had thought that with the torture and execution of Guru Arjan, the Sikhs would have been subdued. Instead, they were becoming stronger and more daring. The guru was dispensing justice amongst his followers, collecting taxes, maintaining armed retainers; like a prince, he went hunting and hawking. His followers addressed him as *sachcha padshah* (true king).

between 1617 and 1619; the exact dates and duration are not certain. The guru had as fellow-prisoners several minor princes and chieftains from various parts of the country. When the time came for his release, he declined to come out unless the other prisoners were simultaneously released. It was agreed that as many as could hold on to his *chola* (a loose ankle length garment) could come out of prison with him. There were fifty-two other prisoners. It is written that the guru had a special *chola* made with fifty-two tassels. All the prisoners were thus able

The Harimandir illuminated at Divali: the festival of lights.

In short, he was acquiring and displaying all the attributes of a political entity; an embryonic state. Emperor Jahangir therefore summoned him to Delhi. On the charge that the fines imposed on his father had not been paid, he was sentenced to imprisonment and incarcerated in the fort at Gwalior.

He remained imprisoned for some months

Facing page: Gurdwaras *are also lit up on Gurpurabs, specially the one falling on Guru Nanak's birthday.*

to gain their freedom with him. That is when he was given the epithet *bandi chhod* (deliverer from bondage).

After his release from Gwalior Fort, Guru Har Gobind travelled to Amritsar. The day coincided with Divali—the festival of lights—observed by illuminating homes. The day acquired a special significance for Sikhs as Amritsar was illuminated to welcome the guru's return. Like Baisakhi, the day became a day of pilgrimage to the seat of the gurus.

Jahangir's attitude towards Guru Har Gobind saw a change; he became more friendly, which enabled the guru to propagate the faith further afield. He travelled in the Panjab, then to Kashmir and later towards the east. In the Garhwal hills he had an encounter with Samarth Ramdas, who later became the Maratha chief Chhatrapati Shivaji's mentor. Seeing the guru fully armed and riding a horse, he asked what kind of a successor he was to Nanak, who had renounced the world. Guru Har Gobind replied that arms meant protection of the poor and resistance against the tyrant. Further, that Baba Nanak had not renounced the world; only *maya* (material wealth) and *homai* (the ego). Samarth is said to have remarked that this answer appealed to him.

Jahangir died in October 1627 and was succeeded by his son Shah Jahan. The detractors and opponents of the guru again became active. They slandered him and carried fabricated tales to the new emperor. Besides, reports reached him of the guru's growing following and of his maintaining armed retainers. These reports added to the consternation at court. Over a period, Shah Jahan's mind was poisoned and he became progressively hostile to the guru.

In the year after his accession, Shah Jahan visited Lahore. Out hunting one day, the emperor's hawk fell into the hands of some Sikhs who took it to the guru. The royal messengers sent to reclaim the hawk were refused its return. The emperor was infuriated and ordered his military commander at Lahore, Mukhlis Khan, to retrieve the bird. The latter marched to Amritsar with a detachment of soldiers. A fight with the Sikhs took place during which Mukhlis Khan was killed. Though this engagement was a minor skirmish, its implications were significant. The Sikhs had, for the first time, militarily challenged the Moghul rulers. Shortly thereafter, Guru Har Gobind left Amritsar, never to return, taking the *Granth Sahib* with him.

There were three further confrontations with the imperial forces—in 1630 with troops of the governor of Jalandhar, Abdullah Khan, at Srigobindpur; the following year at Mehraj with the force of Moghul commander, Kamar Beg; and in 1634 with one of his own renegade soldiers—Painda Khan—who had joined the Moghuls and led an attack on Kartarpur. Soon after these clashes, the guru settled at Kiratpur where he spent the remaining years of his life.

The sixth guru's contributions to the evolution of the faith are significant. First and foremost, the concept of *miri* and *piri* —namely, that the guru, hitherto the spiritual preceptor, would defend the new faith by force of arms when it became necessary.

Then, the introduction of a pennant for his troops, which evolved into the *Nishan Sahib* to be seen at every *gurdwara*; the flag of the Sikhs. It is saffron in colour and displays the Sikh symbol of the *khanda* (double-edged dagger) in black. Even the flagmast is cloaked in saffron cloth. The *nagara*—or kettle drum—used in battle was ultimately to be installed in every *gurdwara*, to be sounded at certain times, for example, when *langar* is ready to be served.

Of Guru Har Gobind's five sons, four had died in his lifetime. The youngest, Teg Bahadur (Mighty of the Sword), had played an important role during the fight at Kartarpur and other conflicts. However, he was retiring by nature and given to meditation and contemplation. The guru later asked his wife to take their son and live in Bakala, a village near Amritsar.

When his time approached, Guru Har Gobind chose his grandson, **Har Rai,** to succeed him. He was the younger son of his eldest, Baba Gurditta, who had predeceased his father. Har Rai acceded to Guru Nanak's spiritual legacy on 8 March 1644. He had been his grandfather's favourite. He was gentle by nature, kind-hearted and devout. He had received guidance and instruction from the Guru himself. He was married in 1640 and had two sons: Ram Rai and Har Krishan.

Guru Har Rai continued to maintain the style of his grandfather, with armed retainers. However, he faced no armed conflict. He took steps to further propagate Guru Nanak's message. He sent several devout and accomplished Sikhs to spread the faith: Bhagat Bhagvan to eastern India, Bhai Pheru to Rajputana and southern Panjab, Bhai Gonda to Kabul, Bhai Nattha to Dhaka and Bhai Jodh to Multan. He himself travelled in the Panjab and Kashmir and attracted more followers. He kept his permanent seat at Kiratpur where he continued the traditions of community prayer, daily discourses, the *langar* and counselling his followers.

Once, when the emperor Shah Jahan fell seriously ill, his son, Aurangzeb, imprisoned him in Agra Fort, and connived with his other two brothers against the eldest, Dara Shikoh, who fled to the Panjab and sought the guru's help.

The latter is said to have deployed a modest force at the ferry at Goindval to delay Aurangzeb's forces who were in pursuit. Dara Shikoh was eventually defeated and killed. Aurangzeb later contrived also to kill his other brothers and ascended to the throne in 1658, while his father was alive. Shah Jahan

Rai went to Dehra Dun where he settled without ever seeing his father again.

Guru Har Rai then nominated his younger son, Har Krishan, to succeed him before he passed away at Kiratpur on 6 October 1661. **Har Krishan** was just over five when he was installed as the eighth guru. Though young in years he displayed an unusual maturity and impressed his followers by his discourses.

His elder brother, Ram Rai, who had been passed over for the succession, sought redress from Aurangzeb for the seeming injustice of his

Nishan Sahib *(flagmast) at Gurdwara Rakab Ganj in New Delhi.*

died in 1666, while still imprisoned.

In addition to the guru's purported action to assist Dara, it was reported to Aurangzeb that the Sikh scriptures contained words derogatory to Islam. Guru Har Rai was summoned to Delhi. He sent instead his elder son Ram Rai. When confronted, Ram Rai distorted a line from the *Granth Sahib* in order, as he thought, to please the emperor. When the incident was reported to the guru, he was incensed and forbade his son ever to appear in his presence. Eventually, Ram

father. The emperor summoned the young guru to Delhi. He arrived in the capital in early March of 1664 and stayed at the house of Raja Jai Singh of Amber. A *gurdwara* known as Bangla Sahib now stands there.

Several instances are recorded to illustrate his intelligence. Cunningham relates one where the child was taken into the royal harem and asked to identify the empress amongst a group of ladies, all equally well dressed. He straightaway identified her and went and sat on her lap.

Another tells of Aurangzeb one day catching hold of both his little hands in one of his and asking what he would do if he were slapped. The guru replied that anyone whose hand the emperor took had nothing to fear; what then had he to be afraid of when the emperor had taken hold of both his hands! Aurangzeb was greatly impressed by his wit and intelligence.

While Har Krishan was in Delhi, an epidemic of small pox broke out in the city. He came out to give aid and succour to those afflicted. In the process, he himself caught the infection. He

conflicts with the Moghul forces. However, he was essentially of an aloof and retiring nature, inclined more towards meditation and contemplation rather than worldly affairs. Nevertheless, he attended to family responsibilities and looked after his mother and his wife. When news reached Bakala of the late guru's dying words, several pretenders set themselves up claiming to be the successor. The most prominent was Dhirmal, the sixth guru's eldest grandson, who had been passed over for succession in favour of his younger brother, Har

Panj Piarey *(with swords) on the steps of Gurdwara Rakab Ganj. Preparatory to leading a Gurpurab procession.*

moved out of Raja Jai Singh's house to a camp on the banks of the river Jamuna. Even while gravely ill he was conscious of his responsibility to name a successor. Before he breathed his last, he uttered the cryptic words 'Baba Bakale'—the Baba, namely, the guru, is at Bakala.

Bakala, a village near Amritsar, is where Guru Har Gobind had sent his wife and youngest son not long before he passed away. Teg Bahadur, in his youth, was an accomplished rider and marksman. He had fought valiantly during the

Rai. There were also others, each with his own *masands*, who were beguiling Sikhs who came in search of the guru.

Makhan Shah, a prosperous Sikh merchant, also came to Bakala. Legend has it that he had vowed an offering of five hundred *mohurs* (gold coins) to the guru for success in a venture. When he arrived at Bakala, he was bewildered

Facing page: *Devotees paying obeisance at Gurdwara Bangla Sahib in New Delhi.*

42

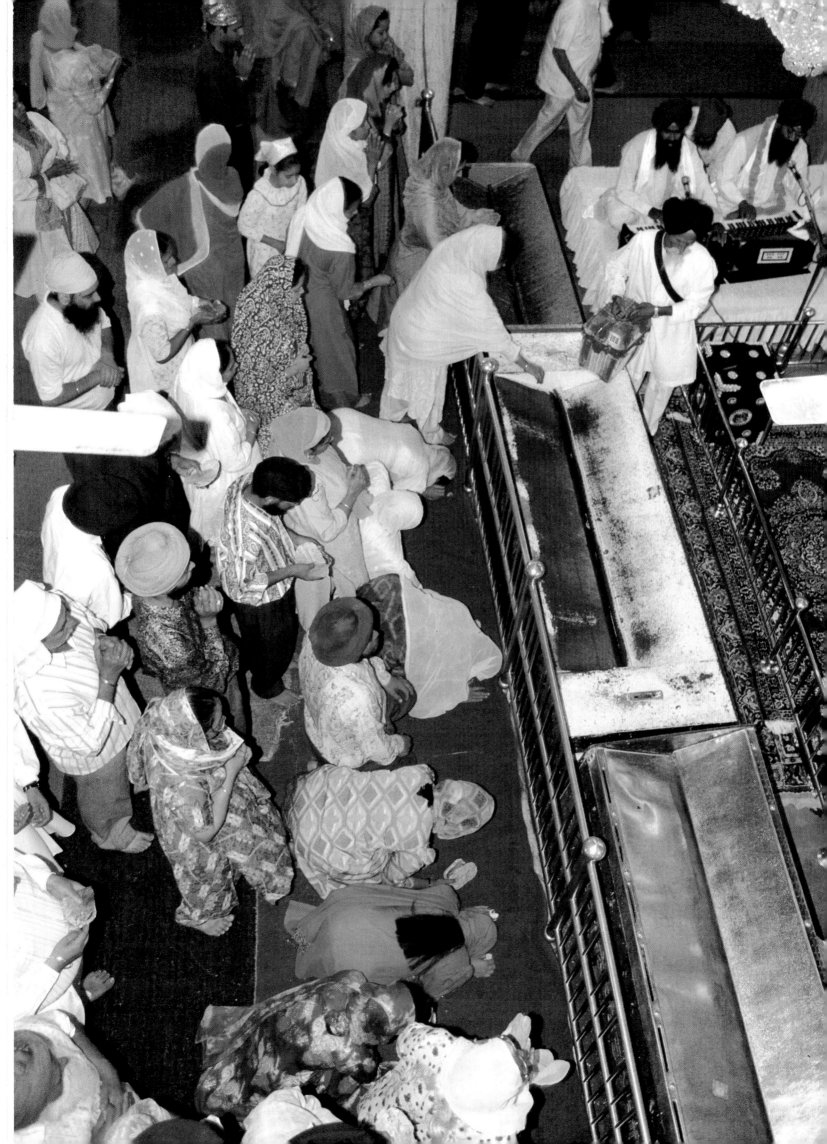

means of securing justice in the name of God. At the commencement of the *Bachitar Natak* he writes:

I bow with devotion to the Holy sword.

The *Jaap* (verse 52) reads: 'I bow to the Wielder of the sword, the Possessor of all weapons; the ultimate in knowledge and the Mother of all people.' In fact, in the *Akal Ustat*, the Almighty has been referred to as *Sarabloh* (All Steel): He is the destroyer of evil and the punisher of the tyrant. God and the sword, in his conception, would appear to have become conterminous. The sword, however, was not meant for aggression or for perpetrating injustice. It was the symbol of self-respect, to be used only in self-defence or in the cause of righteousness and even then only as a last resort.

It would be pertinent to mention here that the battles fought by the sixth and tenth gurus were in self-defence. Also, that the fight was against tyranny and injustice. Never aggressive in nature. Nor against Muslims or Hindus as such. In fact, the gurus' forces often included Muslim and Hindu soldiers. Further, at no point did the Sikh gurus give expression, in word or deed, of antagonism towards any religion. To the extent that reproof may be discernible, it applies only to empty ritual or prayer without single-minded devotion. This admonition is applicable equally to Sikhs.

The rulers of the hill states were receiving reports of the guru's growing following and of their receiving military training. Also, they took exception to his teachings of equality of all men, disregarding caste. Above all, they became apprehensive of his growing strength and influence. Several rajas combined under the leadership of Fateh Chand of Garhwal and marched against him. A battle ensued at Bhangani, a village near Paonta. The battle, fought in September 1688, ended in defeat for the aggressors. The guru's prestige and influence were further enhanced. He was then not quite twenty-two years old.

Previous pages 48-49: 'Nihangs in their panoply.' A procession on the occasion of Hola Mohalla at Anandpur Sahib.

Shortly thereafter he left Paonta and returned to Chak Nanki which he renamed Anandpur (City of Bliss). He proceeded to build forts there—Keshgarh in the centre and Anandgarh, Lohgarh, Holgarh, Fatehgarh and Taragarh at strategic locations on the periphery. In 1691, there was a battle with a Moghul commander, Alif Khan, at Nadaun which ended in victory for the Sikhs. Several other skirmishes followed resulting mostly in favour of the Sikh forces.

Meanwhile, the guru was receiving complaints with increasing frequency from some Sikh *sangats* of the disreputable activities of the *masands*. In 1698 he issued a *hukumnama* directing Sikhs to no longer acknowledge the *masands* but to communicate directly with the guru and to bring their offerings to Anandpur. He addressed them as his 'Khalsa' (from the Persian word *khalisah,* meaning the land belonging to the sovereign as distinct from fiefdoms).

Concrete form was given to this concept (of a direct link) in a dramatic manner on the first day of Baisakh in 1699. People from far and near had gathered on this day, as had become customary since the time of Guru Amar Das, to pay homage to the guru. Since in the previous year Sikhs had been directed to disregard the *masands*, larger numbers had congregated. Sikhs had been asked to come, as far as possible, carrying arms and on horseback. A massive assembly took place at Keshgarh. While the morning service was in progress, the guru appeared with an unsheathed sword in his hand, a look of intense gravity on his face. He announced to the hushed assemblage that his sword thirsted for blood. Would one of his true Sikhs volunteer to offer his head? There was consternation amongst those who heard the guru's words. Then a stunned silence. The guru spoke again but no one stirred. At his third call, Daya Ram, a *kshatriya*, came forward and offered himself to the guru's will. He was led to a tent pitched nearby. A few minutes later, the guru reappeared before the assembly, his sword dripping with blood. He demanded another volunteer willing to sacrifice his life. Many began to leave. Some went to apprise the guru's mother of his capricious behaviour. However, a second Sikh—Dharam Das, a *jat* (a cultivator caste)—came forward. He, too, was led to the same tent from which, after a brief lapse of time, the guru returned with his sword bloodstained.

He made a third, then a fourth and finally a fifth call for a volunteer willing to sacrifice his life. Mohkam Chand, a calico printer, Himmat, a fisherman, and Sahib Chand, a barber, successively came forward in response to the guru's calls. Each was led into the same tent. The congregation was left nonplussed. Those still remaining waited in trepidation.

A while later, Guru Gobind Singh emerged from the tent leading the five Sikhs who had

casteless, martial fraternity. He proceeded next to administer *khande da pahul* or *amrit* (nectar) to them. The five, from different castes, had partaken of *amrit* from the same bowl and been renamed Daya Singh, Dharam Singh, Mohkam Singh, Himmat Singh and Sahib Singh. Caste distinctions had been obliterated and all were given the same suffix 'Singh' (lion) to their names, signifying that they were now brothers. They were required henceforth to wear the five symbols of the Khalsa—*kesh* (unshorn hair), *kirpan* (sword), *kacch* (knee-length drawers),

Leading a school contingent during a procession are five young boys in the garb of Panj Piarey, *with five girls dressed in white.*

volunteered to offer themselves to the guru's sword. They were attired uniformly in saffron coloured robes and turbans of the same colour, each wearing a sword on a belt. The congregation, now much reduced in numbers, stared in disbelief and amazement.

The guru announced that they were the *Panj Piarey* (Five Beloved) who were the culmination of Guru Nanak's revelation. They would form the nucleus of the faith, which he christened Khalsa—'The Pure' or God's Own; a selfless,

kanga (a small comb) and *kara* (a steel bangle). They were enjoined also to worship and have faith in only one God, to protect and help the weak, resist the oppressor, and to consider all human beings as equal regardless of caste or religion. Other articles of faith were also stipulated. Women were admitted to the initiation and given the name suffix 'Kaur' (Prince).

The initiation ceremony completed, the guru stood before the five and, with folded hands

51

requested them to administer *amrit* to him in the same manner. Having been thus initiated, his name was changed from Gobind Das to **Gobind Singh**. This gesture evoked a poet's exclamation: '*Vah vah Gobind Singh apay Gur chela*' (Hail, Gobind Singh, himself the Guru and the follower).

Learning of this development in the organisation of the Sikhs, the chiefs of the feudatory principalities in the hills were further alarmed. They perceived a threat to both their power and their faith from this militant and

forces of the local chiefs, they laid siege to the fort at Anandpur in May 1705.

The Sikhs resolutely withstood the siege, interspersed with assaults. The inmates of the fort were reduced to dire straits, with scarcities of food and other necessities. Many became so dispirited as to want to leave the fraternity and the fort. The guru was disappointed but agreed on condition that they formally disown him. Forty of them did so, giving him a letter declaring that henceforth neither was he their guru nor were they

Inside the gurdwara *at Keshgarh. The alcove on the right displays some of the arms used by Guru Gobind Singh.*

casteless brotherhood, who had forsworn caste distinctions and who were taught to believe in the basic equality of all humans. They endeavoured jointly and severally to evict the guru from Anandpur, located in the territory of Bilaspur State. Repeated efforts, including armed conflicts, between 1700 and 1704 were unsuccessful. Ultimately, they petitioned Aurangzeb for assistance. Under imperial orders, contingents were sent by the governor of Lahore and the *faujdar* of Sirhind. In concert with the

his Sikhs. They then slunk out of the fort.

The aggressors were vexed at their lack of success against the tenacity of the besieged. In the face of this standoff, the Moghul commander offered, on solemn oath, unharmed passage if the Sikhs agreed to evacuate Anandpur. The offer was accepted and the fort evacuated on the night of 5/6 December 1705. However, soon after the Sikhs came out, the rajas and their Moghul allies attacked them in full force. Many Sikhs were killed and much material was lost, including many precious manuscripts of the guru's writings. Fortunately, the guru escaped together with some Sikhs and managed to reach Chamkaur. The pursuing armies caught up with them and a battle ensued on 7 December 1705.

In the fighting at Chamkaur, the guru's two elder sons—Ajit Singh and Jujhar Singh—and all but the guru himself and five Sikhs, fell in action against great odds. That night the five survivors charged him, under the authority he had himself vested in the *Panj Piarey*, to save himself and to reconsolidate the Khalsa. Being thus compelled the guru, along with three of them, escaped in the darkness. When the fighting resumed on the following day, the remaining two put up a heroic fight before they also fell.

The guru's two younger sons, Zorawar Singh and Fateh Singh, and his mother were betrayed after the evacuation of Anandpur to the *faujdar* of Sirhind. Upon their refusal to convert, the two boys, aged nine and six, were executed on 13 December 1705. Their grandmother died of shock after she came to know of their fate.

Guru Gobind Singh reached Dina, near Faridkot. In a matter of a few days, he had lost his mother, all four sons and countless Sikhs. He was forlorn but not despondent. Here he composed the *Zafarnama* (Epistle of Victory) addressed to Emperor Aurangzeb. Consisting of 111 couplets in Persian verse, it is largely critical of the unjust and unworthy acts of the Moghul regime; condemns the false oaths taken on the *Quran* by the emperor's soldiers; and contains a homily on the duty of kings and the sanctity of solemn pledges. He asserts that, when all other means have failed, resort to the sword becomes justified. The letter emphasizes the supremacy of morality in matters of state as in matters of personal conduct and holds that the means are as important as the ends. Two of his followers were sent with the letter to the south, where Aurangzeb was campaigning.

Meanwhile, the guru enlisted some supporters from the Brar clan and continued his march. He was still being pursued by the Moghul forces. He took a position at Khidrana, by a rainwater pond, where a fierce fight took place on 29 December 1705. The attackers failed to capture their quarry and had to retreat. Crucial support unexpectedly came to the guru from the forty who had disowned him a scant four weeks earlier at Anandpur. When they returned to their homes, they had been chided and ridiculed by their families for their cowardice. In their contrition, they arrived at the site of the engagement under the leadership of a brave woman, Mai Bhago, to redeem themselves. In endeavouring to impede the enemy's advance to the guru's position they sacrificed their lives. After the battle, a critically wounded survivor, Maha Singh, asked the guru for forgiveness for them all and requested that the letter of repudiation given at Anandpur be destroyed. He readily conceded both requests and blessed the martyrs. Their heroic act is recalled in the *ardas* (supplication) as the forty who attained salvation (*mukte*, plural of *mukt*). The place was renamed Muktsar where a resplendent *gurdwara* has been constructed and the pond brick-lined.

Guru Gobind Singh then made his way to Talwandi Sabo, in present day Bathinda district, where he had some respite. Many Sikhs—including poets and savants—joined him there. Much literary activity went on. A recension of the *Adi Granth* was undertaken by the guru himself with Bhai Mani Singh as his amanuensis. Since he stayed (or rested) here for about nine months, the town carries the honorific of Damdama Sahib (literally from *dam*, meaning, to rest). In November 1966, the tercentenary of the guru's birth, the town was declared to be a *takht*—the fifth for the Khalsa.

The messengers sent with the *Zafarnama* had not yet returned. The guru decided to travel south himself. He was in Rajputana when he received news that Aurangzeb had died on 20 February 1707. So, he turned towards Delhi, then to Agra where he met the new emperor, Bahadur Shah. The latter was on the point of leaving for the Deccan as his youngest brother, Kam Baksh, had rebelled and become a contender for the throne. The guru travelled south with Bahadur Shah who, after a conciliatory beginning in talks, found himself helpless to change policies in the face of fanatical satraps as, indeed, of his own preoccupation with fighting for his throne. They parted company at Nanded, a town astride the river Godavari.

Here he came across a *bairagi sadhu* (an ascetic), Madho Das, who was reputed to

Sikhs, to include any of his own compositions. (These were collated some years later by Bhai Mani Singh and compiled in what is known as the *Dasam Granth*.)

History provides continuing evidence of this credo. In the troubled and difficult times which the Sikhs faced during the declining years of Moghul rule, when they were ruthlessly persecuted and sought to be exterminated, their most cherished and protected possession was the sacred *Granth*. When Maharaja Ranjit Singh (1780-1839) established a Sikh kingdom, he did

The sanctity of and reverence for the *Sri Guru Granth Sahib* is inculcated in the mind of every Sikh since childhood. At every religious function, it is incumbent after *ardas* to take *hukum* (order or command) from the Holy Book. This entails opening it at random and reading the first *shabad* on the page, whose commencement may at times be on the previous page. Except when it is being read, it is always kept covered. At night, the book is closed, wrapped in one or two layers of cloth and again covered. At all times, it rests on a small bed,

Women devotees ask for blessings by touching the forehead to the ground or by addressing the Supreme Being with folded hands.

so in the name of the Khalsa. His daily routine began with obeisance to and reading from the Book. On festival days, he travelled to the Harimandir in Amritsar for the purpose. After British annexation of the Panjab, Sikh dedication to and belief in the living guru continued. The Gurdwara Reform Movement and other manifestations bear ample testimony to this faith. This tradition continues in independent India. So also wherever in the world Sikhs have made a home.

invariably under a canopy, on a raised platform or plinth. In homes which maintain the *Granth Sahib*, the same procedures are observed. In the more prominent or larger *gurdwaras* the plinth may be embellished with carved marble and have an ornate canopy.

Facing page: *On the steps inside the main entrance devotees gaze upon the Harimandir, in reverence and adoration.*

3000/- DONATED BY S. SURJIT SINGH JI CHADHA
IN MEMORY OF HIS PARENTS S.MALIK SINGH
JI OF M/S MALIK SINGH & SONS CHEMISTS
HALL BAZAR AMRITSAR & SMT. LACHHMIDEVI
EXPIRED ON 9th & 7th JUNE 1984 RESPECTIVELY.
IN MEMORY OF
Rs.1001/-

Profile of the
Sri Guru Granth Sahib

The thirty-six great souls whose lofty ideals and exalted thoughts, expressed in sublime verse, are contained in the Sacred Volume are:

Gurus

Nanak	First Guru	947 *shabads* in 19 *raagas*
Angad	Second Guru	63 *shlokas*
Amar Das	Third Guru	869 *shabads* in 17 *raagas*
Ram Das	Fourth Guru	638 *shabads* in 30 *raagas*
Arjan	Fifth Guru	2,312 *shabads* and *shlokas* in 29 *raagas*
Teg Bahadur	Ninth Guru	59 *shabads* in 14 *raagas* and 56 *shlokas*
Gobind Singh	Tenth Guru	1 *shloka*

Bhaktas and others:

Sadhna	a butcher	1 *shabad*
Surdas	a *brahmin*	2 *shabads*
Sein	a barber	1 *shabad*
Kabir	a weaver	534 *shabads* and *shlokas*
Jaidev	a *brahmin* (author of Geeta Govind)	2 *shabads*
Trilochan	a *vaisha*	5 *shabads*
Dhanna	a *jat*	4 *shabads*
Namdev	calico printer	62 *shabads*
Parmanand	indeterminate origin	1 *shabad*
Pipa	a Rajput noble	1 *shabad*
Sheikh Farid	a *sufi*	123 *shabads* and *shlokas*
Beni	indeterminate origin	3 *shabads*
Bhikhan	a *brahmin*	2 *shabads*
Mardana	rebeck player and the first guru's longtime companion	3 *shlokas*
Ravidas	a *chamar* (leather worker)	40 *shabads*
Ramanand	a *brahmin*	1 *shabad*
Satta and Balwand	bards	8 *vars*
Sunder	third guru's great grandson	6 verses—collectively known as *sud* (beckoning)
Miscellaneous *bhatts*	mostly *brahmins*	123 *swayas*

All gurus haved used the *nom de plume* Nanak for their compositions. At the commencement of a *shabad* or *bani*, the authorship is indicated by the word 'Mehla' (abode) followed by a numeral corresponding to the guru's order in succession. Thus, Mehla 1 would identify the author as Guru Nanak. The compositions of others are identified by individual names. The Holy Book was initially compiled by the fifth guru in 1603-04 and recensed by the tenth guru in 1706. The *Raagmala* at the end is a later addition. The Volume installed in all *gurdwaras* and in homes is identical and has 1,430 pages. The script is Gurmukhi, irrespective of the language of the verse—whether Panjabi, Hindi or any other. Except for the initial thirteen and the concluding seventy-eight pages, the remaining compositions are categorised according to the *raag* in which they should be sung. Singing the *shabads* is *kirtan*. Reciting or reading them is *paath*. Thirty-one *raagas* are included in the Book, though the total number of *raagas* according to ancient texts is eighty-four. Six basic *raagas*, thirty major and forty-eight lesser variations or off-shoots—colourfully described as six males, each having five spouses and eight progeny.

The thirty-one *raagas* which appear in the *Granth Sahib* are: Sri, Majh, Gauri, Asa, Gujri, Devgandhari, Bihagra, Vadhans, Sorath, Dhanasri, Jaitsri, Todi, Bairari, Tilang, Suhi, Bilawal, Gaund, Ramkali, Nat Narain, Mali Gauda, Maru, Tukhari, Kedara, Bhairav, Basant, Sarang, Malar, Kanada, Kalyan, Prahbati and Jaijaiwanti.

Ardas

Ardas is derived from the Persian *arz* meaning supplication and *dast* meaning hands. In other words, a supplication to a higher power, not supported by a written petition. In Sikh practice, it is a solemn part of daily life and also an essential part at all ceremonies, of any type.

Sikhs are enjoined to offer *ardas* twice a day after morning and evening prayers. It is also said at numerous occasions as, for example, at the commencement of a journey, before appearing for an examination, on the first day of a child beginning school, or when embarking on a new venture.

The *ardas* is addressed to the Supreme Being, all those present standing with folded hands. At formal occasions, the gathering faces the *Granth Sahib*, otherwise, in a similar respectful stance facing any direction—God is Omnipresent. The *ardas* consists essentially of four parts. The first is an invocation; the earlier part of which opens with the initial portion of Guru Gobind Singh's *Chandi di Var*. This has been supplemented later by inclusion of his own name and that of the *Granth Sahib*, the living Guru, seeking their blessings.

The second segment is historical in perspective and recalls the heroic sacrifices made by those true to the faith in the cause of righteousness and defense of the *dharma*; the Five Beloved *(Panj Piarey)* the four sons of the tenth guru, the forty martyrs and numerous others who resisted tyranny and injustice, suffering terrible torture and death at the hands of oppressors, without renouncing their faith. Additions from time to time ensure a historical continuum and recognition of a brotherhood transcending time.

The third portion invokes the blessings of God on the Khalsa, on all human beings and particularly asks for benign guidance in daily living; protection against the five evils of lust, anger, covetousness, attachment and pride; the eternal glory of sacred *gurdwaras* and the opportunity to visit them. It seeks the gifts of service, faith, discernment, patience and, above all, of the Name *(Naam)*.

The final portion may be added appropriate to the occasion; by including mention of the specific purpose for which the *ardas* is being offered, such as the birth of a child, the marriage of a couple, or other observance or on the occasion of death. At formal occasions the offer of *kadah prasad* is included, asking for it to be sanctified for distribution among the congregation.

The concluding words ask for the eternal glory of the One True Being and seek His Blessings for the well-being of every one in the world.

The *ardas* concluded, the congregation kneels and bows in obeisance to the *Granth Sahib*. This done, they stand up and say in unison: *'Sri Waheguru ji ka Khalsa, Sri Waheguru ji ki Fateh'* (The Khalsa is of the Wond'rous Lord, Victory also is His).

Finally, the person who has recited the *ardas* says: *'Jo bole so nihal'* (Whoever utters [this] will be fulfilled) and all respond *'Sat Sri Akal'* (True is the Timeless).

THE PHILOSOPHY

Basics

There are many religions in the world, each based on the teachings of great thinkers or founded by inspired souls. Each delineates a way of living and a goal towards which to strive after the end of this life. Also, the manner in which to meet and overcome the problems and temptations encountered during human existence. These ways are *dharma*. Since religion is a route or a way (*path* in Sanskrit), it has come to be known in Panjabi as *panth*. Thus, the Sikh *panth*: one of the several ways or religions.

Some consider that the Sikh faith is a part of the Bhakti movement. This is not entirely so. Although there are similarities, there are also distinct differences between the two. *Bhakti marg* (the way of devotion) is one of the three paths (the others being *karma marg* and *ngyana marg*, respectively the path of action and path of knowledge) expounded in the *Bhagavad Gita* for attaining liberation from the cycle of birth and rebirth. Bhakti took strong roots in South India in the first millennium A.D. It spread to other parts of the country during the first half of the second millennium.

The Sikh *panth* originated with Guru Nanak. It was propagated and evolved by his nine successors. Their teachings are contained in the *Adi Granth*. The basic beliefs summarised below, clearly point to the distinct differences that define the Sikh *panth* from the more

Facing page: Gurdwara Dukh Bhanjan in the parikrama *of Harimandir. Pilgrims paying homage to the* Granth Sahib *(lying open in the foreground).*

amorphous devotions of the Bhakti movement.

The primary objective as taught by this faith is not to look for a heaven or paradise in the hereafter but to aim for ultimate union with the Eternal Lord, described in the *Mool Mantra*, and thus to achieve liberation from the cycle of birth and rebirth. In this endeavour one needs guidance which is provided by the ten gurus, the epitome of which is contained in the *Adi Granth*, the Eternal Guru. Explanation and interpretation of the Sikh *panth* is given in discourses of learned persons. It is beneficial to attend such gatherings in the company of other seekers or *sadh sangat*. The faith is strictly monotheistic.

In the effort to realise the Eternal Lord, an individual has to inculcate purity—of body, mind and soul, both in personal conduct and in relation to society. Hence the advice: *Naam japo* (meditate and pray), *kirt karo* (earn by honest labour) and *vand chhako* (share your earnings). The individual has to live in and as part of this world while resisting temptation. All humans are fellow seekers of salvation.

Emphasis is laid on *udham* (positive action or effort) in any situation. The results are not in one's control. They are dependent on what is ordained which, in turn, is subject to *karmic* forces. Therefore, what is required is acceptance of and surrender to the Divine Will (*Raza* or *Bhana*). Guru Nanak writes in his *Japu*: '. . . countless suffer pain, hunger and adversity; even these, Lord, are Thy Gifts.' He continues: 'Release from the shackles (of the cycle of rebirth) is at the Divine Will; none can say aught else.'

God is not vengeful but benign. Though Omnipotent, He is loving and magnanimous. *Gurbani* names God in some of His infinite qualities and forms: *Daata* (giver), *Pritam* (lover), *Khasam* (husband), *Sahib* (master), *Pita* (father), *Mata* (mother), *Bhandap* (friend), *Bhrata* (brother), *Raakha* (protector), *Meet* (friend), *Yar* (pal), *Karta* (doer), *Thakur* (ruler). In addition, names used by Hindus and Muslims are included: Ram, Rahim, Gobind, Allah, Hari, Rab, Gopal and others. Finally, as *Sargun* (having all qualities) and *Nirgun*

In the endeavour to tread an upright path in an active life, a Sikh is enjoined to be wary of and consciously resist the five elementary temptations or weaknesses of *kaam* (lust), *krodh* (temper), *lobh* (avarice), *moh* (attachment) and *ahankar* (pride).

The essence of the Sikh *panth* then is harmony, universal love, honest labour, moderation in living and complete faith in the One God—the God of all creation; a way which is simple to describe but not easy to follow.

The Granth Sahib *being taken ceremonially from its overnight resting place in the Akal Bunga. to a palanquin on its way to the Harimandir.*

(without any attributes). In short, a universal, caring and just God. The gurus refer to themselves variously as *neech* (lowly), *garib* (poor), *das* (servitor), *nimana* (worthless), *banda* (bondsman), *binwant* (supplicant) and in other such humble terms.

The basics thus indicate the need for a balance between an active and contemplative life—one of a *grahasti* (householder) and seeker of salvation (*moksh*), as an integral member of society and being a good individual.

Moral Code

Precepts governing the code of conduct for Sikhs are collectively known as *rehat-maryada* (*rehat*, observance; *maryada*, custom). The essential tenets are derived from the contents of *Gurbani* included in the *Adi Granth*. Injunctions contained in the *Dasam Granth*, particularly those in the *bani* composed by Guru Gobind Singh, have equal authority.

Bhai Gurdas, an eminent scholar and

propounder of the Sikh faith, composed forty *vars* (epic poems) and five hundred and fifty-six *chhands* and *kabits* (both verse forms), which elaborated on the principles of the Sikh faith. He was the scribe who penned the *Adi Granth* at Guru Arjan's dictation. Bhai Nandlal, a devout Sikh and renowned poet, spent eight years at Anandpur with Guru Gobind Singh. He wrote several books in praise of the gurus and on the Sikh way of life. The writings of these two savants rank after *Gurbani* as indicators of the moral code for Sikh belief and practice.

The Shiromani Gurdwara Prabhandhak Committee (SGPC) came into being in 1920 for the basic purpose of managing all *gurdwaras* in India. (This committee in turn constituted the Shiromani Akali Dal to serve as a central body to co-ordinate the activities of various *jathas*.) Not too long after, the SGPC initiated a project to formulate a unified guide for Sikhs. After extensive consideration and debate, the proposals were finalised in 1945 and published under the title: *Sikh Rehat-Maryada.* This is now accepted as the authentic code of personal conduct for

While singing shabads, the palanquin in which rests the Granth Sahib is carried to the Harimandir on the shoulders of devotees. Men vie for the privilege of lending a shoulder.

Subsequently, several anthologies of and commentaries on Sikh *rehat-maryada* were written during the eighteenth and nineteenth centuries. Some of them exceeded the canons and hence were not acceptable to the orthodox. The more authentic include *Sarabloh Prakash, Tankhanama,* the *Rehatnamas* (of Chopa Singh, Prehlad Singh, Desa Singh and Daya Singh), *Prem Sumarag* and *Mehima Prakash.* Yet all of them remain of secondary authority.

Sikhs. Personal living covers three aspects: prayer, religious observance and *seva* (service).

Prayer: A Sikh is enjoined to recite five *banis* daily: three—the *Japu, Jaap* and the ten *Swaiyas*—in the morning, *Sodar Rehras* at sunset and *Sohila* at bedtime. The morning and evening prayers are to be followed by *ardas.* In addition, a Sikh should, whenever possible, recite or hear *Gurbani* preferably in congregation (*paath* or *kirtan*) and attend *katha* (religious discourse).

Religious observance: To believe in and worship only the One God; to have faith in the teachings of the ten gurus as embodied in the *Sri Guru Granth Sahib*; not to believe in or practice idolatry, caste divisions, untouchability or superstition of any type; to abjure fasting as a religious observance; to abstain from gambling, drugs, tobacco and intoxicants; to keep unshorn hair and not to wilfully harm anyone.

***Seva* or service:** To undertake voluntary social service is an essential part of the Sikh faith. This can be rendered in several ways, such as to clean *gurdwara* premises; cook or serve food and wash utensils in the *langar*; to clean the footwear of persons who gather at *gurdwaras*; and to participate in the construction of or repairs at religious or social premises.

In relation to the religious group or community, a Sikh must be an active and integral part of society and the faith. In this endeavour, he or she is expected to contribute both individually and as part of a group towards the benefit of society; and to participate in or contribute towards the construction and maintenance of *gurdwaras*, schools, hospitals, dispensaries, orphanages and the like.

A Sikh is expected to join the fraternity of the Khalsa by undergoing initiation and imbibing *amrit*. The obligations are strict and onerous. Therefore, this initiation should be accepted only after careful and serious consideration.

The rite *(Amrit Sanskar)* is described elsewhere. The obligations prescribed, in addition to those detailed above, are:

(a) The *amritdhari* is henceforth the child of Guru Gobind Singh. Thus, all *amritdharis* are siblings.

(b) At all times to wear the five K's: *kesh* (unshorn hair and beard), *kirpan* (a sword or its replica in miniature), *kangha* (a small comb), *kaach* (knee-length drawers) and *kada* (iron bangle).

(c) Not to consume the flesh of an animal killed in the manner of *halal* (kosher).

(d) To abjure carnal relations with anyone other than one's spouse.

Facing page: As they step into the sacred precincts, devotees make obeisance to the Harimandir.

(e) To eschew the use of tobacco, drugs and intoxicants in any form.

Social and Religious Structure

In elementary terms, a Sikh is one who believes in one God alone and has faith in and follows the teachings of the ten gurus as embodied in the *Sri Guru Granth Sahib*. Anyone can thus be termed a Sikh if he or she follows the basic precepts of the faith. One who believes in and follows the essentials of the faith is termed a *sehajdhari*. Large numbers of people in Panjab and Sindh, especially before India was partitioned, were *sehajdhari* Sikhs. Many continue to be so.

One who, in addition to observing the basic beliefs and practices, wears uncut hair and beard is a *keshadhari*.

An *amritdhari* is one who has partaken of *amrit* and strictly observes the *rehat-maryada* and other injunctions in his daily life and conduct.

Needless to say, there are renegades and apostates amongst Sikhs as there are in any religious or social group.

There is no ordained priesthood. Indeed there is no religious hierarchy. Any Sikh, man or woman, knowing the procedures and able to read the *Granth Sahib* may conduct a religious ceremony.

The authority to pronounce decisions in religious or social matters, to the extent it may be needed, rests with the *Panj Piarey* (the Five Beloved) with ratification by the *sangat*.

Socially, adherents of the faith are meant to be a fraternity. No divisions are recognised on the basis of caste. (Unfortunately, lapses in this respect continue.) Apostates and descendants or followers of those who challenged or opposed the gurus—such as Minas (followers of Guru Arjan's eldest brother, Prithi Chand), Ramraiyas (followers of Guru Har Rai's elder son), and Dhirmalias (followers of Guru Har Gobind's eldest grandson)—are considered beyond the pale for the orthodox. Apart from these, those who dye their beards, those who give an offspring in marriage in exchange for money (giver or taker of dowry), and those who do not observe the vows they have taken or act against the principles of the faith, are *tankhaias* (offenders meriting religious punishment).

Intermarriage amongst Sikhs and Hindus is common, except amongst the most orthodox of both faiths. Sikhs taking spouses of other religious beliefs is less frequent.

The *rehat-maryada* outlines the manner of considering and imposing penalties for religious offences or misdemeanours. The offender voluntarily presents himself before the congregation, acknowledges his lapse and asks for forgiveness. Minor offences can be condoned by consensus. However, for more serious matters, *Panj Piarey* are selected from amongst the congregation to consider and judge the case. In case an offender does not voluntarily come forward, he can be directed to appear before a gathering of his peers.

Penalties are generally in the form of rendering service to the community, such as cleaning utensils at the *langar* or cleaning the shoes of the congregation outside a *gurdwara*. If the case is serious enough, further penalties can be imposed, such as reciting prayers (in addition to the required religious routine), organising a *paath* (reading of *Granth Sahib*) or, at times, a monetary donation to a religious or social institution.

An appeal can be made to the Akal Takht but this is rare. Occasionally, the Akal Takht itself imposes penalties in the case of Sikh political leaders.

A *Gurmata* can only be considered in matters concerning the basic principles of the faith and not in the case of any religious, educational, social or political matter. Such a *Gurmata* can be adopted only by a special convening of a general assembly of the *panth* (*Sarbat Khalsa*).

A *Hukum Nama* is confined to extremely serious cases and can only be issued by the *jathedar* of the Akal Takht in consultation with the *jathedars* of the other four *takhts*. This is done only in very serious matters and is not a general practice.

Rituals and Ceremonies

There are many stages in a person's life—birth, marriage (if concluded) and death—which are common to all humans. In addition, there are other occasions which have a spiritual or denominational significance and are not shared by all. Or, when shared—for example, naming or christening a child—the rituals vary.

For Sikhs, the basic ritual for all occasions is standard. It is always conducted in the presence of *Sri Guru Granth Sahib*. In other words, the Eternal Guru is present and sanctifies the proceedings, whether in a *gurdwara* or at home. The participants at the occasion, whether invited (for celebrations) or voluntary (for unhappy events), enter the sanctum with footwear removed and heads covered. They present themselves before the *Guru Granth*, which rests on a palanquin under a canopy, with a *granthi* (man or woman) in attendance holding a *chavar* (a whisk). They kneel and bow, touching their foreheads to the floor. While paying obeisance it is customary, though not obligatory, to place an offering. The devotees' offering is invariably monetary, the amount determined by the individual. At times, particularly in rural areas, the offering is in kind, for example, grain, fruit or confectionery.

Having rendered obeisance, the person finds space in the room and sits down cross-legged on the floor in a position facing the *Guru Granth*. *Kirtan* (singing of *Gurbani*) is usually in progress. Its duration is normally one hour from the appointed time. At the conclusion of the *kirtan*, it is obligatory to recite six verses (the first five and the final) of the 'Anand Sahib' composed by the third guru. While *kirtan* is being rendered, a salver containing *kadah prasad* (sacramental food), covered by a cloth, is brought in and placed on a stool alongside the *Granth Sahib*. The *kirtan* concluded, the congregation rises and, standing with hands joined in reverence, in unison recites a verse (Ast. 4; v.8) from the *Sukhmani* of the fifth guru:

Tu Thakur Tum peh ardas. . .
You are the Master, to You we address our prayer;
We who exist by Your beneficence.
You are the Father and Mother; we are Your children;
Your bounty bestows upon us countless blessings.

Facing page: *On the causeway to the Harimandir.*

No one can know Your infiniteness for You are
the highest of the high.
The entire universe is in Your command.
Your creation is subject only to Your order.
You alone are cognizant of Your attributes.
Nanak, thy servitor, ever acclaims Your glory.

The *granthi*, standing before the *Granth
Sahib*, then offers *ardas*. At its conclusion, all
in the congregation bow and sit down. The
granthi returns to his/her earlier position
behind the *Granth Sahib*, with reverence folds

equal measure to all present by the *granthi*
and/or voluntary assistants. The recipients
remain seated and receive the *prasad* reverently
in cupped hands. This marks the conclusion of
the service and those attending make obeisance
and withdraw from the sanctum. This, then, is
the basic ritual.

There are occasions when *kirtan* is not
arranged. However, if *prasad* is to be
consecrated, reciting six verses of the 'Anand
Sahib' is *de rigueur* before the *ardas*.

Kadah is made according to a prescribed

Children at a wedding.

back the covering, and proceeds to take *vaak*
or *hukum* (reciting the first *shabad* on a page
opened at random).

The next step is distribution of *kadah
prasad*. The *granthi* uncovers the salver,
touches the contents with the point of a *kirpan*
and places aside five portions, the symbolic
share of the *Panj Piarey*. These are given to
five *amritdhari* Sikhs in the assembly or, at
times, restored to the salver and mixed with the
bulk. Thereafter, the *prasad* is distributed in

recipe. One measure each of wheat flour
(whether refined, wholewheat, semolina or a
mix), sugar and *ghee* (clarified butter) and three
measures of water. While *kadah* or *halwa* is
being made, the person making it recites the *Japu*
during preparation. It is only after the confection
has been consecrated that it becomes *prasad*.

The basic rite can be performed as an
integral observance or as part of a reading of
the entire *Granth Sahib*. The commencement is
Arambh. The conclusion is *Samapati* or *Bhog*.

The rite is generally conducted both at the commencement and conclusion of the *paath*.

Some events are usually observed with the participation of family and friends. For Sikhs, all observances are generally marked by an element of religion. In the case of certain events, there is a prescribed way. For others, the format is left to individual choice.

Birth: On the birth of a child, whether boy or girl, the basic ritual may be organised. Otherwise, *ardas* is offered as thanksgiving and to seek God's benevolence for the child.

Dastarbandi (tying a turban): No ceremony is prescribed for the occasion when a turban is for the first time draped around a boy's head. However, some families organise a function for the event. The extent of ceremony and festivity depends on the individual choice of the boy's family.

Amrit Sanskar (rite of initiation as Khalsa): The ritual dates back to 1699 when on Baisakhi Guru Gobind Singh introduced the procedure to transform five Sikhs (*Panj Piarey*) into Khalsa and invested them with the authority

Dastar bandi: *draping a turban for the first time.*

Naamkaran (naming): It is customary for a child to be given a name before he/she is forty days old. The procedure, preceded by the basic ritual in full or part, involves the *granthi* opening the *Guru Granth* at random and taking *vaak*. The initial letter of the first word of the *shabad* determines the initial letter of the child's name. The actual name is chosen by the parents or in consultation with the family. A boy's name is suffixed by 'Singh' and that of a girl by 'Kaur'.

inter alia to admit others into the fraternity. The procedure continues to be substantially the same and applies to both boys and girls.

The sacrament is normally administered to initiates in a group, amidst an assembly in the presence of *Sri Guru Granth Sahib*. Five eminent Singhs, appropriately garbed and wearing a *kirpan*, place water and some *patasa* (a confection made of sugar only) in a vessel made of pure iron. They sit around it in *virasan* (the hero's posture) and stir the liquid

69

with a *khanda* (a double-edged dagger). While stirring, they recite five *banis*: *Japu*, *Jaap*, ten *Swayas*, *Chaupai* and 'Anand Sahib'. This procedure is normally completed in less than two hours. The initiates bathe and wash their hair before the ceremony. Wearing clean clothes and a *kirpan*, they are in attendance listening to the *bani*, while the *amrit* is being prepared.

When recitation of the five *banis* is completed, *ardas* is offered. Thereafter, *amrit* is administered in a certain manner. The initiates are seated in a row in *virasan*. Each one, in

The initiation rite is followed by counsel on the responsibilities voluntarily accepted by the novitiates. They are also made aware of the restrictions and restraints to which they are now subject. This discourse is followed by *ardas*, to render thanks to the Almighty, and by distribution of *kadah prasad*. The recipients are now admitted to the ranks of the Khalsa.

Marriage: The Sikh marriage is called *Anand Karaj* (pp. 74-79).

Shukrana (thanksgiving): The basic ritual may be organised by anyone to mark an

Kirtan at Gurdwara Bangla Sahib in Delhi: the ornate canopy over the palanquin on which lies the Granth Sahib. The raagis are with their backs to the camera.

turn, receives *amrit* five times in the cupped palm of the right hand. Each time he or she is told to repeat, '*Waheguruji ka Khalsa, Waheguruji ki Fateh*' (The Khalsa is of the Wondrous Lord, Victory also is His) and they respond five times. Then *amrit* is sprinkled five times on the eyes and five times on the head; each time accompanied by the initiate uttering the dictum. The remaining liquid is drunk out of the same bowl in turn by all initiates, signifying that they are now all bound as siblings.

occasion such as a birthday, an anniversary, success in an examination, moving into a new home, inauguration of a business; indeed, whenever moved by a spiritual urge.

Death: In case of death, it is customary to bathe the body, dress and place it on a plank or container and carry it on the shoulders of relatives or friends or in a vehicle to the place of cremation. After *ardas*, the body is consigned to the flames. *Shabads*, expressing *vairag* (detachment), are sung.

On return to the house, *Sohila* (the final prayer to be said every night) is recited and *kadah prasad* distributed. On the day of cremation a *sahaj* (simple, easy, in stages) *paath* is begun. The ashes need not be taken to any particular place. They may be immersed in a convenient location which has continuously flowing water or in the ocean.

Lamentation, keening or wailing is not permissible. Death is the inevitable conclusion of birth. It should therefore bring no surprise. As Guru Teg Bahadur wrote:

(i) *Sadharan* (simple) or *khula* (open ended) *paath*, a reading of the Holy Book from beginning to end in convenient intervals. Sikhs are expected to practice this always in their daily lives.

(ii) *Akhand* (uninterrupted) reading of the *Granth Sahib*. This ritual is organised at special occasions of joy, sorrow, difficulty or purely out of devotion. The reading from cover to cover is to be completed in forty-eight hours, in relay by a group which need not comprise any specific number of people. Ideally, the *paath*

In the Harimandir a devotee offers a personal ardas.

Chinta ta ki keejiye jo anhoni hoey
Eh marag sansar ko Nanak thir nahin koey
Be concerned about that which is abnormal.
This (death) is the way of the world,
O Nanak, there are no exceptions.

The conclusion of the *paath* is on the tenth day when the basic ritual is organised. No further observance is required.

Basically there are two methods of conducting a *paath*:

should be undertaken by members of a family or a group from the *sangat*. However, this has now given place to *paathis* who are paid to undertake the *paath*.

Another method followed at times is the *Saptah Paath* which is to be completed in seven days by one or more readers.

Following pages 72-73: *Smearing* haldi *(turmeric) paste on a bridegroom . . . part of the pre-wedding revelry.*

71

Anand Karaj
The Sikh Marriage Ceremony

Karaj (derived from the Sanskrit *karya*) means literally work or undertaking. In a solemn sense, it also means 'ceremony'. *Anand* is also a Sanskrit word and means literally 'satisfaction' or 'bliss'.

Marriage according to this rite has been sporadically practised amongst Sikhs since the 17th century. In modern times, legal sanction was accorded to it in October 1909 when the Anand Marriage Act was promulgated.

In the case of arranged marriages, the parents of the boy and girl meet to signify mutual consent to the match and to discuss details of the ceremony. No dowry is demanded or given. (Of course, there are glaring exceptions to this custom in present times. Those observing this rule are, however, still to be found.)

A Sikh marriage is not a sacrament or a contract. It is an act of spiritual union, which is accorded religious sanction, and which is consciously and voluntarily embraced by the boy and girl in the solemn presence of the *Granth Sahib.*

The ceremonial for the marriage begins with the arrival of the *barat* (the bridegroom and his parents, accompanied by relatives and friends) at the place of the marriage (the bride's home or a *gurdwara* or any other designated place). The bride's parents, relatives and friends await them at the entrance to the premises. The bridegroom's party stops a few steps away. The following *shabad* is then recited in unison:

Raag Suhi
(Composed by Guru Nanak)
Hum ghar saajan aye

* * * *

Friends have come to our home;
The True One has brought about this meeting.
Through love have we met by the Lord's Grace, and we derive joy by meeting good souls;
Thus have we attained that for which we yearned.
The wish is to meet every day, my home is blessed;

Within me unending music is sounding, for Friends have come to our home.

After the *shabad* has been recited, *ardas* is offered.

Then the *milni*, or meeting, takes place. Essentially, it is between the father of the boy and the father of the girl. But, in some cases, it is extended to include some corresponding male relatives of the couple-to-be, for example, grandfather, uncles and brothers. The fathers (and any others agreed for *milni*) garland each other and embrace. The *barat* is then escorted into the house.

The party proceeds to the place where the marriage is to be solemnised. The *Granth Sahib* is enthroned on a decorated palanquin. *Raagis* are reciting *shabads* while the congregation gathers and, after paying obeisance before the *Granth Sahib,* sits down on the floor facing the Book. The bridegroom sits at the designated place before the *Granth Sahib.* The bride is escorted in by her brothers, sisters and friends to her place to the left of the bridegroom.

At the outset the following *shabad* is recited:

Sloka in Raag Sri
(composition of Guru Nanak)
Kita lodiye kam so har pai akhiye

* * * *

To seek success in any undertaking, request the Lord.
By the Grace of His teaching, your objective will be fulfilled.
In the company of holy men, imbibe the nectar—the treasury of goodness.
Oh Thou dispeller of fear, protect Thy servitor.
(Sayeth) Nanak, by singing His praises one may realise the Fathomless Lord.

The actual ceremony begins with an offering of a special *ardas* when only the boy, girl and their respective parents stand up while the rest of the congregation remains seated. Upon completion of the *ardas*, those standing pay obeisance to the *Granth Sahib* and sit down.

The *granthi* then takes *vak* (reciting the first *shabad* on a page opened at random, sometimes beginning on the previous page).

Next, the bride's father proceeds to a position behind the couple and places in the hand of his daughter the edge of the *palla*, or stole, which the bridegroom has around his neck. (The symbolism is equivalent to *kanya dan* or the western custom of 'giving away the bride'.) This action is accompanied by the following *sloka* recited by the *raagis*:

Sloka in Raag Ramkali
(Composition of the 5th Guru Arjan)
Ustat ninda, Nanak, ji mai hab vanjayi chodiya hab kichh tiyagi,
Habay sak kudavay ditthe tau pallai tehnde laagi.

* * * *

I have become immune to praise and criticism, O Nanak, and have renounced all;
Having seen all other worldly attachments to be false,
I take hold of your *palla*.

The next stage is the four *lavan* (the four marriage vows in verse form, see I, II, III and IV below) and the circumambulation of the *Granth Sahib*. Each *lav* is first read by the *granthi*, the *raagis* then recite it to music. As they commence, the couple bow to the *Granth Sahib*, get up and walk slowly (clockwise with the boy leading) around the palanquin. By the time they return to their place the recital has been completed. They pay obeisance to the *Granth Sahib* and sit down. Then the second, third and fourth *lavs* are repeated similarly; first read out by the *granthi* and then recited by the *raagis* as the couple walk around the *Granth Sahib*. During the fourth *lav* it has become a custom to shower flower petals on the bridal couple as they walk around.

I

Raag Suhi
(Composition of the 4th Guru Ram Das)
Har pahldi lav parvirti karam dridaya Bal Ram jio

* * * *

In the First Round, the Lord Wishes you to be firm in the performance of your worldly duties;
Regard the Word of the Creator, as the Vedas indicate the path of duty and the manner to avoid wrong-doing.
Be firm in righteousness, meditate upon the Lord's Name which the Smritis (Vedic scriptures) have eulogised.
Worship the True and Perfect Lord whose Grace will free you of all sins.
The Lord's Name will pervade and true bliss will descend on you.
Says Nanak, with this First Round, the marriage has been initiated.

II

Har doojdi lav Satgur purukh milaya Bal Ram jio

* * * *

In the Second Round your God has deigned to unite you with your partner.
Submitting to the Fearless, you shed the taint of the ego by the Grace of the Lord.
Deference to the Divine and singing His praises reveals to you the presence of the Lord.
Within and without every soul dwells the Lord and all beings are fulfilled.
Says Nanak, with the Second Round there is unsung rejoicing within.

III

Har teejdi lav man chao bhiya bairagiya Bal Ram jio

* * * *

With the Third Round the mind yearns for detachment.
In the company of good souls, one is fortunate to discover the Lord.
The pure Lord is attained and one sings His praises.
The good souls see the Great and attempt to describe the Indescribable;
In every soul resounds the Divine song, and one recites the Name if blest.
Says Nanak, with the Third Round (the seed of) detachment sprouts in the mind.

Following pages 76-77: At a marriage . . . the couple making obeisance to the Granth Sahib *(not shown) at the commencement of a* lav.

75

IV

*Har chouthdi lav man sahaj bhiya Har paiya
Bal Ram jio*

* * * *

In the Fourth Round the mind is enlightened
and realisation of the Lord is achieved.
By the Lord's Grace the mind attains bliss as the
sweetness of the Lord's presence pervades
body and mind.
The euphoria of this attachment pleases the Lord
and I am ever drawn closer to Him.
The heart's desire has been fulfilled and I am
felicitated by His Grace.

The first verse expresses rejoicing at
attainment of the Lord.

The second exhorts the being to maintain the
union and never to forget the Lord who is the
Fount of all joys and blessings.

The third beseeches the Lord to bestow the
wisdom never to forget Him.

The fourth advises never to forget the true
Lord, the basic support of all.

The fifth explains that the ability to adore
Him is attained only by good fortune.

The final describes how, by reciting this
bani, one may aspire to union with the

The sarbhala . . . *the groom's 'best man'.*

The Master has ordained this marriage and the
bride's heart is filled with joy.
Says Nanak, with this Fourth Round I have
attained the Eternal Lord.

Immediately thereafter six verses of the
'Anand Sahib' are recited.

Raag Ramkali
Anand bhiya meri maye Satguru mai paiya.

* * * *

Lord, to shed pain and sin, and to attain
bliss.

The next *shabad* to be recited is quoted
below and connotes the joy of the bride in
having acquired a life partner. (Here, again, the
shabad is a tribute to God and expresses joy at
having attained the stage of harmony with the
Almighty. It is adopted as part of the ritual of
Anand Karaj.)

78

Raag Sri
(composition of the 4th Guru Ram Das)
Vivah hoa mere Babula
* * * *

O my father, I am married (for) by the Guru's
  Grace I have attained the Lord.
The darkness of ignorance has been dispelled
  and I forcefully realise the Lord's wishes.
Knowledge of the Guru's wisdom has dawned
  on me, darkness banished and I have found
  the gift of the Divine Jewel.
The blight of ego has disappeared, my pain
  alleviated as I imbibe the Divine knowledge.

Poori asa ji meri mansa
* * * *

O my Lord, all my expectations and desires
  are fulfilled.
I am worthless while you, Lord, possess all
  the virtues.
O my Lord, you embody all virtues, with
  what words can I praise You?
You are oblivious of my doings or faults (but)
  forgive me instantly.
I have been blest with the Nine Treasures (of
  Your Name) and am in bliss.
Says Nanak, I have found my Lord within

Parting is such sweet sorrow . . . . brothers carrying the bride to the doli. *A* doli *is a palanquin in which
a bride was traditionally carried to her new home. Now it is invariably a decorated car.*

I have realised the Eternal and the Indestructible,
  who is Immortal and Omnipresent.
O my father, I am married (for) by the Guru's
  Grace I have attained the Lord.

Then the following *shabad* is recited to
signify that all wishes have been fulfilled by the
Grace of God:

Raag Vadhans
(Composition of the 5th Guru Arjan)

myself and all my sorrows are dispelled.
  At the conclusion, *ardas* is again offered.
Upon completion, the congregation pays
obeisance to the *Granth Sahib* and resumes its
position. A *vak* is then taken by the *granthi*.
Thereafter, while *kadah prasad* is distributed to
all, the couple are garlanded and felicitations
and greetings exchanged. During garlanding,
care is taken that one's back is not turned on
the *Granth Sahib*.

THE FOLK
*

Their Land and Lives

The Panjab (*panj,* five; *ab,* water or river), land
of the five rivers, is the cradle of the Sikh faith.
It is also at a geographical crossroads.
Incursions and invasions into India traversed
this land over the centuries—Greeks, Persians,
Mongols, Turks, Afghans. The epic war of
Mahabharat was fought at Kurukshetra. The
Indus valley civilisation, Buddhist influence in
Mauryan times, Kanishka, all left an imprint.
Thus, ethnically and culturally, the people of
the region are the product of many influences.

The terrain is largely a plain, sloping down
from the sub-Himalayas in the north towards
the Thar Desert in the west. The climate varies
between intense heat and cold interspersed with
summer and winter rains. These factors have
determined the largely farming occupation of
the people and the cropping pattern. The
advent of canal irrigation from the late
nineteenth century onwards augmented water
supply and increased cultivable areas, thereby
benefiting the Panjabi farmer.

It is against the backdrop of this legacy that
the Sikh faith evolved. The great majority of the
estimated eighteen million Sikhs are to be found
in the Panjab. Among those in other parts, it
would be rare to find one not having roots in that
state. Wherever they be they are distinguishable
by their beards and colourful turbans.

The Sikhs share many characteristics with
their fellow Panjabis. Some, however, are
uniquely their own. The historical experience
has made them survivors and hospitable; also

Facing page: *Listening attentively to a discourse at a*
gurdwara.

generous and with a zest for life. This is
expressed in the old saw:

Khada peeta laye da, rehnda Nadir Shahe da
What is consumed has worth, what remains is
for Nadir Shah.

Whatever appeals to a Sikh as a cause becomes
an article of faith, to be pursued at times to the
extreme. There are numerous examples in
history. One of the more notable in recent
times is the Guru ka Bagh *morcha* (agitation) in
1922 when, in pursuit of *gurdwara* reforms, the
Akalis (the political arm of the SGPC) defied the
administration and faced police brutality,
unflinching in their resolve to remain non-
violent. The government finally conceded the
Akali demands. Mahatma Gandhi then sent a
telegram to Baba Kharak Singh: 'The first
decisive battle for independence won.
Congratulations.' Soon after, Pandit Madan
Mohan Malviya, in a speech when visiting
Amritsar, said: 'I cannot resist asking every
Hindu home to have at least one male child
initiated into the fold of the Khalsa. What I see
here before my eyes is nothing short of a
miracle in our whole history' (in Gopal Singh,
1979, p. 657).

Sikhs are generally quick to take offence, also
to accept an apology. An exception is when their
faith or symbols are ridiculed. Otherwise, they
have an inherent sense of humour. It is said that
the majority of jokes about the Sikhs are
authored by Sikhs themselves. They can be
brash, full of confidence and at times aggressive
but with gentleness, reason and coaxing will
agree to a great deal. Peremptory behaviour will
invariably get their backs up.

Historically, Panjab has had an agrarian economy. The people have been good farmers. The Sikhs have also made excellent soldiers. In addition, they are renowned artisans, carpenters, metal workers and mechanics, for they are adaptive, innovative and inventive. They have made agricultural implements and farm machinery at a fraction of the cost of factory manufactured items.

Sikhs have also made a mark in sports, the civil services, industry, the professions, the fine arts—indeed in all aspects of national life and

martyrs. While both considerations are relevant in relation to the Sikh faith, there is a deeper and more fundamental compulsion: complete faith in and devotion to God which is basic to the creed. Love implies sacrifice if not total surrender. If a Sikh is enjoined to love and willingly submit to the One God, he or she must be prepared also to sacrifice everything, including his/her life, for that love. Long before the Sikhs faced hostility and persecution, Guru Nanak wrote (*Adi Granth, shloka* 20, p.1412):

A group of women in a procession at Baisakhi celebrations in Anandpur.

endeavour. In brief, they are an important segment of the diversity, or variety, in which exists the unity of India.

Their Martyrs and Heroes

Every social group has heroes. This would seem to be a necessary focus for the cohesion if not survival of the fraternity. One that has faced adversity and active hostility during its evolution, would also have its

Jau tau prem khelan ka chau. . .
  If you are eager to indulge in (the game of) love come join me with your head placed on the palm of your hand.
  Should you step upon this path,
  Offer your head without regarding it as a favour (to anyone).

Thus, Sikh history recounts tales of many a martyr and many a hero. Guru Arjan was the first martyr of the new faith. Seven decades later, Guru Teg Bahadur became the second. Both could have saved their lives by compromising on principles. Neither succumbed to any temptation. The fifth guru was subjected to fiendish torture before his soul left body. The ninth guru, before he was beheaded, was made to witness the killing by torture of two faithful Sikhs: Bhai Mati Das and Bhai Diala. They all endured their treatment as *Bhana* (the Will of God) and met their end with prayer on their lips.

The *Panj Piarey*, that is, the Five Beloved, who

Singh at Anandpur but some days later returned to assist him at Khidraana (now Muktsar) and were all killed, are referred to as the *chali mukte* (the forty emancipated).

All of them have special mention in the *ardas*.

Banda Singh Bahadur, who was charged personally by the tenth guru in 1708 to continue his mission in the Panjab, fought many a battle with the Moghul forces until he was captured and put to death in Delhi in 1716.

There followed turmoil and conflict in the Panjab during the greater part of the eighteenth

A view of the contingent of the Sikh Light Infantry at a ceremonial parade.

are the nucleus of the Khalsa, are also regarded as martyrs in as much as they volunteered to sacrifice their lives at the call of their guru.

The four sons of Guru Gobind Singh are all martyrs. Ajit Singh and Jhujhar Singh, aged eighteen and fourteen respectively, fell in the Battle of Chamkaur. The two younger ones, Zorawar Singh (nine years) and Fateh Singh (six years), were executed upon their refusal to convert to Islam.

The forty who had disowned Guru Gobind

century. It saw the waning of Moghul power due to a variety of reasons—weak rulers in Delhi, Sikh defiance, the several incursions of Nadir Shah and Ahmed Shah Abdali. The Sikhs were ruthlessly persecuted during much of this time but remained true to their faith. Many were martyred: Bhai Tara Singh, Bhai Mani Singh, Bhai Bota Singh, Bhai Taru Singh, Subeg Singh, Shahbaz Singh, to name a few.

The most hallowed shrine of the Sikhs, the Harimandir, was twice desecrated and avenged

83

each time. First, in 1737, Masse Khan (known as Massa Ranghar), a Moghul official, had the sacred pool filled up and had horses tethered in the precincts. In the sanctum he witnessed performances by nautch girls while smoking a *hookah*. This was avenged by Bhai Mehtab Singh and Bhai Sukha Singh who came to Amritsar, entered the shrine in disguise, killed Massa Ranghar and escaped. They were later captured and killed.

In 1757, the Harimandir was demolished by order of Ahmed Shah Abdali. Baba Dip Singh

Their persecution apparently fuelled their defiance and gave currency to a doggerel (quoted in a Persian manuscript called *Ibrat Namah*):

Manu asadi datri asi Manu de So-ay
Jiyon jiyon Manu vadhada gharin gharin asi hoey
Manu is the sickle and we for Manu the weeds.
The more of us he mows the more we
profilerate in every home.

Then there were the two *ghallugharas* (massacres or holocausts): the *chhota* (small)

Takht Patna Sahib: the birthplace of the tenth guru, Gobind Singh (1666-1708). The gurdwara was constructed later at the direction of Maharaja Ranjit Singh.

and many companions were martyred while leading a Sikh force to avenge this sacrilege. There were times when a price had been put on Sikhs and they were hounded as animals.

In 1748 Muin-ud-Din or Mir Mannu was appointed governor of Lahore and Multan. 'As soon, therefore, as Mir Mannu was firmly established in his authority he addressed himself to the task of suppressing the Sikhs' (G.C. Narang, 1992, p.127). His objective was, as S.M. Latif terms it, 'to extirpate the nation' (quoted by Narang).

and *vaddha* (large) respectively in 1746 and 1762. An estimated 20,000 Sikhs—men, women and children—were killed during the two episodes.

Heroism and sacrifice continued during British rule, whether for national freedom or in religious matters. The Kuka movement, the

Facing page: *In the parikrama of Harimandir Sahib. The spot where Baba Dip Singh fell while leading a Sikh force to avenge the demolition of the Harimandir in 1757 under orders of Ahmed Shah Abdali.*

Ghadar (Revolution) party, the *morchas* (agitations) for *gurdwara* reforms, the *Komagata Maru* episode, the martyrdom of Bhagat Singh and numerous others who went to the gallows or, worse, were sent to *kala pani* (incarceration for life in the Andamans).

The gallantry of the Indian armed forces, both pre- and post-independence, is justifiably renowned. In this record, Sikh officers and men in all three Services occupy a proud place.

The call of the country or the faith has always received a ready response from Sikhs.

with a mart where goods, even animals, are bought and sold. Entertainment does not lag behind. Various shows and games are organised.

There are numerous events in the calendar. Many carry a local emphasis. Others have a wider observance. There are some, however, that are basic and are celebrated wherever there are Sikhs.

Baisakhi is the only festival fixed by the solar calendar. It occurs on 13 April. (Once every thirty-six years it falls on 14 April.) The others

Flowers for the faithful . . . Garlands of marigolds, which had rested on the Granth Sahib, *being given to the devout during a Gurpurab procession.*

Their Festivals

For Sikhs, observing anniversaries of historical events is celebrative in nature. Most occasions are festive while some, commemorating tragic events, are somewhat sedate. Even these carry a festive aura as they recall heroic sacrifice. Because people congregate, the day is termed *mela*, a meeting. At times, especially in rural areas but often even in cities, they attract tradesmen. A *mela* then becomes associated

are all observed according to the lunar calendar, hence the variation in dates every year.

Baisakhi is the first day of Baisakh, the first month of the Bikrami calendar. Apart from ushering in a new year, it has traditionally been observed as a harvest festival in the Panjab.

For Sikhs, the practice of gathering on this day in order to pay homage to the guru was originated by the third guru, Amar Das, almost 450 years ago. Since 1699, the day has an added significance since it marks the day when

Guru Gobind Singh transformed the Sikhs into a new fraternity. It is thus the birth anniversary of the Khalsa.

The occasion is celebrated with enthusiasm. *Akhand paaths* and *kirtans* are held in almost all *gurdwaras*. *Langar* is served. Particularly at larger centres, initiation (*amrit*) ceremonies ·are organised to induct youth (or even older persons) into the Khalsa brotherhood. At some locations, especially in rural areas and smaller towns, fairs are held at which traders set up stalls to sell foodstuffs and merchandise. Trading

November). Since time immemorial, Hindus have observed it as a day to honour and worship Lakshmi, the consort of Vishnu and the goddess of wealth and beauty. The practice of illuminating homes with oil lamps was evidently introduced to ward off the malignant spirits of darkness. It also came to be associated with the return to Ayodhya of Lord Rama, at the end of his fourteen-year exile and after having defeated Ravana in an epic battle—a celebration of the victory of good over evil.

Guru Amar Das had initiated the practice of

Distribution of kadah prasad *at the conclusion of a religious ceremony.*

of cattle, animal races, wrestling contests, and other sporting events are organised.

Subsequent events which occurred on this day have added to its notability. Special mention is merited of Jalianvala Bagh in Amritsar where, on this day in 1919, a group of unarmed civilians, for the major part Sikhs, became targets of imperial bullets.

Divali or Dipavali, the festival of lights, is celebrated on Amavasya (the last day of the waning moon) in the month of Kartik (October-

asking Sikhs to come to Goindval on the occasion of Divali in addition to Baisakhi. Thus the day had already become an annual occasion for Sikhs to congregate at the seat of the gurus.

In the early seventeenth century, around 1620, the return to Amritsar of Guru Har Gobind after his release from the Fort at Gwalior, coincided with this day. The revered Sikh, Baba Buddha,

Following pages 88-89: *Bullock-cart race; part of rural sports.*

established the practice of illuminating the town of Amritsar to commemorate the occasion. *Gurdwaras* and Sikh homes are widely illuminated on the night of Divali.

Hola Mohalla is a fete introduced in the year 1700 by Guru Gobind Singh. Since then it has been an important annual feature in the Sikh calendar.

Holi is an old springtime festival, centred on recalling the frolicking of Lord Krishna. It is observed on the full moon day of the month of Chet (March-April). People traditionally indulge

means the place of attack. Thus, *hola mohalla;* that is attack and the place of attack.

The purpose was to instruct and drill his followers in the art of warfare. Competitions were held in wrestling, archery, manual combat with sword and shield, combat on horseback, dagger play, and so on. War games and competitions took place. Teams were constituted led by renowned captains—one to attack a location defended by the other. The guru himself observed the manoeuvers and adjudged. Thus he prepared his followers for

Preparations for the langar.

in sprinking colour, liquid or powder, on each other in gay abandon, accompanied by other manifestations of gaiety and revelry.

The tenth guru considered this to be somewhat frivolous. Consequently, he decided to introduce a more purposeful observance of the advent of spring. It was designated on the day after Holi and held at Holgarh, a fort at Anandpur. He devised an observance centred on manly pursuits. The word *hola* is adapted from *halla*, meaning attack, while *mohalla*

the challenges of armed struggle which he undoubtedly foresaw to be in the offing.

The day has certainly lost its original military significance. Nevertheless, it has retained the flavour of its origin. Large numbers still assemble especially at Anandpur to celebrate this festival. Nihangs (a particular group of Sikhs) in their panoply, reminiscent of their original role, congregate at Anandpur. Colourful processions are seen. Displays of horsemanship, tent-pegging and mock-combat are held.

90

Competitions in various skills, including *gatka* (a preliminary training for fighting with a mace), are organised. Now a *mela* in essence but with a meaningful historical background, the day is celebrated at other places also though perhaps with lesser display.

Gurpurab is the observance of an event related to the lives of the gurus. Four amongst them have a pre-eminence.

The principal Gurpurab is the birth anniversary of Guru Nanak, the founder of the faith. This is universally celebrated, wherever there are Sikhs, waxing moon in the month of Maghar (November-December). While it is widely observed, the focus centres on *gurdwaras* Sis Ganj and Rakab Ganj in Delhi.

The birth anniversary of Guru Gobind Singh is celebrated on the seventh day of the waxing moon in the month of Poh (December-January).

Other days observed are the anniversaries of the birth, installation and death of the gurus, as also some historic occasions, such as the installation of the *Granth Sahib* in Harimandir. So also the day on which the tenth guru

Holi revelry. Two friends throwing red powder on each other.

on the full moon day of the month of Kartik (October-November).

The anniversary of Guru Arjan's martyrdom falls on the fourth day of the waxing moon in the month of Jesht (May-June). A distinctive feature of this observance is the setting up of *chhabils* (locations where drinking water is available). Cool water, invariably sweetened, is served by volunteers to wayfarers and passersby.

The anniversary of Guru Teg Bahadur's martyrdom occurs on the fifth day of the designated the Holy Book as the eternal Guru and the martyrdom days of the tenth guru's four young sons.

Their Diaspora

The Sikh faith originated and grew in the Panjab. It is in this land therefore that Sikhs, wherever they be, have their roots.

For a variety of reasons, not least their sense of boldness, some ventured out from their homes.

The partition of the country in 1947, when Panjab was divided, gave an impetus to migration to other parts of India and to other countries.

The earliest moves abroad commenced in the latter part of the nineteenth century. Sikhs went to Britain, Canada, and California. Some were taken by the British to Hongkong and Shanghai as policemen. East Africa became a destination in the wake of the railway being built there. Some went to Panama when the canal was being constructed. Many moved to Thailand, Malaysia, Singapore and Indonesia as traders in

other parts of the world: Nepal, Japan, Australia, New Zealand and a scattering in some South American countries.

Wherever they are present in sufficient numbers, they have built *gurdwaras*, more than one in many cities. Where there is an inadequate number, the *Granth Sahib* is likely to be kept in individual homes.

As for their occupations, Sikhs have made an acceptable place for themselves wherever they are. In many countries, they are into the second or even third generation. Many have achieved

A group of young American Sikhs on a visit to Anandpur.

textiles. Sikhs also went to Afghanistan, Iran, Iraq, Burma (now Myanmar), the Philippines, China and to many countries in the erstwhile British Empire. Sikhs are now also to be found in several countries in Europe, like France, Germany, Italy, Belgium. They are also found in

Previous pages 92-93: *Tent pegging. Part of the festival of Hola Mohalla at Anandpur.*
Facing page: *A young girl carrying a* sarangi *(a string instrument) being tuned by the teacher.*

outstanding success. There was a Sikh Member of Congress in the United States. Sikhs are Members of Parliament in London and Ottawa, and members of municipal bodies in some countries. They are successful businessmen, lawyers, judges, physicians, surgeons, architects, engineers and other professionals in many countries, also civil servants in some. Many have made a notable contribution to the societies in which they live.

REFERENCES

Bhai Kahan Singh, *Gur Shabd Ratnakar-Mahan Kosh* (Gurmukhi), Language Department, Government of Panjab, Patiala. First published 1930, reprinted 1974.

Fauja Singh and Kirpal Singh, *Atlas: Travels of Guru Nanak*, Panjabi University, Patiala, 1976.

Harbans Singh, *Encyclopaedia of Sikhism*. Panjabi University, Patiala, 1992.

Sahib Singh, *Japuji Sahib Satik* (Gurmukhi), Singh Brothers, Amritsar, 1973.

W. G. Archer, *Paintings of the Sikhs*, H.M. Stationery Office, London, 1966.

FURTHER READING

Avtar Singh, *Ethics of the Sikhs*, Panjabi University, Patiala, 1983.

G. C. Narang, *Transformation of Sikhism*, Kalyani Publishers, New Delhi. First published 1912, reprinted 1992.

Gopal Singh, *A History of the Sikh People*, World Sikh University Press, 1979.

G. S. Mansukhani, *Life of Guru Nanak*, Guru Nanak Foundation, New Delhi, 1974.

Gunindar Kaur, *The Guru Granth Sahib*, Sterling Publishers, New Delhi, 1981.

Harbans Singh, *Guru Nanak and Origins of the Sikh Faith*, Asia Publishing House, 1969.

—————.*The Heritage of the Sikhs*, Manohar Publications, New Delhi, 1983.

J. D. Cunningham, *History of the Sikhs*, Low Price Publications, Delhi. First published 1849, reprinted 1990.

J. S. Grewal, *The Sikhs of the Panjab*, Cambridge University Press and Orient Longman, New Delhi, 1990.

Khushwant Singh, *A History of the Sikhs*. Vol. I. Princeton University Press, Princeton, 1963.

M. A. Macauliffe, *The Sikh Religion,* 6 volumes, Oxford University Press, 1909. Reprinted.

Shiromani Gurdwara Prabhandak Committee (S.G.P.C), *Sikh Rehat-Maryada* (Gurmukhi), Amritsar.

W. Owen Cole and Piara Singh Sambhi, *The Sikhs—Their Religious Beliefs and Practices*, Vikas Publishing House, New Delhi, 1978.

ACUPUNCTURE TREATMENT FOR MUSCULOSKELETAL PAIN

ACUPUNCTURE TREATMENT FOR MUSCULOSKELETAL PAIN

A TEXTBOOK FOR ORTHOPAEDICS, ANESTHESIA, AND REHABILITATION

Harris Gellman, MD

University of Miami
Florida, USA

TAYLOR & FRANCIS
ALERE FLAMMAM
· Founded 1798 ·

USA	Publishing Office:	TAYLOR & FRANCIS 29 West 35th Street New York, NY 10001 Tel: (212) 216-7800 Fax: (212) 564-7854
	Distribution Center:	TAYLOR & FRANCIS 7625 Empire Drive Florence, KY 41042 Tel: 1-800-624-7064 Fax: 1-800-248-4724
UK		TAYLOR & FRANCIS 27 Church Road Hove E. Sussex, BN3 2FA Tel: +44 (0) 1273 207411 Fax: +44 (0) 1273 205612

ACUPUNCTURE TREATMENT FOR MUSCULOSKELETAL PAIN

1 2 3 4 5 6 7 8 9 0

Printed by McNaughton & Gunn, Inc, Saline, MI, 2002.

A CIP catalog record for this book is available from the British Library.
   The paper in this publication meets the requirements of the ANSI Standard Z39.48-1984 (Permanence of Paper).

Library of Congress Cataloging-in-Publication Data
CIP information available from publishers.

ISBN 90-5702-516-7

I thank my wife for her support and patience without which I could not have completed this book; To my children, I thank them for their unconditional love; To my mentors and teachers, I thank them for their friendship and the stimulation to seek knowledge; and to the contributors, I thank them for the willingness to share their knowledge and give of their time to make this an outstanding work.

CONTENTS

PREFACE

In today's changing medical environment, physicians are being called upon to provide more comprehensive care—by patients as well as their insurance carriers. Patients expect more from us as physicians in our ability to manage both acute and chronic pain. Many of our patients are becoming aware of such treatment alternatives as acupuncture, homeopathy, and Chinese herbal medicine, and expect that we, as physicians, should also have an understanding of these techniques. Until recently, many physicians have ignored the techniques used in China for thousands of years to treat pain and other maladies, however, many United States medical schools now include courses in acupuncture and alternative medicine in their curricula.

I personally have been interested for many years in the use of alternative methods to treat patients who have been treatment failures, in an attempt to achieve at least some measure of improvement. Many of these patients have valid complaints of pain. The inability to cure or even improve these complaints has led to a search for a way to help. We, as western trained physicians, tend to focus on specific complaints that we can rapidly identify and treat, ignoring the ones we feel are unrelated. Eastern philosophy is much different. The relationships between the organ systems are well recognized, allowing seemingly unrelated sets of complaints to be identified as a weakness or overactivity of energy within a single organ system or group of organ systems.

Western physicians are traditionally taught that the body's physiologic functions are mediated by hormones, polypeptides, and neurotransmitters that are released and transported through the blood. The Chinese, or eastern, philosophy of medicine and healing is based on the body's energy or *Chi*. This system or paradigm of medicine is different than ours, but in many ways, just as valid. To understand and use acupuncture for the treatment of disease and pain, one must accept some of the basic philosophies of Chinese medicine.

Traditionally, western trained physicians initially have trouble understanding the concept of chi or energy flow. Interestingly, these same physicians have no trouble understanding the ability to measure the electrical energy of the heart using EKG monitoring, or the brain with an EEG. The use of electricity to augment fracture healing when a non-union or delayed-union is present has become an accepted technique. A natural extension of this is the understanding that all of the body's organs are surrounded by an electric field, which we are capable of measuring, should we so choose. Extending these concepts to include the concept of chi, we realize that, not only is there an electric field that surrounds the body, but also one that flows within the body. These energy fields flowing within the body move through meridians or channels. This is a very basic explanation of the concept of chi. The energy within and around each organ system can affect other organs and organ systems. The organ systems are related to each other by radiant energy fields very similar to the harmonics of radio waves.

Blockage of energy flow results in disease and pain. Unblocking the flow of energy helps to cure disease and alleviate pain. This is one area where the western and eastern medical systems differ. We have been taught that to cure disease and alleviate pain medications with measurable pharmacological levels must be used. Although we are not yet able to fully measure the effect of acupuncture in stimulating the neuro-endocrine system the effect is readily apparent in the patient's response. Studies have shown that neurotransmitters and endorphins are released during electrical stimulation of acupuncture needles.

While practicing hand surgery in Southern California, I have had the opportunity to observe and interact with many practitioners of acupuncture and Chinese medicine. During this time I saw dramatic improvement in some of my patients with refractory pain after receiving acupuncture treatments. This improvement renewed my interest in other methods available to use when treating these patients. This book is written in an attempt to impart some of this information, in the hope that it will be useful in patient care. The purpose of this text is not to draw anyone away from their present treatment regimens, but to add to the armamentarium of available techniques for patient care. As you read this text, you will progress on a journey through healing in a way which will serve as a useful adjunct to the procedures and medications currently in use.

LIST OF CONTRIBUTORS

C. Chan Gunn, MD
Medical Director, Gunn Pain Clinic
Vancouver, BC Canada

Clinical Professor, Multidisciplinary Pain Center
University of Washington
Seattle, WA USA

President ISTOP, Institute for the Study and Treatment of Pain
Vancouver, BC Canada

May C. M. Pian-Smith MD, MS
Department of Anesthesia and Critical Care, Massachusetts General Hospital
Harvard Medical School
Boston, MA USA

Francis W. K. Smith, Jr, DVM, DACVIM (Medicine, Cardiology)
Managing Member, Veterinary Consultants LLC
Lexington, MA USA

Lang Ha Pham MD
Anesthesia Associates of New Mexico
New Mexico Pain and Wellness Center
Albuquerque, NM USA

Mark D. Seem, PhD, LAc
Founder and President of the Tri-State College of Acupuncture
Former President of the National Council of Acupuncture Schools and Colleges
Maintains a private practice in Manhattan, NY USA

Stephen M. Taylor, DO
The Center for Pain Management
Fort Worth, TX USA

PART I

BASICS OF ACUPUNCTURE

1

INTRODUCTION TO ACUPUNCTURE AND CHINESE MEDICINE

Harris Gellman, M.D.

The Chinese system of medicine uses a different paradigm than that of western medicine. Although eastern and western systems of medicine may seem diametrically opposed, they *can* be used together to complement each other and provide a more complete treatment program for the patient.

Traditional Chinese medicine recognizes that the body is divided by a series of meridians or channels into an orderly network. These lines form a longitudinal course around the body. This complex system of channels and their connecting vessels act as the distribution system that carries *Chi* (energy), blood, and the body fluids around the body. One must not be tempted to think of the meridians or channels in the same way in which we think of blood vessels because conventional anatomy and physiology would not be able to identify these pathways in the same physical sense.

The origins of acupuncture are impossible to define because they lie in periods before recorded history. The acupuncture channels and their corresponding points were described as early as 200 BC in the classic ancient work on acupuncture, the *Huang Di Nei Jing*. The channels (meridians) were compared to the great rivers in China, extending to all parts of the country, keeping it alive by providing the essential water and nutrients.

According to traditional concepts, Chi is the dynamic vital energy present in all living things which flows through these channels, regulating the body's functions. These channels connect the interior of the body with the exterior. This interlacing network of meridians is the essence of traditional acupuncture. A basic principle of acupuncture is that by stimulating points on the surface of the body, an effect occurs that is transmitted through the meridians and ultimately into the interior of the body. Therefore, by utilizing the external or surface acupuncture points, it is possible to exert a direct therapeutic effect on the channels and organs, and thus the body's internal functions. Chi has five major functions in the body. Movement, including involuntary movements and activities like thinking and dreaming; protection of the body from pathological and environmental agents; transformation of food into blood and urine; governing retention of the body's substance by holding organs in their proper place; and lastly, warming the body.

Chinese medicine sees all illness as a process of energetic disharmony. Modern western medicine tends to be divisive, looking at individual body parts and functions without always considering their relation to the body as a whole. Chinese medicine works in a circular way, believing that there are many factors that create a pattern of imbalance, disharmony or disease. The heart of Chinese medicine lies in recognizing these patterns of disease. Acupuncture tries to reestablish this harmony, stimulating the body's own natural healing ability.

THE ORGANS

The concept of organs in Chinese medicine is quite different from that of traditional western medicine. Understanding this difference is very important because the pathophysiology and pathology of the organs is fundamental to the understanding and treatment of disease. The salient characteristic of the Chinese concept of the organs is the lack of emphasis on the physical structure. Although many of the terms for the organs are similar to their western counterparts, they do not refer to the specific tissue, but to concepts which are complexes of closely interrelated groups of functions. These functions, which are described in traditional texts, are not based on surgical correlates, but on clinical observation of patients over many hundreds of years.

There are 11 organs: six hollow or *Fu* organs that are considered *yang*. These include the large intestine, small intestine, gallbladder, stomach, urinary bladder and Sanjiao. The remaining five *Zang* organs are solid and considered to be *yin*. These include the lung, heart, pericardium, spleen, kidney, and liver. Although heart and pericardium are considered as part of a single functional system, they lie on separate channels. One yin and one yang organ form a single functional unit. The functional units run parallel to each other in the limbs.

The treatment itself consists of stimulating acupuncture points with needles (acupuncture), pressure (acupressure), electricity (electroacupuncture) or heat (moxibustion).[1] The acupuncture points are regions containing a rich supply of nerve endings.[2] Dung[3–6] pointed out that about one third of the points coincide with the motor end points of the underlying muscle. Bossy[7] described the anatomical features of acupoints, while Rosenblatt[8] showed lower electrodermal resistance at acupuncture points, which is the basis of all acupoint locating devices. Zhu[9], in 1984, showed that during electrical excitement of one distant acupuncture point, the entire connected channel demonstrated low impedance. In 1984, DeVernejoul et al.[10] demonstrated that radioactive tracers would migrate along the meridians after being injected into an acupuncture point. This work was challenged however, by Lazorthes et al.[11] Darras et al.[12] produced further evidence of the tracer migration along the meridians in 1992. Heine[13] described anatomical features of the two central meridians, the Ren Mai and the Du Mai, claiming his findings could explain the control and coordination function of these two meridians as described in TCM (traditional Chinese medicine) (Table 1.1).

Table 1.1. Basic Meridian Theory

The Twelve Principle Meridians			
Principle Meridian	Yin/Yang	Location	Coupled Pair
LUNG	YIN	ARM	Tai Yin
LARGE INTESTINE	YANG	ARM	Yang Ming
STOMACH	YANG	LEG	Yang Ming
SPLEEN	YIN	LEG	Tai Yin
HEART	YIN	ARM	Shao Yin
SMALL INTESTINE	YANG	ARM	Tai Yang
URINARY BLADDER	YANG	LEG	Tai Yang
KIDNEY	YIN	LEG	Shao Yin
PERICARDIUM	YIN	ARM	Jue Yin
SANJIAO	YANG	ARM	Shao Yang
GALLBLADDER	YANG	LEG	Shao Yang
LIVER	YIN	LEG	Jue yin

Lung

The lungs are yin organs. Their main meridian is the lung meridian of the hand (Tai Yin).

Large Intestine

The large intestine is yang meridian. Its main meridian is the large intestine meridian of the hand (Yang Ming).

Stomach

The stomach is a yang organ. Its main meridian is the stomach meridian of the foot (Yang Ming).

Spleen

The spleen is a yin organ. Its main meridian is the spleen meridian of the foot (Tai Yin).

Heart

The heart is a yin organ. Its main meridian is the heart meridian of the hand (Shao Yin).

Small Intestine

The small intestine is a yang organ. Its main meridian is the small intestine meridian of the hand (Tai Yang).

Urinary Bladder

The bladder is a yang organ. Its main meridian is the bladder meridian of the foot (Tai Yang).

Kidney

The kidney is a yin organ. The main meridian is the kidney meridian of the foot (Shao Yin).

Pericardium

While the pericardium is not considered an organ in the true sense, it is classified as yin in character. Its main meridian is the pericardium meridian of the hand (Jue Yin).

Sanjiao (Triple Heater)

The triple heater meridian is considered a yang meridian. Its main meridian is the triple heater meridian of the hand (Shao Yang).

Gallbladder

The gallbladder is a yang organ. Its main meridian is the gallbladder meridian of the foot (Shao Yang).

Liver

The liver is a yin organ. Its main meridian is the liver meridian of the foot (Jue yin).

There are eight additional meridians known as the *extraordinary* meridians. Two of these are of particular importance: The first is the **"Du-Mai"** also known as the **"Governor Vessel"** (see Fig. 4.16), runs along the midline of the back. The du channel is not linked to any particular organ, but it has a controlling or "governing" influence on all the other yang channels and is closely related to the central nervous system. The Du Mai has significant influences on the functions of the central nervous system. Du in Chinese means "the governor".

The second is the **"Ren-Mai"** also known by the names **"Jenn Mo"** or **"Conception Vessel"** (see Fig. 4.17). It which runs along the midline on the ventral surface or front of the body. The ren channel is not linked to any definite internal organ. It has however a controlling influence over all the yin channels and the anteriorly situated alarm points of certain internal organs. The Ren Mai influences the genital organs, hence the name Conception Vessel.

Modern practice is to classify these two channels with the 12 paired channels to make up fourteen channels. These 12 coupled "main" meridians and the two "extraordinary" meridians (Ren Mai and Du Mai) make up the system of 14 meridians on which the 361 classical acupuncture points are located.

Extra Points

These are additional points, found after the categorization of the 361 classic acupuncture points, which are not on the principle or extra meridians, but are of importance because of their specific actions.

MUSCULOSKELETAL PATHOLOGY AS RELATED TO MERIDIANS AND THE ORGAN SYSTEMS

Tendons

Liver yang energy sends liver blood to nourish and support **tendons and muscle functions**. The liver is on the Jue Yin meridian. Strong healthy muscles, which are supple in movement, are an indication of good liver (and spleen) blood and Qi (energy). **Muscular spasm, tremor or numbness of the limbs**, and other signs of tendon malnutrition point to insufficient liver blood and an imbalance of liver yang energy.

Nails: The ancient philosophers considered the nails to be extensions of the tendons. When the **liver blood** is healthy, the nails are strong and pink; a decrease in blood and energy is reflected in soft pale nails. Brittle nails are often a reflection of liver disease.

Muscles

Spleen energy and muscle health are closely related. Deficient spleen energy reduces muscle tone and results in **weakness and muscle wasting** of the extremities. The spleen is on the Tai Yin meridian.

Lumbar Back Pain

This is due to a deficiency of **kidney** energy, while **heel pain, leg pain, and knee pain** are due to a deficiency of **kidney** yin. The kidney is on the Shao Yin meridian.

Hair

Good growth and richness of color are indications of strong **kidney** energy. As kidney energy weakens, the hair falls out.

Growth and Development

Kidney energy is responsible for controlling growth, development and reproduction. Kidney energy nurtures the **growth and development of the bones** and marrow, and when necessary, aids in their repair.

2

THE NEUROPHYSIOLOGIC BASIS OF ACUPUNCTURE

May C. M. Pian-Smith, MD, Lang Ha T. Pham, MD and Francis W. K. Smith, Jr., DVM

In many Western cultures, any positive effects of acupuncture therapy were often attributed to the placebo effect or hypnosis, despite the fact that a placebo effect could not account for the successful use of acupuncture for veterinary medicine for over a thousand years in China. In traditional Chinese medicine, acupuncture therapy is thought to cure diseases by balancing energy within the meridians through stimulation of specific acupuncture points, but "Scientific" interest in acupuncture began in the 1950s, under the Chairman Mao's direction. After 1972, in the setting of improved diplomatic relations between China and the Western world, reports from China indicated that acupuncture could produce a surgical plane of analgesia. Since then, a great deal of research has been performed on both hemispheres to elucidate the mechanisms of acupuncture analgesia. This chapter reviews the research, which has focused on the relationship between the acupuncture point and the neuroendocrine system and its role in pain control. Also describes culture studies that have explored acupuncture points and meridians as vessels for transport of bioelectric energy.

THE PAIN PATHWAY

To understand many of the theories of acupuncture requires an understanding of the central nervous system (CNS), especially as it relates to the transmission, perception and inhibition of pain. Pain results from a noxious stimulus applied to pain receptors in the skin or in musculoskeletal or visceral structures. Pain receptors are free nerve endings that transmit information regarding mechanical, chemical or thermal stimuli.

The neurons that transmit pain impulses are components of the sensory nervous system and are referred to as A-delta and C-fibers. A-delta fibers are thin and poorly myelinated. C-fibers are one-tenth the diameter of A-delta fibers, are unmyelinated, and transmit impulses ten times more slowly than A-delta fibers.[14]

C-fibers have a higher threshold for stimulation and transmit a more unpleasant pain sensation.[14]

A-alpha sensory neurons located in the muscles and joints are important for proprioception. A-beta sensory neurons are mechanoreceptors involved in perceptions of light touch and the bending of hairs. A-alpha and beta sensory neurons transmit sensory information much faster than A-delta or C-fibers. They are not involved in pain transmission but may play a role in some mechanisms of acupuncture.

Stimulation of A-delta and C-fibers results in propagation of a nerve impulse along the peripheral nerve corresponding to the spinal cord (Fig. 2.1).[15] Somatic and visceral sensory neurons enter the dorsolateral funiculus and Lissauer's tract, from which impulses can be transmitted to several spinal segments cranial and caudal to the point of entry.[16] Sensory neurons then synapse on projection neurons and inhibitory and excitatory interneurons in the substantia gelatinosa of the dorsal horn gray matter. Excitatory interneurons probably release glutamate or substance P, whereas inhibitory interneurons contain endorphins.[14]

In primates, the projection neuron travels in the contralateral spinothalamic tract in the ventrolateral funiculus. The location of the spinothalamic tract and the degree of

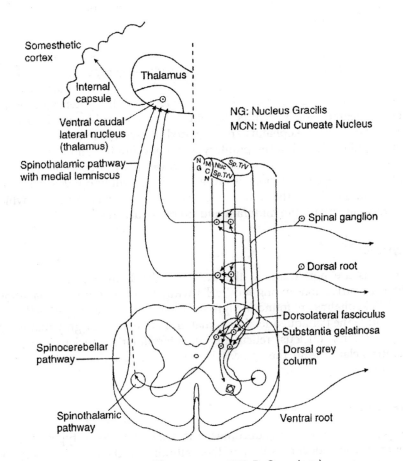

Figure 2.1 Ascending pain pathway[15] (Courtesy of W. B. Saunders.)

crossing vary among species.[15] Unlike primates, most other animals have a diffuse, bilateral, and multisynaptic pathway for conduction of pain impulses to the brain.[15] These interspecies variations in anatomy could account for some of the conflicting results of studies that use spinal cord lesions to study acupuncture analgesia.

The spinothalamic tract consists of several tracts that project to different higher brain centers (reticular formation, periaqueductal gray matter, thalamus, limbic system, somatosensory cortex).[14] Pain perception is believed to occur at the thalamic and cortical levels.[17]

Endorphins

Transmission of information within the nervous system is modulated by neurotransmitters. Though many neurotransmitters (endorphins, serotonin, norepinephrine, acetylcholine) are involved in pain transmission and inhibition, endorphins inhibit pain and have been implicated as a cause of the analgesia and some of the systemic effects induced by acupuncture.

There are at least eighteen endogenous peptides with opiate-like activity, commonly referred to as endorphins.[14] They are derived from three precursor molecules. Proopiomelanocortin is the precursor for B-endorphin and adrenocorticotrophic hormone (ACTH). Proenkephalin is the precursor for met-enkephalin and leu-enkephalin. Prodynorphin is the precursor for dynorphin and related peptides.[14]

B-endorphin and the enkephalins differ in many respects. B-endorphin is a larger polypeptide containing thirty amino acids, as compared with enkephalins, which contain only five.[18] B-endorphin is 10–100 times more potent than morphine, while the enkephalins have less than 1% of the potency of morphine.[18] The rate of degradation also differs significantly. B-endorphin circulates for several hours, whereas the enkephalins are degraded in seconds to minutes.[19]

B-endorphin is found in the pituitary gland and brain.[18] In the pituitary gland, highest concentrations occur in the pars intermedia, lower concentrations occur in the adenohypophysis, and none is present in the neurohypophysis.[20] In the brain, B-endorphin is found in the arcuate nucleus of the hypothalamus, from which long nerve tracts innervate the midbrain and limbic structures.[7]

Enkephalins

Enkephalins are not found in the pituitary gland. In the brain, they have a multifocal distribution among local cells with short nerve tracts emanating from them.[18] Enkephalins are found in highest concentrations along pain pathways. The areas include the periaqueductal gray matter, periventricular gray matter, nucleus raphe magnum, nucleus reticularis gigantocellularis, nucleus caudalis, and substantia gelatinosa in the spine.[19] Dynorphin is found in interneurons in the spinal cord.[21]

Neurotransmitter Receptors

There are several types of endorphins, and there are several types of endorphin receptors.[22] The endorphins vary in their afffinity for the different receptors. The effects of naloxone (a morphine antagonist) also vary with the receptor type involved. For example, it takes 10 times more naloxone to reverse the effects of enkephalins than the effects of morphine.[22] A 1.5-fold larger naloxone dose is needed to reverse dynorphin analgesia than that of morphine.[21] This fact calls into question some studies that concluded that naloxone did not reverse acupuncture analgesia. It could be that in those studies the investigators were dealing with an enkephalin system and not a B-endorphin system. As is the case with endorphins, the receptor-rich areas of the CNS are associated with regions of pain perception and modulation (periaqueductal gray matter, medial thalamus, nucleus raphe magnum, substantia gelatinosa).[19]

Brain Levels of Endorphins

Brain levels of opioid peptides display a circadian rhythm. Acupuncture stimulation has different effects on brain levels of endorphins, depending on the time of day. Stimulation at one time may increase levels in one brain area while decreasing them when performed at a different time of day.[23] This adds credence to the principle of traditional Chinese medicine that recommends treatment of different conditions at different times of day.

THE ACUPUNCTURE PATHWAY

The acupuncturist communicates with the body through specific acupuncture points. Acupuncture points are cutaneous areas containing relatively high concentrations of free nerve endings, nerve bundles and nerve plexi, mast cells, lymphatics, capillaries and venules.[16] Different points contain various proportions of different types of nerve endings and different relationships to major nerves. Acupuncture points and channels are characterized as skin areas with lower electrical resistance than is found in surrounding skin and may be points of locally positive direct current (DC) potentials.[16,24–26]

The acupuncture stimulus is transmitted from the acupuncture point to the spinal cord by afferent peripheral nerves. Several lines of evidence support this claim. If the acupuncture point is first injected with procaine, analgesia will not result from stimulation of that point.[27] Procaine, because it is a local anesthetic, prevents electrical transmission. Further, acupuncture performed on the paralyzed limb of paraplegics and hemiplegics does not result in analgesia.[27] The most profound analgesia tends to be induced by stimulation of points overlying major peripheral nerves.[28] From the acupuncture point, the afferent neuron enters the spinal cord and follows pathways similar to those of the pain pathway.[29]

NEURAL MECHANISMS OF ACUPUNCTURE

The Gate Theory and Segmental Acupuncture Analgesia

One of the earliest theories developed was the gate theory, proposed by Melzack and Wall.[30] They theorized that stimulated A-beta fibers, rapidly carrying nonpainful sensory information to the substantia gelatinosa, synapsed on inhibitory interneurons that would close the "gate" to ascending pain transmission before pain impulses arrived from slowly conducting C-fibers (Fig. 2.2) This would prevent pain impulses from reaching higher brain centers for conscious

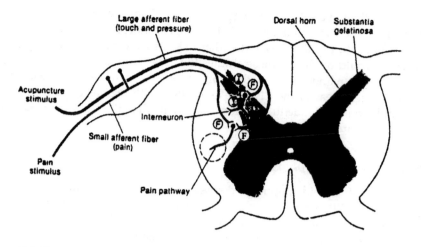

Figure 2.2 The gate theory. Acupuncture stimulus carries impulses to interneurons in the substantia gelatinosa of the spinal cord. A painful stimulus also sends impulses to same area. 1 = inhibition, F = facilitation. Acupuncture stimulus facilitates interneuron action, which causes inhibition of pain afferent synapse with the pain pathway to the brain.[80] (Courtesy of W. B. Saunders.)

perception. This type of pain control would also be expected to induce regional analgesia as the sensory afferents are transmitted cranially and caudally several spinal segments within the dorsolateral fasciculus before entering the dorsal horn gray matter.[24]

Gerhart,[14] however, was unable to demonstrate a pain-inhibiting effect from selective stimulation of A-beta fibers. It is more likely that the gate is closed by A-delta fibers.[16] Milne[31] showed that, whereas C-fibers and large myelinated fibers are not important for acupuncture effects, small myelinated fibers are essential. Though A-delta fibers stimulate enkephalin-secreting interneurons in the substantia gelatinosa, which inhibit C-fiber synaptic potentials,[32] the interneurons are inhibited by C-fibers.[33] The importance of A-delta fibers in pain modulation is evident in clinical conditions with loss of peripheral A fibers, such as herpes zoster. With this condition, even innocuous stimuli result in severe pain.[24]

Selective inhibition of A-delta fibers has been shown to inhibit first pain but then to potentiate the more noxious second pain that is transmitted by C-fibers.[14] Therefore, it is important to recruit as many A-fibers as possible to stimulate the interneurons. According to this theory, acupuncture would induce analgesia by preferential stimulation of A-fibers over C-fibers.[24]

There is abundant evidence that acupuncture can induce segmental analgesia, possibly through a gate mechanism. In Milne's model of acupuncture analgesia, A-delta fibers are essential, and analgesia was not abolished in spinalized rats, showing that analgesia can be produced locally in the spine.[31] Acupuncture points with the highest proportion of A-fibers to C-fibers provide the best segmental analgesia.[34] Analgesia produced by this mechanism has been shown to inhibit the discharge of cells in the dorsal horn adjacent to the substantia gelatinosa.[27] The analgesia is only partially inhibited by lesions in the dorsolateral funiculus cranial to the afferent input, which suggests that higher brain centers are not essential for pain control.[35]

Clinically, segmental analgesia is evoked by high-frequency, low intensity electro-acupuncture stimulation. This analgesia is generally characterized by a rapid onset after stimulation of the acupuncture points, diminishes rapidly after cessation of stimulation, and is not reversed by naloxone. It is not inhibited by hypophysectomy.[36] Analgesia is segmentally related to the peripheral nerve carrying the impulse from the acupuncture point. The segmental effect is produced by the propagation of acupuncture impulse cranially and caudally in the tract of Lissauer, exerting its pain-inhibiting effect over several spinal segments.[32]

It is difficult to define the segments, since inhibitory and facility systems determine the margins of the segment at any given time.[32] These segmental effects also have an ipsilateral nature. The segmental analgesic effects of acupuncture are limited predominantly to the same side as the acupuncture stimulation.[29] These findings are compatible with spinal neural interactions involving nonopiate neurotransmitters that are rapidly degraded in the synapse.

Investigators have demonstrated non-naloxone-reversible segmental analgesia using low-frequency stimulation for dental analgesia,[37] whereas others have demonstrated segmental analgesia that is naloxone reversible.[31] These discrepancies may reflect differences in naloxone dosing, as early investigators were not aware of the differences in receptor binding and involvement of enkephalins and dynorphin in the spine. They also may reflect differences in stimulation type and point selection or the presence of endorphin-mediated and nonendorphin-mediated segmental effects.

The gate control theory has been criticized in part because acupuncture of points on the face can induce analgesia. Sensory afferents are processed in the trigeminal nucleus in the brainstem and were not believed to communicate with the substantia gelatinosa.[38] Therefore, multiple gates were proposed, with gates in the thalamus and even the cerebral cortex. Hypothesizing the presence of additional gates is probably not necessary because more recent research has shown that the trigeminal nucleus does communicate with the substantia gelatinosa to the level of the fourth cervical segment in the spine.[39] Though gating mechanisms may account for some of the effects of acupuncture, they do not explain the delayed onset of some of the effects or the results of cross-circulation studies that will be discussed later.

THE ROLE OF ENDOGENOUS OPIOID PEPTIDES IN THE CNS

Segmental analgesia has been well documented and at least initially was believed to be unrelated to the endogenous opiate system. However, naloxone, a competitive antagonist of morphine, was found to reverse acupuncture analgesia in many cases.[40] Numerous sophisticated studies have supported the importance of opiates in acupuncture analgesia. For example, microinjection of naloxone into the periaqueductal gray matter[41] or intrathecally over the spinal cord[42] inhibits acupuncture-induced analgesia in rat and rabbit models. Naloxone injection into sites that do not contain endorphins had no effect.

Intrathecal injections of cholecystokinin (CCK), a peptide in spinal cord thought to act like naloxone, blocks morphine and acupuncture induced analgesia[43,44] and antisera to CCK blocks acupuncture analgesia. More recently, enhanced release of immunoreactive CCK has been demonstrated from rat spinal cord.[45]

It has been determined that cross-tolerance can develop between acupuncture and morphine,[46] and tolerance develops in prolonged acupuncture analgesia.

Levels of met- and leu-enkephalin increase in the brain after electro-acupuncture.[48] Furthermore, when captopril, an inhibitor of the degradation of metenkephalin-arg6-phe7 (MEAP, a metenkephalin precursor), is injected into the periaqueductal gray matter, acupuncture analgesia is enhanced.[49] The captopril effect is abolished by antisera to MEAP.

Levels of the opiate peptide NAGA and B-endorphin were shown to increase in the brain and cerebrospinal fluid (CSF) after acupuncture.[50] A linear correlation between percentage increases in B-endorphin in CSF and pain threshold or pain tolerance has been demonstrated. Acupuncture analgesia is enhanced when endorphins are protected from enzymatic degradation in rats[51] and in humans.[52] Conversely, acupuncture is less effective in animals bred with a congenital deficiency of endorphin receptors.[53]

By injecting dynorphin and antidynorphin antiserum into various area of the CNS, it was found that this opiate induces analgesia only in the spinal cord. Intrathecal injections of antidynorphin also decrease acupuncture analgesia.[21] Other studies showed that electroacupuncture uses B-endorphin and enkephalins in the periaqueductal gray matter to mediate analgesia, whereas in the spine enkephalins and dynorphin and not B-endorphin are important for the acupuncture effect.[54] An exhaustive review of the evidence for the role of endorphins in acupuncture is beyond the scope of this chapter, and the reader should refer to excellent reviews of the subject by He[55] and Pomeranz.[56]

DESCENDING INHIBITION OF PAIN

Afferent impulses from acupuncture points parallel pain pathways, traveling up the ventrolateral funiculus and projecting on the reticular formation, periaqueductal gray matter, thalamus, limbic system and somatosensory cortex.[57-59] Interruption of this sensory pathway anywhere from the acupuncture point to the brain may decrease the effectiveness of acupuncture.[59] Lesions in the dorsolateral fasciculus, cranial to the site of acupuncture stimulation, can also decrease the analgesic effect.[35] The dorsolateral fasciculus carries efferent impulses from the brain. These findings support involvement of the brain in acupuncture analgesia and suggest that the pain may be modulated by descending inhibition. Though nuclei in the limbic lobe or basal ganglion systems, or application of procaine to the somatosensory cortex, can attenuate acupuncture analgesia, the most important areas for descending control are in the brainstem.[29]

Important nuclei for mediating the descending inhibition of acupuncture are the periaqueductal gray matter, dorsal raphe nucleus, arcuate nucleus of the hypothalamus, locus ceruleus, nucleus raphe magnum, and caudate nucleus.[29,55] These nuclei are interconnected by complex feedback-modulating pathways (Fig. 2.3). The periaqueductal gray matter and nucleus raphe magnum may function as a unit, with the periaqueductal gray matter serving as a major integrating center for impulses from higher brain centers and the spinal cord, and mediating both ascending and descending inhibition.[42] Endorphins, serotonin and catecholamines are the predominant neurotransmitters between these nuclei.[29,55] Endorphins act to inhibit inhibitory interneurons, resulting in the disinhibition of the nuclei.[55] The serotonin neurons may also carry enkephalins.

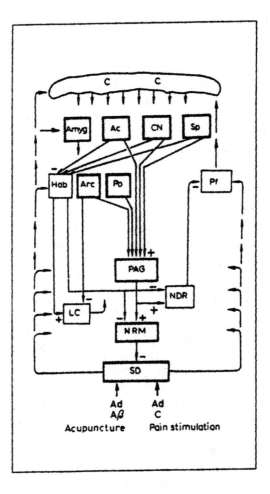

Figure 2.3 Possible central circuits through which the endogenous opioid peptidergic system mediates acupuncture analgesia. Abbreviations: Ac = n. accumbens; Amyg = n. amygdala; Arc = arcuate n.; CC = cerebral cortex; CN = caudate n.; Hab = habenular n.; LC = locus ceruleus; NDR = n. raphe dorsalis; NRM = n. raphe magnus; PAG = periaqueductal gray; Pf = parafiscicular n.; Po = preoptic area; SD = dorsal horn of spinal cord; Sp = septal area.[45] (Courtesy of *Pain*.)

The nucleus raphe magnum is the final integration site in descending inhibition and stimulates a pain-inhibiting pathway in the dorsolateral funiculus that consists primarily of serotonergic neurons.[29,35] Serotonergic nerves within the nucleus raphe magnum are stimulated by B-endorphin and enkephalins, and this effect is blocked by naloxone[65] Other brainstem nuclei involved in descending inhibition include serotonergic and norepinephrine fibers.[29] These neurons project on interneurons in the substantia gelatinosa, which release enkephalins to inhibit transmission of impulses by the pain-transmitting neuron in the dorsal horn and induce muscle relaxation.[29,40]

The type of endorphin acting in the spinal cord varies with the frequency of the acupuncture stimulus.[60] Low-frequency stimulation (<5 Hz) stimulates predominantly A-delta fibers and met-enkephalin release at the spinal cord.[29,31] High-frequency stimulation (> 100 Hz) stimulates C-fibers preferentially and dynorphin release in the spinal cord.[29,31] High-frequency stimulation analgesia (200 Hz) is mediated by serotonin and norepinephrine.[31]

Norepinephrine-containing neurons also descend in the dorsolateral funiculus and synapse directly on nociceptive fibers in the dorsal gray matter, gamma motor neurons and preganglionic sympathetic fibers. Norepinephrine exerts an inhibitory effect on these neurons, and the effects are not naloxone reversible.[27] Inhibition of gamma motor neurons causes muscle relaxation and would be helpful in relieving muscle spasm.

ASCENDING INHIBITION OF PAIN

The integration and perception of pain at the thalamic level may also be altered by a neural opiate mechanism. Pain responses in certain neurons in the nucleus parafascicularis and nucleus centralis lateralis can be suppressed by stimulating specific acupuncture points.[61] The electrical activity in the same neurons was suppressed by intravenous admnistration of morphine.[24] Stimulation of the midbrain raphe nuclei, including the nucleus raphe dorsalis, caused inhibition of nociceptive responses of parafascicular neurons even after transection of the dorsal funiculus.[55] The dorsal raphe nucleus receives impulses from the periaqueductal gray matter and then sends efferents to the parafascicular nucleus, suggesting that ascending inhibition may be mediated from the periaqueductal gray matter.[55] Acupuncture stimulates caudate and amygdala nuclei that are rich in endorphins.[62] These nuclei connect with the medial thalamus and may have an inhibiting function on the central, nonspecific projective system.[62]

Endorphins have received most of the attention as mediators of acupuncture analgesia. However, from the previous discussion, it is clear that other neurotransmitters are involved in the effects of acupuncture.

Serotonin

Many studies have demonstrated the importance of serotonin in acupuncture analgesia.[63] Decreases in morphine analgesia parallel decreases in serotonin levels, whereas restoring serotonin levels with tryptophan reestablished analgesia.[63]

An important relationship appears to exist between endorphins and serotonin. Intraperitoneal injection of pCPA, an inhibitor of serotonin synthesis, decreases brain serotonin levels and increases endorphin levels. Conversely, administration of naloxone inhibits the effects of endorphins and increases brain levels of serotonin.[64]

The effect of these changes on acupuncture analgesia was observed in another series of experiments. Intraventricular injections of naloxone or intraperitoneal injections of pCPA had a minor inhibitory effect on acupuncture analgesia. However, if administered simultaneously, they had a profound inhibitory effect. Further, intraventricular injection of naloxone sufficient to reduce acupuncture analgesia by 50% had no inhibitory effect when administered to rats that had previously been given pargyline to increase their serotonin levels.[65] These interactions suggest a model of acupuncture analgesia with a fair degree of plasticity in rats.

The main source of serotonin is the nucleus raphe magnum.[40] As mentioned earlier, endorphins stimulate release of serotonin to modulate nociceptive input in the dorsal horn by activation of inhibitory interneurons. Because increases in serotonin can compensate for a lack of endorphins, other pathways or other ways to stimulate this pathway must exist. Studies suggest that serotonin may be involved in an ascending pathway from the nucleus raphe magnum to the forebrain.[65]

Adrenergic Compounds

Catecholamines are also important neurotransmitters in acupuncture analgesia. Alpha-adrenergic stimulants decrease analgesia, whereas B-adrenergic stimulants potentiate acupuncture analgesia.[64] Catecholamines act in the spinal cord and brain. Iontophoretic injection of norepinephrine on nociceptive dorsal horn neurons eliminated pain impulses.[40] Intraventricular[65] and intraperitoneal[48] injections of phentolamine (an a-agonist) and propranolol (a B-blocker) decrease acupuncture analgesia.[48,65] Levels of norepinephrine in those parts of the brain associated with analgesia increased after electroacupuncture therapy.[66]

There is evidence that stimulation of adrenergic neurons in acupuncture analgesia is mediated, at least in part, by endorphins. Opiate administration results in stimulation of a nucleus in the vicinity of the lateral reticular nucleus, which sends axons down the dorsolateral funiculus and increases norepinephrine metabolites in the dorsal horn.[40] The same nucleus is similarly activated by acupuncture stimulation.[65] Norepinephrine, like serotonin, appears to modulate pain perception by interactions with forebrain structures, such as the habenula, periaqueductal gray matter, and nucleus accumbens.[65]

Other Neurotransmitters

Cholinergic compounds are also involved in acupuncture analgesia. Atropine (an anticholinergic compound) decreases acupuncture analgesia, whereas eserine (a parasympathomimetic) increases acupuncture analgesia.[64] Acupuncture stimulation causes release of acetylcholine from the hypothalamus, which may be important for release of endorphins.[67] Substance P, histamine and cGMP also potentiate the analgesic effect of acupuncture.[29] Gamma aminobutyric acid (GABA) and cAMP are antagonists of acupuncture analgesia.[29]

HUMORAL ACUPUNCTURE MECHANISMS

A humoral mechanism for acupuncture analgesia was first postulated after it was found that transfer of CSF[27] or brain tissue[68] from one animal under acupuncture analgesia to an animal not receiving acupuncture resulted in analgesia in the recipient. This property is not limited to the CSF. When the carotid arteries and jugular veins of 2 rabbits were cross-connected, acupuncture in one rabbit resulted in an increased pain threshold of the other rabbit.[68] Opioid peptides were implicated when this change in the pain threshold of the other rabbit was found to be reversed by naloxone.[68] A 20- to 30-minute induction period is needed to achieve optimal analgesia, and the analgesia persists for hours after stimulation of the points has ceased.[27] The analgesia is generalized and reversed by naloxone.

Many researchers believe that the humoral component is B-endorphin released from the pituitary. Evidence for this includes the finding that hypophysectomy can eliminate acupuncture analgesia. Also, administration of dexamethasone decreases pituitary B-endorphin levels and decreases acupuncture analgesia.[65] Adrenalectomy increases pituitary B-endorphin levels and analgesia.[65] These findings are controversial in that other investigators have found hypophysectomy and adrenalectomy to have no effect on acupuncture analgesia.[29]

Though the pituitary gland may be important in humoral analgesic mechanisms and plasma endorphin levels rise during acupuncture, some researchers doubt that B-endorphin is the humoral component responsible for the analgesia. They argue that the plasma levels of B-endorphin necessary to produce analgesia are not achieved under physiologic conditions.[65] Studies have also shown that B-endorphin levels in the plasma and CSF change independently after acupuncture.[69] In horses, B-endorphin and cortisol levels increased during acupuncture, but the increases did not correlate consistently with the degree of analgesia.[70] Another study found that acupuncture did increase serum ACTH and B-endorphin levels but that pretreatment with hydrocortisone could significantly decrease these hormone levels without affecting analgesia.[71] One investigator demonstrated a drop in serum B-endorphin levels without a drop in ACTH levels during acupuncture, suggesting that acupuncture increased peripheral uptake of B-endorphin rather than increased pituitary secretion.[72] Though B-endorphin is released by acupuncture and may be contributing to analgesia, it is not always essential for acupuncture analgesia.

These conflicting findings have led some investigators to conclude that pituitary release of B-endorphin is more a function of stress analgesia rather than a requirement of acupuncture analgesia.[72] Some of these discrepancies may also be related to differences among species, differences in point selection, frequency of stimulation, assay techniques, and types of endorphins assayed.

Serotonin is important in mediating the CNS effects of acupuncture. Serotonin concentrations increase 30–40% in the systemic circulation after acupuncture.[38]

Though opiates are most commonly thought of for their analgesic properties, they have numerous systemic effects that can be correlated with systemic effects of acupuncture. For example, opiate receptors are present in the gut and decrease peristalsis while increasing segmental contractions. Commercial opiate products effectively control diarrhea. B-endorphin receptors are also present on blood vessels and may contribute to the vasodilation observed with acupuncture.[73]

B-endorphin is not the only humoral factor involved in the acupuncture effect. The precursor protein for B-endorphin also produces ACTH and B-LPH. ACTH acts on the adrenal cortex to stimulate release of cortisol. Acupuncture increases serum cortisol levels[74] and urinary catecholamine levels.[38] This increase in cortisol could explain the stress leukograms and increases in blood glucose seen in many acupuncture patients.[38] B-LPH may act as a precursor of other opiates or may stimulate the adrenal gland.[29]

Acupuncture facilitates the function of the neuroendocrine system by improving blood supply to the hypothalamo-pituitary system, as well as by increasing enzyme concentrations within these capillary beds.[67] Acupuncture can cause release of growth hormone in chronic pain patients through stimulation of opiate pathways.[75] Acupuncture stimulates prolactin release from the pituitary gland and oxytocin from the hypothalamus.[76] Acupuncture modulates thyroid function, depending on the functional state of the gland at the time.[76] Ovarian function is affected by luteinizing hormone release induced by acupuncture.[76] The role of acupuncture in modulating parathyroid and pancreatic function is not clear.[76]

Humoral immunity is enhanced by acupuncture.[77] Phagocytic activity, lymphocyte transformation, and the rate of T-cell rosette-formation are increased. White blood cell counts increase.[16,77] There is often a decrease in eosinophil numbers. Immunoglobulin and antibody levels increase[77] as do interferon levels.[78] Some of these effects may be mediated by opiates because opiate receptors are also found on lymphocytes and platelets. The effects that increase WBC numbers require an intact nervous system.[77]

ACUPUNCTURE INTERACTIONS WITH THE AUTONOMIC NERVOUS SYSTEM

Numerous viscerosomatic relationships have been described. Type A-delta visceral and somatic fibers have a similar distribution in the dorsal gray matter and tract of Lissauer in the dorsolateral funiculus.[29] Visceral and somatic inputs also converge in the spinothalamic tract. Visceral A-delta fibers also form reflex arcs with propriospinal afferents, causing muscle cramping secondary to visceral inflammation.[29] Visceral and somatic sensory afferents can also induce antidromic activation of each other.[29] Consequently, conditions of somatic pain can also cause visceral manifestations of disease. These interactions account for the phenomenon of referred pain and explain the results of studies that have demonstrated the modulation of the parasympathetic and sympathetic nervous system through somatic stimulation of A-delta and C-fibers.[32]

Stimulation of acupuncture points can cause a reflex arc, resulting in sympathetic-induced segmental superficial and visceral vasodilation.[29,79] This also explains how acupuncture of somatic structures can be effective in treatment of internal organ dysfunction (Fig. 2.4). An important point is that studies have demonstrated a segmental nature to this somatovisceral reflex. Acupuncture points MH-6 and ST-36 are known to exert strong influences over the heart and stomach, respectively. Studies have demonstrated that the somatovisceral afferents from these points and the respective organs overlap in the dorsal horn gray matter.[29] Autonomic tone can also be modulated centrally by acupuncture.[80,81]

Acupuncture increases cAMP levels through stimulation of the CNS and release of catecholamines from the adrenal medulla.[82] The increase in cAMP confirms binding of the catecholamine to its target receptor. Cyclic AMP is a common second messenger and affects many cellular functions, including vasodilation and bronchodilation.

LOCAL EFFECTS OF ACUPUNCTURE

Acupuncture patients are aware of reactions at the needle site. Correct stimulation of the acupuncture point produces a sensation that the Chinese refer to as "*Deqi*". This is a feeling of heaviness, distention, cramping, soreness, warmth, numbness and sometimes pain. One hypothesis is that this sensation is predominantly caused by stimulation of A-delta fibers,[31] followed by C-fibers, and finally Group-2 fibers.[29] This sensation is not obtained with stimulation of placebo acupuncture points and

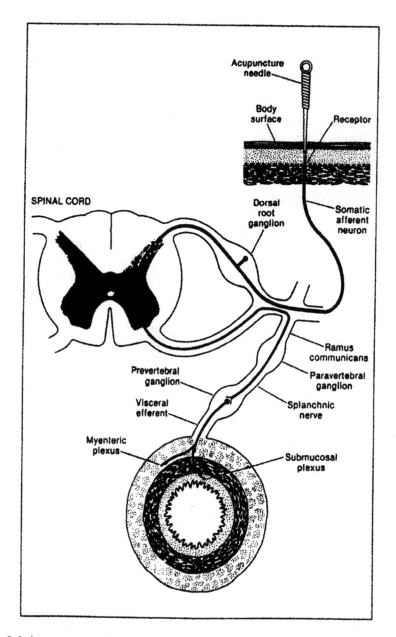

Figure 2.4 Acupuncture stimulation of somatovisceral reflex to affect organ function.[80] (Courtesy of W. B. Saunders.)

requires an intact somatic nervous system.[83] Injection of procaine into the deep tissue underlying the acupuncture point eliminates this sensation and can prevent acupuncture analgesia.[59] The analgesic effect of acupuncture has been correlated with the intensity of the needling sensation.[58] The feeling of warmth is caused by vasodilation and a measurable increase in skin temperature.[38]

Needling stimulates a local defense reaction that involves an integrated immune, visceral and somatic response. The needle sensation causes a muscle reflex that induces ipsilateral flexion, contralateral extension, and muscle contraction around the needle. The composition of acupuncture points makes them very reactive to microtrauma caused by needling. Local immune-inflammatory systems are stimulated,[84] which include release of Hageman factor XII with subsequent stimulation of the coagulation cascade, plasminogen, kinins and complement system.[16] Prostaglandins have also been implicated in the local tissue response.[38] Mast-cell damage causes release of histamine, heparin and kinin protease, enhancing vasodilation.[16] Vasodilation is further enhanced by changes in autonomic tone resulting from segmental spinal reflexes.[16] Bradykinin, released at the stimulation site, is a very potent vasodilator and increases local vascular permeability to allow other inflammatory mediators access to the area.[38]

The vasoactive effects of acupuncture follow a time course. There is a short vasoconstrictive phase (lasting 15–30 see), followed by a quasi-control state (lasting 10 sec to 2 min) and then a vasodilation phase (lasting 2 min to 2 weeks).[38] The tissue reaction occurs with several time-dependent phases that include vasodilation, nociceptive potentiation, chemotaxis, solubilization, tissue repair and inactivation of the reaction (Table 2.1).[16] This results in a heightened local tissue immune status, improved local tissue perfusion, and muscle and tissue relaxation. This local reaction can cause acupuncture needles to be expelled during treatment. Pain is relieved as a result of improved perfusion and relief of muscle spasm caused by local effects of needling and somatovisceral reflexes.

Local effects of acupuncture are not limited to stimulation of acupuncture points. However, because of the high concentration of nerve endings and dense microvasculature, the effects are greater if acupuncture points are used.[38] The neurohumoral and local effects of acupuncture are depicted in Figure 5 (Fig. 2.5).

BIOELECTRIC MODELS OF MERIDIANS AND ACUPUNCTURE EFFECTS

Acupuncture points have special characteristics that allow them to be identified.[25,26] Stimulating the points induces local and neuroendocrine responses that can have profound effects on the patient. The existence and role of acupuncture meridians have been more controversial.

Acupuncture meridians or channels have been localized in the stratum corneum. The stratum corneum is generally thinner along the acupuncture channel. The channels have a lower AC impedance than does the surrounding skin,[25] which permits an induced electrical current to preferentially flow along the channel. Acupuncture points are points along meridians that have increased local conductivity, and not all points can be located in all persons using their conductance.[26]

Before meridians could be identified by electrical impedance, their paths were deduced by the phenomenon of *propagation of sensation along the channels*. This is a sensation that radiates from the stimulated acupuncture point along its meridian, and is caused by stimulation of A-delta fibers, followed by C-fibers and finally Group-2 fibers. These afferent Group-2 fibers were shown to be proprioceptive intrafusal fibers of the muscle spindles.[16] Group-2 fibers enter the tract of Lissauer and then the dorsal horn gray matter before synapsing on the motor neurons.[16] Group-2 fibers, along with A-delta and C-fibers, then transmit impulses antidromically over dorsal root fibers above and below the point of stimulation.

Table 2.1. Mediators involved in local reaction to needle insertion. 1, 2, 3, and 4 predominate during the initial phase of the reaction; 5 and 6 predominate during the intermediate and latter phase of the reaction.[16] Copyright *American Journal of Acupuncture* **1989. Reprinted with permission.**

Mediators	Function
1. Vasodilatory	
Histamine, leukotrianes (LT C, D, E), prostaglandin E$_1$, E$_2$, bradykinin	Vasopermeability; egress of immune cells, antibody, complement and factor XILA-dependent reactants, smooth muscle contraction and bronchospasm
Kinin protease	Amplification of vasocative phase
Acetylcholine	Stimulate cGMP and hence histamine, heparin and SRS-A release
2. Nociceptive excitation	
Bradykinin	Excites A-delta and C fibers (Substance P)
Substance P fibers	Antidromic or axon reflex vasodilation
3. Chemotactic	
ECF-A, NCF-A, kallikrein, bradykinin, LT B$_4$, PGD$_2$, PGI$_2$, C3, C4, C5	Eosinophilis; arylsulfatase B and histaminase, neutrophils; release of lysosomal enzymes, monocytes; phagocytosis, lymphocytes; antibody production and lymphokines and basophils; amplification of vasoactive phase
4. Solubility	
Plasmin	Activation of C3, C1 and C5 and lysis of fibrin
Heparin	Inhibits production of thrombin
Prostacyclin (PGI$_2$)	Disaggregation of platelets
Lysosomal enzymes, C9	Clearance of needle damage products
5. Tissue repair	
Platelet activating factor (PAF)	Brochoconstriction and aggregation and degranulation of platelets
Adanosine diphosphate	Degranulation and attraction of platelets
Thromboxanes (TX) A$_2$	Aggregation of platelets
Serotonin (5HT)	Vasoconstriction
Thrombin	Converts fibrinogen to fibrin to form clots
6. Inactivation	
Plasmin	Degradation of Hageman factor XILA
Arylsulfatase B	Inactivation of SRS-A (LT C$_2$ D$_2$ E)
Histaminase	Breakdown of histamine
Endoglucuronidase	Degradation of heparin and heparan sulfate
Epinephrine (EP), PGE, histamine (H$_2$)	Stimulates cAMP that inhibits release of histamine, heparin and SRS-A
Histamine	Stimulates adrenal medulla to produce EP
Corticosteroids	Inhibits formation of arachidonic acid

If enough proprioceptive and nociceptive fibers are stimulated, sensation is propagated along the channel. Impulses are preferentially conducted along the meridians because of their low impedance.[16] The value of propagation of sensation is demonstrated in that analgesia is most successful when the propagated sensations reach the affected area of the body.[29]

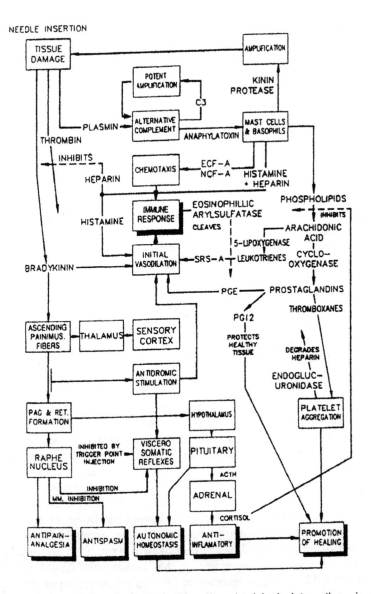

Figure 2.5 Simplified block diagram illustrating the physiologic interactions involved in needle stimulation to produce the beneficial responses to acupuncture. Copyright *American Journal of Acupuncture* 1989. Reprinted with permission.

Becker and Reichmanis proposed a healing and analgesic system based on DC electrical signals generated and propagated by Schwann's cells, and satellite and glial cells of the nervous system.[85] In this system, acupuncture points boost the DC signal being carried by the acupuncture meridian. If this theory is correct, insertion of a metal needle into an acupuncture point would short circuit the current and block the pain impulse.

Studying the electrical properties of the LI and MH meridians, Reichmanis found that half of the acupuncture points did act as DC power sources, and these points were present in all patients studied.[85] It was also demonstrated that meridians conducted current with flow toward the CNS. Acupuncture points were demonstrated to be positively charged in relationship to their surroundings and to display a unique electrical field. The field strength of the acupuncture points varied on a 15-minute cycle that was superimposed on the 24-hour circadian rhythm of the body's overall DC system.[85]

Studies of bone fracture repair confirmed the value of DC potentials in healing.[85] Becker and Selden proposed that acupuncture meridians carried injury potentials to the brain, which in turn directed an appropriate DC impulse to the area to stimulate healing. DC currents are carried over the perineurium at relatively slow speeds, which could explain why acupuncture analgesia can have a 20-minute induction period. Under general anesthesia the DC potentials are reversed, with the spine and brain becoming negative and the extremities positive. With local anesthetics, only the potential in the injected area changes. Use of an electromagnetic field can reverse the normal DC potential and induce analgesia. All of these findings suggest that acupuncture analgesia and healing properties may be mediated by changing electromagnetic fields in the body.[85]

A similar energetic view is held by Nordenstrom, who proposed that acupuncture interacts with the vascular-interstitial closed circuit system to cause movement of electric energy. He postulated the existence of a circulatory system other than blood for electrogenic transport between blood and tissue. This interstitial channel would be analogous to meridians in acupuncture. Insertion of an acupuncture needle into an acupuncture point changes the electric charge in the subcutis by causing a capacitive flow of current to equalize the potential difference between the skin and the needle. This current and change in tissue charge are believed to result in physiologic changes in the organism.[87]

Takase proposed that acupuncture meridians are conduits for sodium ions.[88] Acupuncture induces a flow of sodium to deficient areas and thereby corrects metabolic abnormalities. He postulated that pain occurs secondary to acidosis and hypoxia caused by poor circulation. These changes cause an inhibition of active transport and activation of endogenous buffer systems that result in local sodium depletion. Loss of extracellular sodium causes an osmotic balance because of failure of active transport that causes cells to swell and burst. This, in turn, causes release of inflammatory mediators and pain. Takase maintained that this type of pain is best treated by providing sodium to help reestablish active transport. He supported his theory by demonstrating that injections (0.05–0.1 ml) of sodium hydroxide (NaOH) at concentrations of 10^{-9} g/ml into acupuncture points are more effective than traditional needling in controlling pain and that measurements of tissue pH and sodium are increased after treatment. Using radioisotopes of sodium (^{24}NaOH), calcium (^{47}CaCl$_2$) and thallium (^{201}TlCl$_2$) injected into ST-36, he was able with a scintillation counter to show that the ^{24}Na flowed to points ST-36 and ST-41, whereas there was no movement of the ^{47}Ca or the ^{201}Tl. Whether other electrolytes can be transported in these meridians has not been explored. He also noted that the time course of propagation of sensations paralleled the time course of movement of sodium along the meridian.

IMPLICATIONS FOR ACUPUNCTURE THERAPY

It is clear from the previous discussion that the mechanisms involved in acupuncture are complex, are often interrelated, and exhibit a great deal of plasticity. Acupuncture analgesia can be induced by multiple neural and non-neural mechanisms. The degree of involvement of each mechanism depends on the type of stimulus and the location of the acupuncture point relative to the site of desired analgesia or pathology. This heterogeneity of acupuncture mechanisms has a number of therapeutic implications, including point selection, duration of stimulation, intensity and frequency of stimulation, and frequency of treatments.

Location of Stimulus

Studies of foot shock-induced analgesia in rats showed that stimulating different parts of the body produces different types of analgesia. Short-duration shock on the forefeet produces analgesia that is reversible with naloxone.[89] The same shock applied to the hind feet produces analgesia not reversible by naloxone.[89] Further, shock-induced analgesia in morphine-tolerant rats was significantly reduced in the forefeet but unaffected in the hind feet.[89] In these studies, the site of the pain stimulus was the tail. The hind limbs shared a segmental relationship with the site of analgesia, whereas the forelimbs were distant from the site of analgesia. In this case, the shock-induced analgesia of the forefeet follows a neural-opiate mechanism, while shock-induced analgesia of the hind feet follows a segmental nonopiate mechanism. This finding implies that the same stimulus applied to different anatomic locations can produce analgesia by two different mechanisms.

A similar phenomenon has been observed in acupuncture analgesia. Acupuncture points that are segmentally related to the spinal segments where analgesia is desired produce better analgesia and are less affected by nalexone than points that do not bear a segmental relationship to the desired site of analgesia. This suggests that local points are acting predominantly through a segmental nonopiate mechanism to produce analgesia. Distant points produce analgesia that is reversible with naloxone by activating neural-opiate and hormonal-opiate mechanisms.

Differences in analgesic properties of points in the same segment or meridian have also been demonstrated. One study showed GB-30 to produce effective analgesia, whereas GB-2 on the same meridian did not.[28] Similarly, ST-36, which is on the same segment as GB-30, did not produce effective analgesia in this model.[28] Use of a distal point, GV-26, produced analgesia almost as potent as stimulation of GB-30. There is a high density of nerve endings at GV-26.[28] The degree of analgesia produced by stimulation of the sural nerve was equivalent to stimulation of GB30,[28] suggesting that the analgesic value of an acupuncture point is related to the abundance of nerves at the point.

Acupuncture points also bear different relationships to the autonomic nervous system and therefore exert different physiologic responses. Stimulation of ST-36 stimulates the parasympathetic nervous system, which causes a decrease in blood pressure.[90] Stimulation of GV-26 activates the sympathetic nervous system, which causes an increase in blood pressure.[91]

Point selection, therefore, is very important in achieving the desired effect. Random selection of acupuncture points is unlikely to be helpful. Whenever possible, points should be chosen to include points with a segmental relationship to the area of pathology or desired analgesia. Points with properties that are known to be helpful for the particular ailment should also be selected.

Stimulation Type

Another interesting finding from foot shock experiments is that, if the hind foot is shocked for a short period, the resultant analgesia is not reversible with naloxone, whereas analgesia induced by hind foot shock of long duration is reversible with naloxone.[89] This suggests that, by changing the stimulus, different pain-controlling mechanisms can be evoked. Similar findings have been detected in acupuncture analgesia. Segmental analgesia is induced rapidly, whereas generalized opiate-mediated analgesia requires an induction period of 20–30 minutes.

Some of the effects of needle insertion occur rapidly. These include direct neural interactions and local inflammatory responses. Longer stimulation induces humoral responses, including the opiate system, and favors generalized analgesia and antiinflammatory responses. These findings are consistent with principles of traditional Chinese medicine that maintain that brief needling has a stimulating effect, whereas prolonged needling has a sedating, energy-dispersing effect.

The stimulation frequency is also important. Low-frequency stimulation (< 5 Hz) stimulates predominantly A-delta fibers and met-enkephalin release at the spinal cord.[29–31] High-frequency stimulation (> 100 Hz) stimulates C-fibers preferentially and dynorphin release in the spinal cord.[16,18] Very-high-frequency stimulation analgesia (200 Hz) is mediated by serotonin and norepinephrine.[18]

The intensity of the stimulus is also important. Stimulation of ST-36 with 1.4 volts at 50 Hz did not produce analgesia, whereas stimulation with > 2 volts at 50 Hz produced good analgesia.[28]

The traditional model of acupuncture analgesia involves a stimulus of low frequency (approximately 1–5 Hz) and an intensity sufficient to cause muscle fasciculations. This stimulation results in generalized analgesia with a prolonged induction period and aftereffect, and involvement of endorphins.[52] High-frequency (100–1,000 Hz) and low-intensity stimulation of acupuncture point results in local segmental analgesia[79] that is often not reversible with naloxone.[76]

Time of Day

There is a circadian rhythm to endorphin levels and different classes of endorphins have different circadian rhythms. Also, there is a circadian rhythm to DC potentials.[72] As acupuncture effects are probably mediated at least in part by endorphins and DC potentials, treatment at different times of day may have varying effects. This may lend credence to the principle in traditional Chinese medicine that disorders in different body systems should be treated at different times of day.

Frequency of Treatment

Because many of the neurohumoral effects of acupuncture are transient, treatments should not be spaced far apart. Because patients can develop tolerance to serotonin, endorphins and norepinephrine, the treatments should not be too frequent or last for long periods. Treatments once a day or every other day are generally effective. Treatments once a week can also be very effective.

ADJUNCTIVE THERAPIES BASED ON ACUPUNCTURE MECHANISMS

Use of tryptophan[50] to increase serotonin levels, and D-phenylalanine and bacitracin[80] to inhibit endorphin metabolism can enhance analgesia of acupuncture.

The Chinese term for physics is Wu Li, which means "patterns of organic energy". Acupuncture is essentially an energy medicine, acting upon the body's subtle energy system to bring about change. In order to understand and accept acupuncture in western terms we must accept the interchangeable nature of energy and mass ($E = mc^2$), and of mind and body.

3

ACUPUNCTURE BASICS

Harris Gellman, M.D.

MATERIALS

Acupuncture Needles

Initially, acupuncture needles were sterilized and re-used, and this remains the most common practice in China today. In the United States however, disposable, sterile needles are readily available at a cost that makes their use practical. There are many kinds of filiform needles of different sizes in clinical use today. The most commonly used lengths are 0.5 to 5 inches, the caliber ranging from 26 gauge to 32 gauge.

gauge:	26	28	30	32
diameter (mm.)	0.45	0.38	0.32	0.26

TECHNIQUES OF NEEDLE PLACEMENT AND MANIPULATION

Acupuncture treatment utilizes several different needle manipulation techniques to regulate the energy flow in the meridians. In general the needle should be inserted with the use of both hands. The right hand is used as the puncturing hand, while the left hand is used as the "holding" or "pressing hand". The right (puncturing) hand holds the needle handle and performs needle manipulation while the left hand is used to fix the location of the point on the skin and to grip the needle body helping the puncturing hand to insert the needle.

Finger Press Technique

This technique involves insertion of the needle aided by the fingers of the pressing hand. Press on the acupuncture point with the nail of the thumb, index, or middle finger of the left hand. Hold the needle with the right hand, keeping the needle tip closely against the border of the nail of the left hand. Insert the needle into the skin. This method is most suitable for inserting short needles (Fig. 3.1).

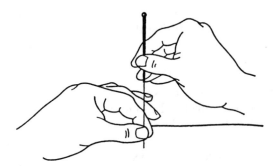

Figure 3.1 Needling techniques—holding the needle

Pinch Needle Method (Fig. 3.2)

With this technique the needle tip is grasped using a sterile cotton ball to hold and stabilize the needle tip. The left hand is used to pinch the tip of the needle with the cotton ball while the right hand presses the needle downward. As the right hand keeps a constant pressure of the needle against the skin, the left hand swiftly inserts the needle shaft through the skin. This method is best for inserting long needles (Fig. 3.2).

Skin Pinching Technique

Pinch the skin up around the point of the needle with the thumb and index finger of the left hand while holding the needle with the right hand. The needle is then inserted into the pinched-up skin. This method is best when inserting a needle into an area where the muscle and skin are thin.

Skin-Spreading Technique

Place the thumb and index fingers, or the index and middle fingers against the skin where the acupuncture point is located. Separate the two fingers that are pressing against the skin, thereby spreading and tensing the skin. With the skin

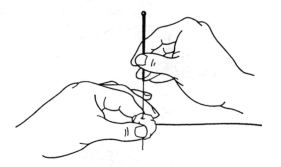

Figure 3.2 Needling techniques—pinch needle method

tightly stretched, hold the needle with the right hand and insert it into the point. This method works well for puncturing the skin in areas where the skin is loose.

Tube Insertion (Fig. 3.3)

Many needles come individually packaged in sterile tubes. With these needles, insertion is most easily accomplished by holding the tube against the skin with the left hand, thereby tensing the skin. The right hand then pushes the needle into the skin with a swift pressing motion. This is the most sterile of the needle techniques. This technique works best with shorter needles.

   Experience will aid both in choosing the correct point and in minimizing discomfort during needle insertion.

NEEDLING TECHNIQUES

Lifting and Thrusting

Insert the needle to the correct depth for the particular acupuncture point. Using one hand to hold pressure on the skin and hold the body of the needle, the puncturing hand grasps the handle of the needle and lifts it from the deep position to just below the surface of the skin. When the needle is in the deep position and is pressed downwards further, it is called "thrusting" the needle. This movement should be limited to a depth of 2–5 mm only, moving the needle either perpendicularly up and down or obliquely in and out. The theory behind this technique is that, when the needle is lifted, it opens the gate allowing energy to flow forward along the meridian, while thrusting the needle deeper closes the gate. Lifting the needle should therefore increase energy while thrusting it should decrease or block energy flow. This technique is most useful for removing blood stasis and obstructions in local regions. Puncturing too strongly or at too great an angle must be avoided.

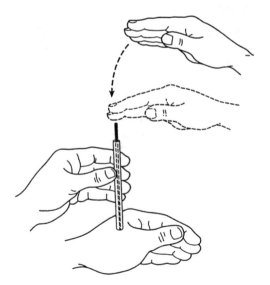

Figure 3.3 Needling techniques—tube insertion

Twirling or Rotating

While holding or pressing the skin to stabilize the body of the needle with one hand, the other hand grasps the handle of the needle and rotates the needle clockwise and then counterclockwise. At the same time the needle is advanced to the correct depth to locate the acupuncture point. Needle rotation is of primary importance in manipulation and is the most frequently used needling technique. Twirling or rotating can be used for point location, increasing or decreasing energy flow in the meridian, relieving muscle spasm, relieving pain in local areas, and controlling needle sensation.

TIMING OF ACUPUNCTURE TREATMENT

The needles are left in place for varying lengths of time depending on the desired effect, but usually the time is not longer than 20 minutes. When treating children, the needle may be placed and then immediately withdrawn. For children laser acupuncture or acupressure is also effective.

NEEDLE DIRECTION AND DEPTH

The direction and depth of needle penetration depend mostly on the anatomic location of the point being needled. Special care should be taken when points are directly over nerves or arteries.

NEEDLE STIMULATION

Electrical Stimulation (Electroacupuncture)

Electroacupuncture developed by adding an electrical stimulator to the inserted needles. Electroacupuncture has been in use in China since the early 1930's. Current is applied to the needle after it has been inserted into the skin and the needle sensation (De Qi) has been felt. Therapeutic effect is achieved through acupuncture stimulation aided by the electric current. The electric current helps stimulate the flow of Qi through the channel where the needle is placed. Several pairs of needles can be connected at the same time to a stimulator. Varying the frequency and strength of the electrical impulse will help to achieve the desired result.

Advantages of using electricity over manual stimulation are (a) it substitutes for prolonged hand manipulation of the needle, (b) stronger and more consistent stimulation can be produced, and (c) the amount of stimulation can be easily modified by adjusting the current as necessary.

POSITIONING THE PATIENT

Usually the supine position is best for needling the points of the frontal and facial regions, chest and abdomen, and the anterior aspect of the extremities. A prone position is preferable for occipital, neck, lumbo-sacral regions, and the posterior aspect of the lower extremities. For the points on the head, back, and upper extremities, a comfortable sitting position is also suitable.

METHODS OF POINT LOCATION

1. Anatomic Landmarks

Anatomic or body surface landmarks allow rapid and easy identification of points. Most acupuncture points are generally found in depressions in muscles or around bones or joints. Points are often sensitive to pressure. Most of the important points are located on, or at, a prominence or depression over bone, joint, or muscle. There are many other points however, which are located at non-musculoskeletal locations such as a skin crease or hairline, at the side of a finger or toe nail, nipple, umbilicus, or eye, etc. Most points on the back are located with reference to the spine.

Anatomic landmarks may be divided into two types: (1) the fixed, immobile landmarks such as bony prominences, fingernails, or toenails, and (2) movable landmarks such as spaces and depressions that will appear while the muscles and joints move voluntarily.

Many points are found after first finding another easier to locate point, and then finding the desired point relative to the easier to find point.

2. Proportional Measurement: Cuns

The length or width of the different sections of the body is divided into a specific number of equal parts: each part being termed *one cun*. This is the most standard method of measurement (Fig. 3.4).

A system using body landmarks and a relative unit of measurement called a body inch, or *cun*, was developed in ancient China and remains the standard today. The length or width of various sections of the body is divided into a specific number of equal parts, each part being called one cun. One of the difficulties in using this system lies in the fact that body inches (*cuns*) vary in size according to the section of the body being measured as well as the size of the patient being measured.

The hand is usually used to measure body inches. A commonly used criterion for determining one cun (one body inch) is the distance between the two ends of the creases of the proximal and distal interphalangeal joints of the index finger when flexed. The width of the distal phalanx of the thumb from the interphalangeal joint to the tip of the thumb can also be taken as one cun. The breadth of the index and middle finger is 1.5 cuns, and the breadth of the four fingers at the proximal interphalangeal joints when held side-by-side is equivalent to 3 cuns. Obviously there will be variation between the size of different examiner's (and patient's) hands. In truth, however, most acupuncture points are zones, rather than discrete points, and a sensitive feel is required. When locating acupuncture points from physical landmarks, a system of unit measurement is applied. The length of a unit is relative to the physical proportions of the individual (Fig. 3.5).

3. Location by Measurement of Skin Resistance Using a Point Locator

Acupuncture points can also be identified using a commercially available point locator. The point locator is an electronic device which detects changes in skin

Finger measurements
(in CUNS)

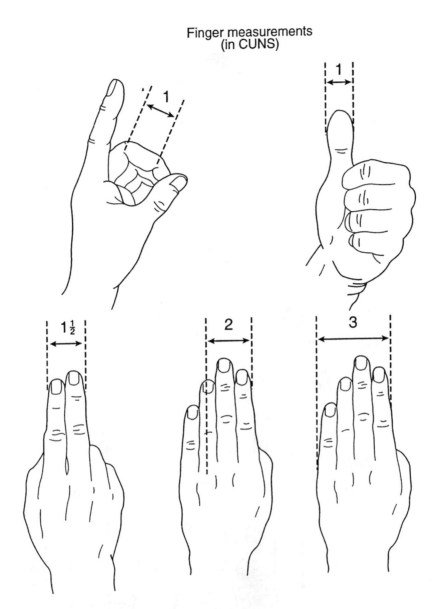

2 CUN = 2½ finger breadths (of the patient).
5 CUN = 6½ finger breadths (of the patient).

Figure 3.4 Anatomic landmarks—measurements in CUNS

resistance. The points are then localized by finding areas or zones of decreased surface resistance or conductivity.

4.   *Ear Points*

Acupuncture points corresponding to the musculoskeletal system are also located on the external ear. Appropriate ear points to stimulate can be identified using a

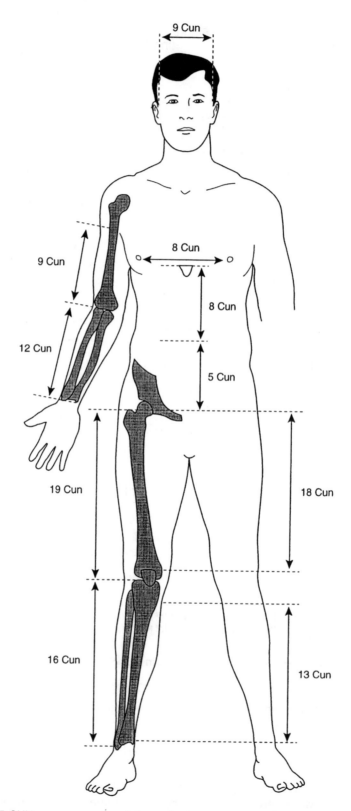

Figure 3.5 CUN measurements relative to body parts (extremities, etc.)

point locator. Moving the point locator around the ear identifies points which need to be stimulated through an increase in the sound heard. Many point locators also have a stimulate mode so that once the point is identified, it can be stimulated without removing the stimulator.

5. Ah-Shi Points

These are painful, sensitive, or tender points on a meridian. Often, when there is a musculoskeletal injury, local or distant points on the same or related meridian will be tender. When a point is sensitive to palpation, this is an indication that there is energy blockage at the point and that the point will need to be needled.

HOW TO DECIDE WHETHER TO STIMULATE OR DISPERSE A POINT OR MERIDIAN

Most acute musculoskeletal pain problems are due to an excess or blockage of Chi. Chronic pain however, may be due to *either* an excess or deficiency of Chi. Pain improved by icing is usually due to an excess or stagnation of Chi, while pain improved with heat may be due to a deficiency state. A chronic deficiency in kidney Chi is often the cause of chronic arthritis such as is seen with chronic knee pain when attempting to walk. These patients are usually best treated by tonifying (increasing) kidney energy. A common protocol would be Ki 3 (–) to Ki 10 (+) stimulated electrically, to tonify kidney energy. An additional needle is placed in UB 60 to balance the circuit. Acute injuries: back sprains, fractures, surgery, and other musculoskeletal problems of relatively short duration will respond better to dispersion of the excess or stagnant energy. In general, reducing or dispersing excess Chi (energy) is achieved by deep insertion of the needle. When treating muscle or ligament pain, insert the needles obliquely across the direction of the fibers and use a relatively strong stimulation. Needles placed without stimulation will usually result in a dispersion of energy. When the needles are placed in a zone of excess energy it is not uncommon to see a red area of skin surrounding the needle similar to a histamine response. As the energy of the point dissipates the redness will disappear. Leaving the needles in place for approximately 20 minutes, without any stimulation to the needle, will usually result in adequate dispersion of the excess energy at the point.

NEEDLING PRECAUTIONS

Practitioners should be familiar with the locations of the internal organs and the appropriate safe needling depths associated with points in those areas. This precaution especially includes the sense organs (i.e., eyes) and the sex organs. Familiarity with the location of major blood vessels and nerves in the area of the acupuncture points will help to avoid accidental puncture and injury. Some circumstances where acupuncture is contraindicated are in hemophilia and pregnancy. Caution should be exercised when treating patients with severe psychosis.

Needling is prohibited at the following sites: the fontanels in infants, the nipples and breast tissue, the umbilicus, and the external genitalia.

Electroacupuncture should **not** be used in patients with **pacemakers,** and used with *extreme caution* in patients with a history of significant cardiac abnormalities.

COMPLICATIONS OF ACUPUNCTURE

While major complications such as nerve or vessel injury are rare, minor complications such as hematoma formation, pain, and fainting are not. Needle breakage rarely occurs and can be minimized by using new, disposable needles. Although systemic infections are uncommon, Izatt and Fairman[94] reported a case of knee acupuncture followed initially by septicemia, and later by septic arthritis of the elbow and wrist. Kirschenbaum and Rizzo[95] recently reported a case of glenohumeral joint pyarthrosis due to Staphylococcus Aureus following acupuncture of the ipsilateral shoulder. Bacterial endocarditis has also been reported after acupuncture in patients with cardiac valve abnormalities.[96,97] Antibiotic prophyllaxis should be considered for patients with known cardiac abnormalities before skin procedures are undertaken.[97] Strict attention to sterile needle technique and cleansing the skin with alcohol prior to needle insertion should prevent infections. Common sense should be used; needles should not be placed into or through, pimples or pustules when present on the skin. In addition, needles should not be placed directly into an area of a hematoma or an open wound. These areas can be safely treated by surrounding the hematoma or wound with the needles leaving a margin of intact or uninvolved skin. Caution must also be exercised regarding the depth of needle penetration. Gray et al.[98] reported two cases of pneumothorax resulting from the insertion of needles too deeply into the paraspinal muscles at bladder point 43. A thorough knowledge of the anatomic structures in the area where needles are to be placed is essential.

POINT SELECTION

There are approximately 361 points on the body, most of which have a specific energetic function. Some points tend to move energy towards the interior of the body while others bring energy to the surface. The choice of acupuncture points differs with each patient, and often with each treatment, although certain key points tend to be used repeatedly. Acupuncture formulas may need to be changed with each treatment until improvement is seen. Points are chosen for their specific actions, and they may be close to a particular area of discomfort or at some distance from it. Certain points are chosen because specific meridians are useful to treat specific problems, or because of the proximity of a point to a painful area. Points on the lower leg, for example, are often chosen to treat headaches, or points on the forearm to treat problems of the chest. Many acupuncture points on the back, for example, are found with reference to the spinal column. Sometimes there is an obvious connection via the channels and meridians, but points may also be used for their specific action, such as tonification of the blood, to remove dampness, or to strengthen digestion. Each meridian has a series of command points, which are located either between the toes and the knees, or between the finger tips and elbows. These points are the ones most frequently used in treatment since their energetic qualities are very specific, and the flow of *Chi* (energy) in the meridians is most active in these portions of the extremities.

CHOOSING THE RIGHT POINTS

1.   Ah Shi Points

These are tender points over, or very close to, the affected area. The name is mandarin for *Ah YES!*—a typical exclamation of a patient who has had one of theses points pressed upon by the examiner causing or reproducing pain. These are not necessarily points on a specific meridian or channel. Their use is especially indicated if one can reproduce or aggravate symptoms or pain by pressure on one of these points. Ah-Shi points should not be directly needled if there is obvious swelling or redness at the point. In this circumstance the point should be surrounded by needles just outside of the red or swollen zone.

2.   Local Points

These are points on a principle meridian or are known "extra points" closest to an affected area. Almost every treatment for musculoskeletal disorders will involve the use of local points. Because local points, unlike Ah Shi points, are established points along known meridians, it should be possible to elicit a strong clear sensation of t'eh Chi (a deep, dull pain known as *needle sensation*) when they are needled. If Chi is weak, persistent needle manipulation may be required to achieve the desired effect. Once a good t'eh Chi sensation has been elicited, you should try to direct the sensation toward the affected area by angling the needle.

3.   Intermediate Points

These are usually meridian points along a principle meridian (or "extra points") that are in the general vicinity of the problem area but not as close as local points. These points can be used to reinforce the action of the local points and can also have an effect on the general Chi circulation along the meridian. Their level of action is intermediate between that of the local and the distal points. You should choose points both above and below a problem area in order to help clear any obstruction to energy flow existing between them.

4.   Distal Points

These are main meridian or "extra" points that are on the meridian most involved in the disorder but distant to the involved area. The points used are usually those positioned between the elbows and fingers, and knees and toes. These points affect the flow of Chi in their meridian. If the first and last points on the meridians are used, these points traditionally affect the Tendino Muscular Meridians (TMM), which affect the muscles and joints without disturbing the deeper energy circulation of the principle meridians. These points are most useful for acute or superficial problems such as sprains or bruises.

5.   Corresponding Acupoints[99,100,101]

Clinically, some disorders cannot be treated with local points because of open wounds, or the desire or need to move the affected extremity during treatment. For acute injuries *corresponding, mirror, or crossing points* may provide rapid relief.[100] *Corresponding or mirror* acupoints refer to points in other parts of the body which are homologous, contralateral, or otherwise related to the limbs, joints or soft tissues that have suffered injury, sprain, or contusion. The expected effect when using these points should occur rapidly (within a few minutes).[100]

PRINCIPLES FOR SELECTING CORRESPONDING (MIRROR) POINTS

Ipsilateral Corresponding Anatomical Area (Top to Bottom)[99]

These points are on the same side of the body as the painful area, but are at a distant corresponding point of the corresponding, ipsilateral extremity. For example:

- Digital joints of the foot correspond to digital joints of the hand.
- The ankle joint corresponds to the ipsilateral wrist joint. The medial malleolus to the styloid process of the radius, and the lateral malleolus to the styloid process of the ulna.
- The knee corresponds to the ipsilateral elbow joint. The patella to the olecranon; the patellar ligament to the biceps tendon; the medial femoral condyle to the lateral humeral epicondyle; and the lateral femoral condyle to the medial humeral epicondyle.
- The hip joint corresponds to the ipsilateral shoulder joint. The anterior superior iliac spine corresponds to the ipsilateral acromion.
- The corresponding point of lumbar sprain is at *Ren 17*, midway on the line joining the two nipples. (This is a front-back correspondence.)
- The corresponding points on the limbs are at the equivalent points of the locations of trauma. For example, the corresponding acupoint for pain in the dorsum of the hand is on the dorsum of the ipsilateral foot.

Contralateral Correspondence (Right to Left)

This is simply the mirror point on the other side of the body. For example, the corresponding points for pain in the right wrist would be found on the left wrist in the same anatomic area.

Crossed Correspondence or Reverse-Mirror (Diagonal)[99,100,101]

This is a combination of up-down (ipsilateral) and right-left (contralateral) correspondence. For example, the corresponding point for pain in the right ankle would be the left wrist, and left scapular pain would correspond to a point on the right hip. The palm corresponds to the sole, the elbow to the knee, and fingers to toes.

Specific points are selected according to the following principles:[101]

- Select points from yin channels if the disorder is on the medial aspect, and points from the yang channels if the disorder is on the lateral aspect.
- Select points on the right side of the body to treat disorders on the left and vice-versa. Select points from the arm yangming channel to treat the leg yangming channel and vice versa, the arm shaoyang channel to treat the leg shaoyang channel, etc.

For example, for a disorder affecting LI 15 on the right shoulder, ST 31 on the left hip would be selected; for a disorder affecting GB 40 on the left ankle, SJ 4 on the right wrist would be selected.

- If the disorder covers many channels, points are selected from all of the corresponding channels. *Selecting the right channel takes priority over point selection.*
- The patient should move the affected limb while the needles are being manipulated.
- Treatments are usually of the reducing or energy decreasing type because most of these problems are due to blockage or stagnation of Qi (energy) or blood (used in the Chinese medicine definition of the word) in the meridians.[101]

The most tender or painful point in the region of the trauma is taken as the basis for identification of a corresponding point.[99] There is usually one point which is more tender than any other, even in a large diffuse area of injury. This point is used to guide the search for the corresponding point in the related part of the body. When there are two tender or painful points, two corresponding points should be chosen. Interestingly, when the tender or painful point moves, the corresponding point also changes location. Searching for a corresponding point can be done by pressure, kneading, or pinching and pulling. To search by pressure the thumb is moved with moderate force over the corresponding area looking for a point of abnormal sensation. Pressure at the corresponding point should alleviate the pain at the original site. Three types of corresponding points may be identified:

- a positive point is one that gives sensations of soreness, numbness, or pain on pressure;
- a negative point is one symmetrical to the positive point, eliminating soreness, numbness, or pain on pressure;
- a beneficial point is one that relieves the pain from injury on pressure.

Acupuncture at either the negative or the beneficial point will produce a curative effect. The needle is inserted rapidly into the corresponding point. Once an effect is achieved, the patient is told to move or exercise the injured extremity while the needle is manipulated (twirled or heated). The needle is then retained for 20 to 30 minutes.

Many patients and practitioners have been astonished by the dramatic and rapid relief of pain and limitation of movement that can be achieved using the crossing method of point selection with a reported success rate as high as 98%.[101] This technique is useful for acute sprains and contusions, as well as most musculoskeletal conditions.

Special Points

Certain points can be added to any treatment regimen because they have special functions:

UB 60—useful for the pain of acute trauma
St 38—highly specific for the shoulder
St 431—one of the best analgesic points in the leg
SI 6—excellent point for acute stiff neck
UB 11—may be used in all bone, joint, and cartilage disorders

UB 40—important point: Needle this point in severe acute back pain; influences the lower area of the back
UB 60—painful disorders of the ankle
SJ 5—arthritis of the wrist and finger joints
SJ 14—painful disorders of the shoulder joint
GB 30—a very effective point for treating sciatica
GB 34—special point for muscles and tendons
GB 39—important distal point for torticollis
LI 10—a good general tonification point
Du 20—*one of the most important governing and harmonizing points. It is therefore indicated for every acupuncture treatment.*

Certain points can be added to any treatment because of their general qualities. Two protocols which may be a useful addition to any treatment are (1) LI 4 and St 36 needled bilaterally, and (2) Ki 3, Ki 10, and UB 60. Stimulate Ki 3 and Ki 10 electrically, connect the negative lead to Ki 3 and the positive lead to Ki 10, stimulate at 2–5 hz. Turn the stimulator amplitude up slowly until the threshold of sensation is reached, stimulate for 20 minutes. This will tonify (strengthen) kidney energy. This treatment is useful in almost all musculoskeletal disorders.

Hand Points

These are points on the hand that are useful for treating specific areas of the musculoskeletal system such as the low back, shoulder, neck, and arm.

Ear Points

These points affect a corresponding anatomic area of the body. An ear point will be tender if the associated anatomical area is involved. These points will usually cause a decrease pain when needled and stimulated.

Finding the appropriate ear point to stimulate can be done using any commercially available point locator. The locator/stimulator is moved along the ear until an area of maximal sensitivity is found with the locator. The point is then stimulated for 30 seconds at threshold of sensation. For pain, complete treatments can sometimes be done using ear points alone. If the patient's pain responds well to ear point stimulation, small ear electrodes can be left in place for up to one week and then removed. *Because of the risk of infection, caution should be exercised when leaving any needle in place, particularly in an avascular area like ear cartilage.*

DIAGNOSIS OF PATIENT PROBLEMS: A CHINESE PERSPECTIVE

When evaluating a problem from the Chinese medicine perspective, certain questions will help to identify the meridian(s) involved with the underlying problem. Chinese diagnosis is largely a process of pattern recognition allowing an accurate diagnosis.

Certain complaints or physical signs will alert the examiner to an imbalance in a particular meridian system. Problems may be due to either a deficiency or excess of energy. In Chinese medicine the color of the body and face can often be correlated with a particular organ system. Typical representative skin colors and their related meridian systems are (1) White—skin, respiratory system, lungs; (2) Red—blood vessels, heart, brain; (3) Black—kidneys, bladder, endocrine glands; (4) Yellow—spleen, pancreas, stomach, lymphatic system; (5) Green—liver, nervous system.

SYSTEMIC SYMPTOMS BY ACUPUNCTURE MERIDIAN[102]

These symptoms, while not specific for the musculoskeletal system, will help to guide the practitioner to the correct meridian. When taking a history from the patient, questions regarding these symptoms are appropriate to narrow down the choice of meridian(s) for treatment.

1. Liver: Exerts Influence over Nerves and Muscles and Part of the Musculoskeletal System

Symptoms of involvement of the Liver (Jue Yin) meridian include irritability, numbness in the limbs, muscle cramps, pain under the diaphragm, easy chilling, coarse brittle nails and hair, dry eyes, weak or blurred vision, tinnitus, and hypersensitivity of the genital organs.

2. Heart

Patients with imbalance of the Heart meridian may complain that they are easily confused, have increased anxiety, mood swings, insomnia, restlessness and fatigue, and palpitations.

3. Spleen

Slow digestion is a common complaint in those with imbalance of the Spleen meridian. Many complain of lingering hunger after meals. They are easily worried, have difficulty focusing, and often jump from one topic to another. They are overwhelmed by details and upset by change. Other common problems include hemorrhoids; tender muscles; and easy or frequent bruising.

4. Lung: The Lung Meridian has a Strong Influence on the Skin

Patients may complain of frequent colds or coughs, allergies, and morning attacks of coughing or sneezing with clear mucous discharge.

5. Kidney: The Kidney Meridian is Felt to Control the Joints

Weakness of kidney energy is one of the most frequent problems in our fast paced, industrialized society. Patients report loss or thinning of hair, *pain in the low back, sacrum, or hips, and weakness or soreness of hips, knees, ankles, or feet.* Weakness of kidney energy results in lack of stamina, where patients run out of energy quickly, have diminished motivation, forgetfulness, *puffiness and swelling of the feet and ankles,* puffiness around the eyes, decreased hearing, and tinnitus. Hearing loss and tinnitus are most often related to the kidney meridian.

4

ACUPUNCTURE POINTS AND INDICATIONS

Harris Gellman, M.D.

NEEDLE PLACEMENT AND DEPTH OF NEEDLE PENETRATION

Before describing point locations and uses, a few words must be said about needle placement and depth of needle penetration. Typically, needles are inserted through the skin into the muscle underlying the skin at the acupuncture points. Often, an important neurovascular structure is in the vicinity of the acupuncture point, and is therefore at risk for penetration by the needle; any such risk will be noted in the discussion of each acupuncture point. In general, needles should be inserted such that the direction of insertion coincides with the direction of flow of the meridian. Never place a needle unless you are familiar with the anatomy in the area of the point.

The purpose of this text is for the treatment of musculoskeletal disorders. Points that are not generally useful in the treatment of musculoskeletal problems will be listed for reference to anatomic location only. The depth of penetration suggested is only a general recommendation and should be used with caution and common sense. In most instances you will want to insert the needle to a depth whereby the needle enters the muscle. However, many locations have little subcutaneous tissue, and therefore needle placement must be more superficial. Additionally, because of the size variation between individuals, the depths are relative to the patient's size and must be adjusted by experience and judgement. As mentioned above, sterile technique is important to prevent superficial or systemic infection.

The most frequently used points are listed in **bold** type.

LUNG MERIDIAN (LU)

The lung meridian is a Yin meridian. The lung and spleen meridians together make up the **Tai Yin** axis (Fig. 4.1).

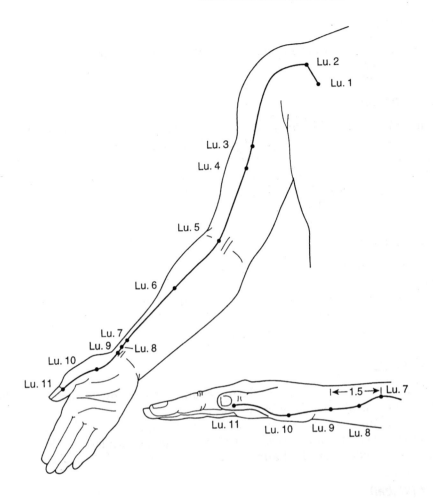

Figure 4.1 Lung Meridian
Modern acupuncturists do not generally employ Lu 8, as it is situated directly over the radial artery.

General

The lungs are the principle components of the respiratory system. They synthesize all body energies, facilitate blood circulation, contribute to body fluids and metabolism, equalize internal temperature changes, and balance body energy with external changes of temperature.

If lung energy is weak, then exposure to wind, damp, and cold results in obstruction of the local meridian energy flow. Numbness, pain, chill at the local area, and sensations of aching and heaviness are felt throughout the body.

Superficial Course

The superficial course of the lung meridian starts on the lateral side of the thorax in the first intercostal space, descends along the radial side of the upper arm and forearm to the wrist joint, and ends at the radial corner of the thumb nail.

Clinical Applications

Clinical applications include diseases of the upper extremities, lung, skin, and respiratory system.

Lu 1 (Zhongfu)

Location: In the infraclavicular fossa 1.5 cun below the midpoint of the clavicle.
Indications: Pain in the chest, upper back, and shoulder area.
Recommended depth of needle penetration: 0.5 inch, toward lateral aspect of chest.
Anatomic precaution: This is considered a **dangerous point,** as the lung lies directly under this point. Inserting the needle deeply into this point may result in collapse of the lung. **Artery:** Thoracromial artery above; Axillary artery inferiorly.

Lu 2 (Yunmen)

Location: At the inferior margin of the clavicle, between the pectoralis major and deltoid muscles.
Indications: Upper back and shoulder pain and inflammation.
Recommended depth of needle penetration: 0.5 inch, obliquely.
Anatomic precaution: **Superolaterally Axillary artery.**

Lu 3 (Tianfu)

Location: On the medial aspect of the upper arm, 3 cun below the anterior axillary fold, on the radial side of the biceps muscle.
Indications: Pain in the medial aspect of the upper arm.
Recommended depth of needle penetration: 0.5 inch, perpendicularly.
Anatomic precaution: **Brachial artery.**

Lu 4 (Xiabai)

Location: On the medial aspect of the upper arm, on the radial side of the tendon of the biceps muscle, 1 cun below lung 3.
Indications: Pain in the medial aspect of the upper arm.
Recommended depth of needle penetration: 0.5 inch, perpendicularly.
Anatomic precaution: **Brachial artery.**

Lu 5 (Chize)

Location: At the level of the elbow crease, on the radial border of the biceps tendon. This point is more easily found with the elbow flexed about 45°.
Indications: Pain and swelling of the elbow and arm. Arthritis of the elbow joint.
Recommended depth of needle penetration: 0.5 inch, perpendicularly.
Anatomic precaution: **Radial recurrent artery.**

Lu 6 (Kongzui)

Location: 5 cun distal to lung, 7 cun proximal to the wrist crease.
Indications: Pain and motor impairment of the elbow and arm.
Recommended depth of needle penetration: 0.5 inch, perpendicularly.

Lu 7 (Lieque)

Location: When the index fingers and the thumbs of both hands of the patient are crossed, this point is under the tip of the upper index finger. Alternatively, 1.5 cun proximal to the distal wrist flexion crease on the radial, lateral border of the forearm.

Indications: Occipital headache, pain and stiffness neck, cervical spondylosis, local disorders such as arthritis of the wrist or tenovaginitis, DeQuervain's tendonitis.

Recommended depth of needle penetration: 0.5 inch, obliquely upward.

Lu 8 (Jingqu)

Location: 1 cun above the transverse fold of the wrist, over the volar aspect of the radial styloid process.

Indications: Pain in the wrist and hand.

Recommended depth of needle penetration: 0.3 inch, perpendicularly or obliquely.

Anatomic precaution: **Point covering the Radial artery.**

Lu 9 (Taiyan)

Location: At the outer end of the wrist crease, on the lateral side of the radial artery.

Indications: Diseases of the wrist joint, pain in the back and shoulder.

Recommended depth of needle penetration: 0.3 inch, perpendicularly or obliquely.

Anatomic precaution: **Radial artery.**

Lu 10 (Yuji)

Location: On the palm, at the midpoint of the first metacarpal, at the junction of the "red and white" border of the skin.

Indications: Pain and numbness of the hand as a consequence of peripheral vascular disorders, arthrosis of the thumb joint.

Recommended depth of needle penetration: 0.3 inch, perpendicularly.

Lu 11 (Shaoshang)

Location: 0.1 cun proximal to the radial corner of the thumb nail.

LARGE INTESTINE MERIDIAN (LI)

The Large Intestine meridian is a Yang meridian. The large intestine meridian and the stomach meridian together make up the **Yang Ming** axis (Fig. 4.2).

General

The principal activities of the large intestine are to process residual food matter and expel it from the body. Disturbance of these functions is usually caused by excessive heat and dryness in the large intestine. Symptoms of excessive heat due to dysfunction of the large intestine include acne, rosacea, dermatitis, eczema, and other skin and nasal disorders.

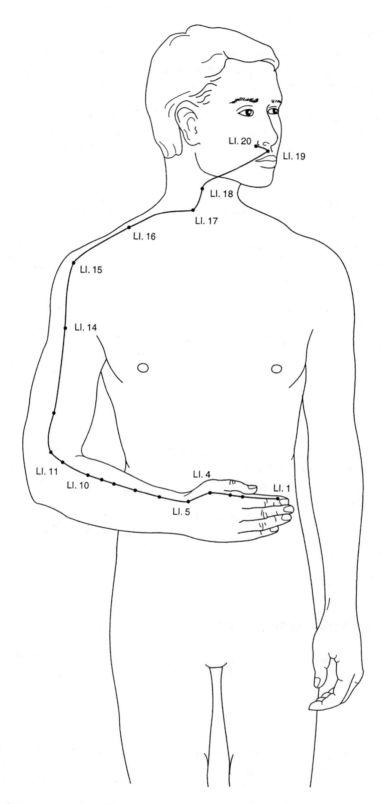

Figure 4.2 Large Intestine Meridian

Superficial Course

The large intestine meridian runs from the radial corner of the index fingernail along the radial border of the hand, radial and dorsal forearm, to the radial side of the elbow crease. It continues along the lateral side of the upper arm, ascending to the shoulder, continuing along the anterior neck, over the chin and crossing under the nose to the opposite nasolabial fold.

Clinical Applications

Clinical applications include diseases of the upper extremities, throat, head, face, teeth, and mouth.

LI 1 (Shangyang)

Location: 0.1 cun proximal to the radial corner of the base of the index fingernail.

LI 2 (Erjian)

Location: In the depression distal to the second metacarpalphalangeal joint, on the radial side of the MCP joint. Close the fist to locate point.
Indications: Shoulder and back pain.
Recommended depth of needle penetration: 0.2 inch.

LI 3 (Sanjian)

Location: On the radial side of the index finger in a depression proximal to the head of the second metacarpal bone. Close fist to locate point.
Indications: Redness and swelling of the fingers and back of hand.
Recommended depth of needle penetration: 0.3 inch.

LI 4 (Hegu)

LI 4 is the best analgesic point in the body and most frequently used acupuncture point to relieve pain in all parts of the body.
Location: In the dorsal first web, between the thumb and index finger.

1. When the forefinger and the thumb are adducted, at the highest point of the muscles on the back of the hand (Fig. 4.3).
2. At the midpoint of a line drawn from the junction of the first and second metacarpals to the middle point of the border of the web.
3. Place the distal-most crease of one thumb against the web between the opposite thumb and forefinger. Where the tip of the former thumb rests when flexed, is the LI 4 point of the opposite hand.

The point is over the motor point of the adductor pollicis and first dorsal interosseous muscles.
Indications: Disorders of the thumb, forefinger, and wrist joint, pain and paralysis of the upper extremity, pain in all parts of the body. Analgesic point for the body.
Recommended depth of needle penetration: 0.5 inch, perpendicularly.

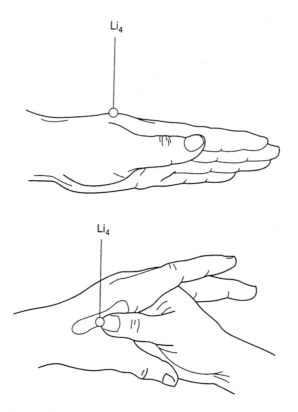

Figure 4.3 Finding the location of LI 4.
a.) When the thumb and index finger are adducted LI 4 is at the highest point over the **muscles on** the back of the first web-space.
b.) Place the distal-most crease of the thumb against the web between the opposite thumb and index finger. LI 4 is at the tip of the thumb.

LI 5 (Yangxi)

Location: On the radial side of the dorsum of the wrist. When the thumb is abducted, it is in the hollow between the tendons of the extensor pollicis brevis and longus.
Indications: Pain and arthritis of the wrist and hand.
Recommended depth of needle penetration: 0.3 inch, perpendicularly.
Anatomic precaution: **Deep branch of the Radial artery**.

LI 6 (Pianli)

Location: 3 cun proximal to LI 5.
Indications: Pain and edema in the forearm.
Recommended depth of needle penetration: 0.3 inch, obliquely.

LI 7 (Wenliu)

Location: 5 cun proximal to LI 5, on a line connecting LI 5 and LI 11.
Indications: Aching of the shoulder and arm.
Recommended depth of needle penetration: 0.5 inch, perpendicularly.

LI 8 (Xialian)

Location: 4 cun distal to LI 11.
Indications: Pain in the elbow and arm.
Recommended depth of needle penetration: 0.5 inch, perpendicularly.

LI 9 (Shanglian)

Location: 3 cun distal to LI 11.
Indications: Aching in the shoulder and back, tingling and numbness of the upper extremities.
Recommended depth of needle penetration: 0.5 inch, perpendicularly.

LI 10 (Shaosanli)

Location: On the lateral aspect of the forearm, 2 cun distal to LI 11. This point lies over the motor point of the brachioradialis.
Indications: Tennis elbow, arthritis of the elbow, pain or paralysis of the shoulder and forearm. **This is a good general tonification point**. This is also a shiatsu massage point used to relieve pain.
Recommended depth of needle penetration: 1 inch, perpendicularly.

LI 11 (Quchi)

Location: At the lateral end of the elbow crease when the elbow is semi-flexed, midway between Lu 5 and the lateral epicondyle of the humerus.
Indications: Disorders of the elbow; tennis elbow; paralysis of the arm; pain in the shoulder, elbow, and arm.
Recommended depth of needle penetration: 1 inch, perpendicularly toward H 3.

LI 12 (Zhouliao)

Location: Superior to the lateral epicondyle of the humerus, on the lateral border of the humerus.
Indications: Pain, contracture, and numbness of the elbow and arm.
Recommended depth of needle penetration: 1 inch, perpendicularly.

LI 13 (Wuli)

Location: On the antero-medial border of the humerus, 3 cun above the elbow crease.
Indications: Pain in the elbow and arm.
Recommended depth of needle penetration: 1 inch.
Anatomic precaution: **Brachial artery**.

LI 14 (Binao)

Location: On the lower border of the deltoid muscle, on a line connecting LI 11 and LI 15.
Indications: Pain and impaired movement of the elbow and arm, disorders of the

shoulder joint and its surrounding soft tissues.
Recommended depth of needle penetration: 0.3 inch, perpendicularly.

LI 15 (Jianyu)

Location: In a depression just lateral to the anterior tip of the acromion process.
Indications: Disorders of the shoulder joint and the surrounding tissues. Frozen shoulder, arthrosis of the shoulder joint.
Use with SJ 14 and SI 9 and LI 4 for frozen shoulder.
Recommended depth of needle penetration: 0.5 inch, perpendicularly, when the arm is abducted.

LI 16 (Jugu)

Location: In the depression between the acromioclavicular joint and the spine of the scapula.
Indications: Pain in the shoulder, back, and upper extremities.
Recommended depth of needle penetration: 1 inch, laterally obliquely.

LI 17 (Tiandling)

Location: 1 cun below LI 18 at the posterior border of the sternocleidomastoid muscle.

LI 18 (Neck-Futu)

Location: 3 cun lateral to the prominence of the thyroid cartilage (Adam's apple).
Anatomic precaution: The great vessels of the neck and the vagus nerve are located in this area.

LI 19 (Nose-Heliao)

Location: 0.5 cun lateral to Du 26 after the channel has crossed the midline.
Indications: Trigeminal neuralgia, toothache.
Recommended depth of needle penetration: 0.3 inch, obliquely.

LI 20 (Yingxiang)

Location: In the horizontal line drawn from the outermost point of the ala nasi as it crosses the nasolabial groove.
Indications: Trigeminal neuralgia, toothache.
Recommended depth of needle penetration: 0.3 inch, obliquely.

STOMACH MERIDIAN (ST)

The stomach meridian is a Yang meridian. The stomach channel and the large intestine channel (also yang) make up the **Yang Ming** axis (Fig. 4.4)

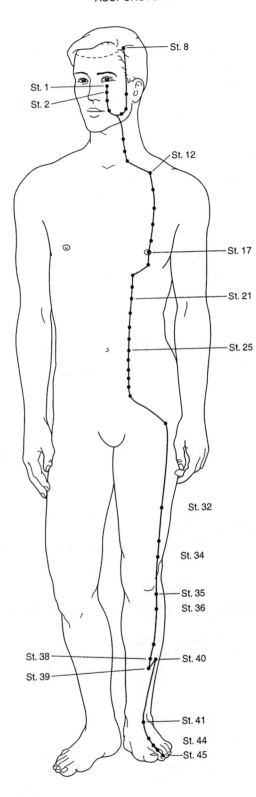

Figure 4.4 Stomach Meridian

General

The main function of the stomach is to receive and digest food before directing nutrients to the spleen, and the partially digested waste matter to the small intestine. When disorders of the stomach result in an excess of undigested food, the various distress signals include upper abdominal pain, abdominal distension, nausea, vomiting, and loss of appetite.

Superficial Course

The stomach meridian starts below the center of the eye (pupil) at the midpoint of the lower margin of the orbit, then coursing in a U-turn down to the lower jaw and then back up to the temple to St 8. A further branch courses downward from St 5 on the cheek along the throat to the supraclavicular fossa, to the clavicle (St 12). The meridian then follows the mamillary line along the thorax to the abdomen, where it moves 2 cun lateral to the midline and continues on the anterior side of the thigh to the lateral side of the knee and lateral border of the tibia to the dorsum of the foot. The channel ends at the lateral corner of the 2nd toenail (St 45).

Clinical Applications (Migraine, Trigeminal Neuralgia)

Stomach points on the lower extremity are useful in the treatment of paralysis, joint disorders, and shoulder disorders (St 38).

St 1 (Chengqi)

Location: Below the eyeball at the midpoint of the lower margin of the orbit.

St 2 (Sibai)

Location: 0.7 cun below St 1 in the infraorbital foramen.
Indications: Trigeminal neuralgia, headache.
Recommended depth of needle penetration: 0.2 inch, perpendicularly.

St 3 (Juliao)

Location: Directly below St 2, at the lower border of the ala nasi, lateral to the naso-labial groove.
Indication: Trigeminal neuralgia, toothache.
Recommended depth of needle penetration: 0.3 inch, obliquely.

St 4 (Dicang)

Location: 0.4 cun lateral to the corner of the mouth.
Indications: Trigeminal neuralgia, toothache.
Recommended depth of needle penetration: 0.5 inch, obliquely.
Anatomic precaution: **Facial artery**.

St 5 (Daying)

Location: Anterior to the angle of the jaw, at the lowest point on the anterior border of the masseter muscle.
Indications: Trigeminal neuralgia, toothache, trismus.
Recommended depth of needle penetration: 0.5 inch, perpendicularly or obliquely.
Anatomic precaution: **Facial artery**.

St 6 (Jiache)

Location: At the most prominent point of the masseter muscle, felt while clenching the jaws. This is a motor point.
Indications: Trigeminal neuralgia, toothache, spasm of the masseter muscle.
Recommended depth of needle penetration: 0.3 inch, perpendicularly.

St 7 (Xiaguan)

Location: In the depression on the lower border of the zygomatic arch, anterior to the condyloid process of the mandible.
Indications: Arthritis of the temporomandibular joint, trigeminal neuralgia, toothache.
Recommended depth of needle penetration: 0.5 inch, perpendicularly.

St 8 (Touwei)

Location: 0.5 cun lateral to the lateral margin of the hairline, at the corner of the forehead.
Indications: Migraine.
Recommended depth of needle penetration: Subcutaneously.

St 9 (Renying)

Location: Posterior to the common carotid artery, on the anterior border of the sternocleidomastoid muscle, lateral to the thyroid cartilage.
Anatomic precaution: **Bifurcation of the internal and external carotid artery**.

St 10 (Shuitu)

Location: On the anterior border of the sternocleidomastoid muscle, midway between St 9 and St 11.

St 11 (Qishe)

Location: Directly below St 9 on the superior border of the clavicle.
Indications: Stiff neck.
Recommended depth of needle penetration: 0.3 inch, perpendicularly.

St 12 (Quepen)

Location: In the middle of the supraclavicular fossa, on the mammillary line.
Indications: Intercostal neuralgia, pleuritis.
Recommended depth of needle penetration: 0.3 inch, perpendicularly.
Anatomic precaution: **Subclavian artery and brachial plexus**.

St 13 (Qihu)

Location: Below the midpoint of the clavicle, 4 cun lateral to Ren 21.
Indications: Back pain.
Recommended depth of needle penetration: 0.5 inch, obliquely.

St 14 (Kufang)

Location: In the first intercostal space, 4 cun lateral to Ren 21.
Indications: Costal pain.
Recommended depth of needle penetration: 0.5 inch, obliquely.

St 15 (Wuyi)

Location: In the second intercostal space, 4 cun lateral to Ren 19.
Indications: Costal pain.
Recommended depth of needle penetration: 0.5 inch, obliquely.

St 16 (Yingchuang)

Location: In the third intercostal space, 4 cun lateral to Ren 18.
Indications: Costal pain.
Recommended depth of needle penetration: 0.5 inch, obliquely.

St 17 (Ruzhong)

Location: This point is the nipple. The anatomic location is the level of the fourth intercostal space, 4 cun lateral to the midline.
Note: **This point is prohibited for acupuncture. It is used as a landmark only**.

St 18 (Rugen)

Location: Directly below the nipple line, in the fifth intercostal space.
Indications: Chest pain, mastitis, intercostal neuralgia.
Recommended depth of needle penetration: 0.5 inch, obliquely.

St 19 (Burong)

Location: 6 cun above the umbilicus, 2 cun lateral to Ren 14.
Indications: Intercostal neuritis.
Recommended depth of needle penetration: 0.5 inch, perpendicularly.

St 20 (Chengman)

Location: 5 cun above the umbilicus, 2 cun lateral to Ren 13.
Indications: Pain and spasm of the rectus abdominus.
Recommended depth of needle penetration: 0.5 inch, perpendicularly.

St 21 (Liangmen)

Location: 4 cun above the umbilicus (vertically proximal to St 25), and 2 cun lateral to Ren 12. This point overlies the gallbladder.

St 22 (Guanmen)

Location: 3 cun above the umbilicus, 2 cun lateral to Ren 11.
Indications: Edema.
Recommended depth of needle penetration: 0.5 inch, perpendicularly.

St 23 (Taiyi)

Location: 2 cun above the umbilicus, 2 cun lateral to Ren 10.

St 24 (Huaroumen)

Location: 1 cun above the umbilicus, 2 cun lateral to Ren 9.

St 25 (Tianshu)

Location: 2 cun lateral to the umbilicus.
Indications: Paralysis of the abdominal muscles.
Recommended depth of needle penetration: 0.5 inch, perpendicularly.

St 26 (Wailing)

Location: 1 cun below the umbilicus, 2 cun lateral to Ren 7.

St 27 (Daju)

Location: 2 cun below the umbilicus, 2 cun lateral to Ren 5.

St 28 (Shuidao)

Location: 3 cun below the umbilicus, 2 cun lateral to Ren 4.

St 29 (Guilai)

Location: 4 cun below the umbilicus, 2 cun lateral to Ren 3.
Indications: Pelvic pain.
Recommended depth of needle penetration: 0.5 inch, perpendicularly.

St 30 (Qichong)

Location: 5 cun below the umbilicus, 2 cun lateral to Ren 2.
Anatomic precaution: Superficial epigastric artery, laterally the inferior epigastric artery.

St 31 (Biguan)

Location: Directly below the anterior superior iliac spine, on a line level with the lower border of the pubic symphysis. Point is at the meeting points of a vertical line from the anterior superior iliac spine and a horizontal line from the lower border of the symphysis pubis.
Indications: Osteoarthritis of the hip, sensory disorders of the lower limb, paralysis (hemiplegia) of the lower limb, hemiplegia.
Recommended depth of needle penetration: 1 inch, perpendicularly.

St 32 (Femur-Futu)

Location: 6 cun proximal to the superior-lateral border of the patella.
Indications: Paralysis of the lower extremities, arthritis of the knee, wasting and weakness of the quadriceps, knee pain, and disorders of the knee joint.
Recommended depth of needle penetration: 1 inch, along lateral border of the femur.

St 33 (Yinshi)

Location: In a depression 3 cun above the superior lateral border of the patella.
Indications: Knee pain and disorders of the knee joint.
Recommended depth of needle penetration: 1 inch, perpendicularly.

St 34 (Liangqui)

Location: In the depression 2 cun proximal to the lateral end of the proximal border of the patella, directly above St 35.
Indications: Disorders of the knee joint.
Recommended depth of needle penetration: 1 inch, perpendicularly.

St 35 (Dubi)

Location: In the depression below the patella, on the lateral side of the patellar tendon. It is best located with the knee slightly bent.
Indications: Arthritis of the knee, sprain and strain of the knee, painful disorders of the knee joint.
Recommended depth of needle penetration: 0.5 inch, obliquely and medially.

St 36 (Zusanli)

Location: One finger breadth lateral to the distal end of the tibial tuberosity, 3 cun below St 35.
Indications: Paralysis of the lower limb, polyneuropathy of the lower limb.
Recommended depth of needle penetration: 1 inch, perpendicularly.

St 37 (Shangjuxu)

Location: 3 cun distal to St 36, one finger breadth lateral to the anterior border of the tibia.
Indications: Paralysis of the lower limb.
Recommended depth of needle penetration: 1 inch, perpendicularly.

St 38 (Tiakou)

Location: 5 cun distal to St 36. One finger breadth lateral to the anterior border of the tibia.
Indications: Frozen shoulder, peri-arthritis of the shoulder.
This point is highly specific for the shoulder.
Recommended depth of needle penetration: 1 inch, perpendicularly.

St 39 (Xiajuxu)

Location: 3 cun distal to St 37.
Indications: Paralysis of the lower limb.
Recommended depth of needle penetration: 1 inch, perpendicularly.

St 40 (Fenglong)

Location: 8 cun below the knee, one finger breadth lateral to St 38.
Indications: Paralysis and numbness of the lower extremities.
Recommended depth of needle penetration: 1 inch, perpendicularly.

St 41 (Jiexi)

Location: On the dorsum of the ankle, midway between the tips of the malleoli, along the ankle crease, between the extensor digitorum longus and extensor hallucis longus tendons.
Indications: Disorders of the ankle joint and soft tissues of the area, paralysis of the leg, drop foot, hemiplegia.
Recommended depth of needle penetration: 0.3 inch, perpendicularly.

St 42 (Chongyang)

Location: 1.5 cun distal to St 41, at the highest point of the dorsum of the foot, dosalis pedis pulse can be felt here.
Indications: Pain in the dorsum of the foot.
Recommended depth of needle penetration: 0.3 inch, perpendicularly.
Anatomic precaution: **Avoid dorsalis pedis artery.**

St 43 (Xiangu)

Location: In the depression just distal to the bases of the second and third metatarsals.
Indications: Analgesic point of the leg for surgery of the lower limb, pain and swelling of the dorsum of the foot. **This is one of the best analgesic points in the leg.**
Recommended depth of needle penetration: 0.3 inch, perpendicularly.

St 44 (Neiting)

Location: 0.5 cun proximal to the web margin between the second and third toes.
Indications: Best analgesic point for the lower limb for arthritis of the toes and feet.
Recommended depth of needle penetration: 0.3 inch, perpendicularly.

St 45 (Lidui)

Location: On the lateral side of the second toe; 0.1 cun posterior to the corner of the nail.

SPLEEN MERIDIAN (SP)

The spleen meridian is a Yin channel. The spleen channel and the lung channel together make up the **Tai Yin** axis (Tai Yin = Large Yin) (Fig. 4.5).

General

Spleen energy penetrates all aspects of the digestive system; forms the blood; protects its passage through the body; and nourishes the muscles, extremities, mouth, and lips.

Spleen energy, together with correct exercise, results in strong and firm body muscle. Insufficient spleen energy or a spleen disorder reduces muscle tone, results in weakness of the extremities and fatigue, and eventually causes the body to become wasted.

Superficial Course

The spleen meridian starts on the medial side of the great toe, then runs along the medial side of the foot and leg ascending to the groin, and crosses at the groin to the lateral side of the abdomen. The spleen meridian then runs from the abdomen to the lateral and upper side of the thorax. The meridian then courses downward and lateral to end at the axillary line at the sixth intercostal space (Sp 21).

Clinical Applications

The spleen system is traditionally believed to regulate blood and water metabolism, to influence the skeletal muscles, and to nourish the lips and tongue. Points of the spleen meridian are indicated in disorders of the skin, edema, and ascites.

Sp 1 (Yinbai)

Location: On the medial side of the great toe, 0.1 cun posterior to the corner of the nail.

Sp 2 (Dadu)

Location: On the medial side of the great toe, anterior and inferior to the 1st metatarsophalangeal joint, at the junction of the "red and white" skin.

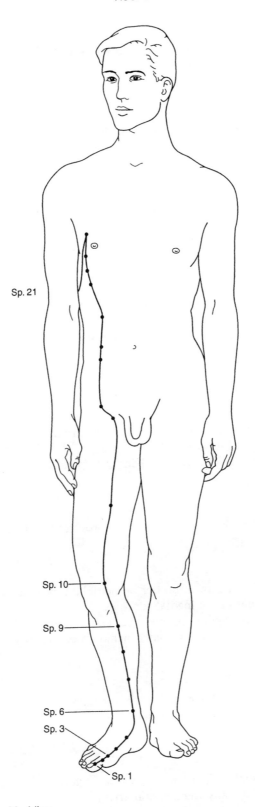

Sp. 21

Sp. 10

Sp. 9

Sp. 6

Sp. 3

Sp. 1

Figure 4.5 Spleen Meridian

Sp 3 (Taibai)

Location: On the medial side of the foot, posterior and inferior to the head of the first metatarsal, at the junction of the "red and white" skin.

Sp 4 (Gongsun)

Location: On the medial side of the foot in a depression below the base of the first metatarsal, at the junction of the two colors of the skin on the medial border of the foot.

Sp 5 (Shangqiu)

Location: Anterior to the inferior border of the medial malleolus.
Indications: Pain in the ankle joint, arthritis.
Recommended depth of needle penetration: 0.3 inch, perpendicularly.

Sp 6 (Sanyinjiao)

Location: 3 cun proximal to the tip of the medial malleolus on the medial border of the tibia.
Indications: Lower limb disorders, muscle disorders, disturbances of blood flow to the lower extremities, lower leg ulcers.
Recommended depth of needle penetration: 0.5 inch, perpendicularly.

Sp 7 (Lougu)

Location: 3 cun proximal to Sp 6 at the posterior border of the tibia.
Indications: Numbness of leg and knee.
Recommended depth of needle penetration 1 inch, perpendicularly.

Sp 8 (Diji)

Location: 3 cun distal to Sp 9 at the posterior border of the tibia.

Sp 9 (Yinlingquan)

Location: At the level of the lower border of the tibial tuberosity, in the depression below the lower border of the medial condyle.
Indications: Edema and swelling of the lower extremities.
Recommended depth of needle penetration: 1 inch, perpendicularly.

Sp 10 (Xuehai)

Location: 2 cun proximal to the medial end of the patella, at the highest point of the prominence of the vastus medialis muscle.

Sp 11 (Jimen)

Location: 6 cun proximal to Sp 10, medial to the sartorius muscle.
Anatomic precaution: Laterally the Femoral artery.

Sp 12 (Chongmen)

Location: On the lateral border of the femoral artery, 3.5 cm lateral to the midpoint of the superior border of the symphysis pubis.
Anatomic precaution: **Medially the Femoral artery.**

Sp 13 (Fushe)

Location: 0.7 cun proximal to Sp 12, 4 cun lateral to midline.

Sp 14 (Fujie)

Location: 1.3 cun below Sp 15, 4 cun lateral to the abdominal midline.

Sp 15 (Daheng)

Location: 4 cun lateral to the umbilicus, on the nipple line, on the lateral side of the rectus abdominus.

Sp 16 (Fuai)

Location: 3 cun proximal to Sp 15, 4 cun lateral to Ren 11.

Sp 17 (Shidou)

Location: In the sixth intercostal space, 6 cun lateral to the abdominal midline.

Sp 18 (Tianxi)

Location: In the fourth intercostal space, 6 cun lateral to the abdominal midline.

Sp 19 (Xiongxiang)

Location: In the third intercostal space, 6 cun lateral to the abdominal midline.

Sp 20 (Zhourong)

Location: In the second intercostal space, 6 cun lateral to the abdominal midline.

Sp 21 (Dabao)

Location: In the midaxillary line, in the sixth intercostal space.
Indications: General aching and weakness of limbs.
Recommended depth of needle penetration: 0.5 inch, obliquely.

HEART MERIDIAN (H)

The heart meridian is a Yin meridian. The heart meridian and the small intestine meridian together make up the **Shao Yin** axis (Fig. 4.6).

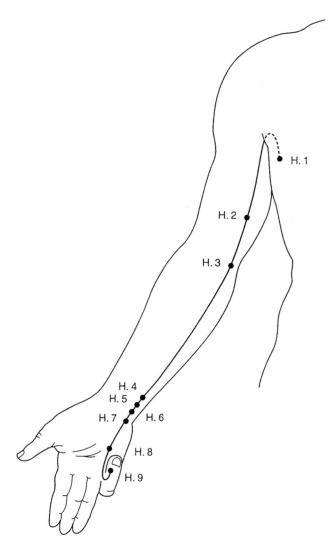

Figure 4.6 Heart Meridian

General

Heart energy controls the blood and blood vessels, affects the complexion, nourishes the tongue, and is a focus for the spirit (shen). The Chinese perception of the Heart relates primarily to the activity of the central nervous system but is also connected to the autonomic nervous system and circulation.

Superficial Course

The heart meridian descends from the axilla along the medial and posterior border of the arm, ulnar to the palm ending on the radial nail corner of the small finger (H 9).

Clinical Applications

Clinical applications include diseases of the heart, chest, and upper extremities.

H 1 (Jiquan)

Location: At the center of the axilla, on the medial side of the axillary artery.
Indications: Pain in the arm, paralysis of the upper extremities, disorder of the shoulder joint and surrounding tissues.
Recommended depth of needle penetration: 0.5 inch, perpendicularly.
Anatomic precaution: **Axillary artery**.

H 2 (Qingling)

Location: 3 cun above the elbow, in the groove medial to the biceps muscle.
Indications: Shoulder and arm pain.
Recommended depth of needle penetration: 0.5 inch, perpendicularly.

H 3 (Shaohai)

Location: Midway between the medial end of the elbow crease and the medial epicondyle of the humerus when the elbow is fully flexed.
Indications: Disorders of the elbow, numbness of the upper limb, medial epicondylitis, arthritis of the elbow joint.
Recommended depth of needle penetration: 0.5 inch, perpendicularly.
Anatomic precaution: Brachial artery and median nerve.

H 4 (Lingdao)

Location: On the radial side of the flexor carpi ulnaris tendon, 1.5 cun above H 7.
Indications: Ulnar nerve neuralgia, joint pain.
Recommended depth of needle penetration: 0.3 inch, perpendicularly.
Anatomic precaution: **Ulnar artery**.

H 5 (Tongli)

Location: 1 cun proximal to H7, on the radial side of the tendon of the tendon of the flexor carpi ulnaris.
Indications: Pain in the wrist and arm.
Recommended depth of needle penetration: 0.3 inch, perpendicularly.

H 6 (Yinxi)

Location: 0.5 cun proximal to H7, on the radial side of the tendon of the tendon of the flexor carpi ulnaris.
Indications: Neurasthenia.
Recommended depth of needle penetration: 0.3 inch, perpendicularly.

H 7 (Shenmen)

Location: On the radial side of the tendon of the flexor carpi ulnaris muscle, at the wrist flexion crease, on the posterior border of the pisiform bone.

H 8 (Shaofu)

Location: In the palmar surface of the hand, between the tips of the ring and small fingers, when the fingers are brought into the palm when making a fist.
Indications: Disorders of the palm, rheumatoid involvement of the hand and wrist, dupuytren's contracture, pain in the hand, Raynaud's phenomenon.
Recommended depth of needle penetration: 0.3 inch, perpendicularly.

H 9 (Shaochong)

Location: 0.1 cun proximal to the radial corner of the nail of the little finger.

SMALL INTESTINE (SI)

The small intestine meridian is a Yang meridian. The small intestine meridian and the urinary bladder meridian together make up the **Tai Yang** axis (Fig. 4.7).

General

The main function of the small intestine is to complete digestion; ingested nutrients and water are absorbed through its walls into the blood. The main disorders of the small intestine are related to indigestion and malabsorption, with symptoms such as abdominal pain and distension, diarrhea, decreased urination, and enuresis.

Superficial Course

The small intestine meridian starts at the ulnar corner of the fingernail of the small finger and courses proximally along the ulnar and dorsal side of the arm to the dorsal side of the shoulder. The meridian then runs along the shoulder in a zigzag line and continues on the lateral side of the neck and cheek to the ear. A connecting branch runs from the cheek along the nose to UB 1.

Clinical Applications

Clinical applications include the treatment of painful disorders along the meridian, arthritis of the shoulder and neck, and upper extremities.

SI 1 (Shaoze)

Location: At the ulnar side of the small finger, approximately 0.1 cun posterior to the corner of the nail.
Indications: Headache.
Recommended depth of needle penetration: 0.1 inch, perpendicularly.

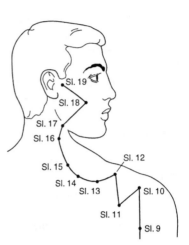

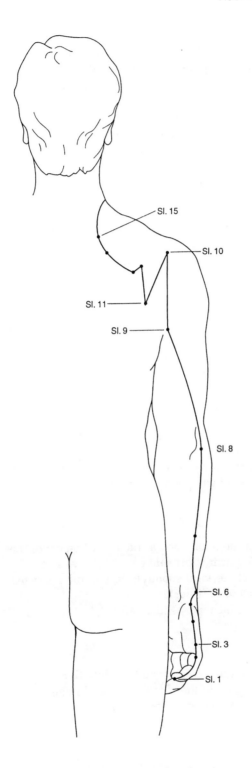

Figure 4.7 Small Intestine Meridian

SI 2 (Qiangu)

Location: In the depression anterior to the ulnar side of the fifth metacarpal-phalangeal joint. When a fist is formed, the point is on the junction of the "red and white" skin of the transverse crease distal to the metacarpalphalangeal joint.
Indications: Pain in the arm, numbness of the fingers.
Recommended depth of needle penetration: 0.2 inch, perpendicularly.

SI 3 (Houxi)

Location: At the medial end of the main transverse crease of the palm when making a fist.
Indications: Acute stiffness of the neck, acute low back pain, paralysis of the upper extremities, restricted motion of the shoulder, peripheral neuropathy.
Recommended depth of needle penetration: 0.5 inch, perpendicularly.

SI 4 (Hand-Wangu)

Location: At the ulnar side of the border of the palm in the depression between the base of the fifth metacarpal and the hamate.
Indications: Arthritis of the elbow, wrist, and finger joints.
Recommended depth of needle penetration: 0.3 inch, perpendicularly.

SI 5 (Yanggu)

Location: At the ulnar side of the wrist in the depression between the styloid process of the ulna and the pisiform bone.
Indications: Pain in the lateral aspect of the arm and wrist.
Recommended depth of needle penetration: 0.3 inch, perpendicularly.

SI 6 (Yanglao)

Location: On the dorsum of the wrist, in the depression at the lateral aspect of the styloid process of the ulna, when the forearm is pronated.
Indications: Wrist and back pain, stiff neck, cervical spondylosis, painful, restricted shoulder motion. **Excellent point for acute stiff neck.**
Recommended depth of needle penetration: 1 inch, perpendicularly.

SI 7 (Zhizheng)

Location: 5 cun proximal to the wrist, on a line connecting SI 5 with SI 8.
Indications: Rigidity or stiffness of neck, pain in the elbow, arm, and fingers.
Recommended depth of needle penetration: 0.5 inch, perpendicularly.

SI 8 (Xiaohai)

Location: In the posterior aspect of the elbow joint, in a depression between the olecranon of the ulna and the tip of the medial epicondyle of the humerus with the elbow flexed.

Indications: Pain in the small finger, elbow joint, shoulder, and back.
Recommended depth of needle penetration: 0.3 inch, perpendicularly.

SI 9 (Jianzhen)

Location: 1 cun proximal to the highest point of the posterior axillary fold with the arm adducted to the side.
Indications: Frozen shoulder, sprains and strains of the shoulder muscles, paralysis of the upper limb, periarthritis of the shoulder.
Recommended depth of needle penetration: 1 inch, perpendicularly.

SI 10 (Naoshu)

Location: With the arm at the side, it is directly proximal to the posterior axillary fold, on the lower border of the scapular spine.
Indications: Pain and weakness of the shoulder and arm, periarthritis of the shoulder.
Recommended depth of needle penetration: 1 inch, perpendicularly.

SI 11 (Tianzong)

Location: In the center of the infrascapular fossa, forming a bilateral triangle with S.I. 10 and S.I. 9.
Indications: Pain in the shoulder and posterolateral aspect of the arm.
Recommended depth of needle penetration: 0.5 inch, perpendicularly.

SI 12 (Bingfeng)

Location: In the center of the suprascapular fossa, directly above S.I. 11, in the depression formed when the arm is abducted.
Indications: Pain in the shoulder joint, numbness and aching of the upper extremities.
Recommended depth of needle penetration: 0.5 inch, obliquely.

SI 13 (Quyuan)

Location: On the medial end of the suprascapular fossa, midway between S.I. 10 and the spinous process of the second thoracic vertebrae.
Indications: Pain and contracture of the shoulder joint.
Recommended depth of needle penetration: 0.5 inch, obliquely.

SI 14 (Jianwaishu)

Location: 3 cun lateral to the lower border of the spinous process of the first thoracic vertebrae (Du 13).
Indications: Aching of the scapular joint, stiffness and pain in the neck and/or shoulder.
Recommended depth of needle penetration: 0.5 inch, obliquely.

SI 15 (Jianzhongshu)

Location: 2 cun lateral to the lower border of the spinous process of the seventh cervical vertebrae (Du 14).
Indications: Pain in the shoulder and back, stiffness and pain of the neck, cervical spondylosis.
Recommended depth of needle penetration: 0.5 inch, obliquely.

SI 16 (Tianchuang)

Location: On the posterior border of the sternocleidomastoid, 0.5 cun posterior to LI 18.
Indications: Rigidity and stiffness of neck.
Recommended depth of needle penetration: 0.5 inch, perpendicularly.
Anatomic precaution: **Ascending cervical artery**.

SI 17 (Tianrong)

Location: On the anterior border of the sternocleidomastoid, at the level of the angle of the jaw.
Indications: Arthrosis of the temporomandibular joint.
Recommended depth of needle penetration: 0.5 inch, perpendicularly.

SI 18 (Quanliao)

Location: In the depression below the prominence of the zygomatic bone on a vertical line from the outer canthus of the eye
Indications: This is a regional analgesic point for head and neck surgery.
Recommended depth of needle penetration: 0.3 inch, perpendicularly.

SI 19 (Tinggong)

Location: In the depression between the tragus and mandibular joint when the mouth is slightly opened.

URINARY BLADDER (UB)

The urinary bladder meridian is a Yang meridian. The urinary bladder meridian and the small intestine meridian together make up the **Tai Yang** axis. The bladder meridian is the longest in the body.

General

The function of the bladder is relatively simple: by storage and excretion of waste body fluids, it assists kidney energy in regulating water metabolism. Common disorders include dysuria, oliguria, anuria, and hematuria.

Superficial Course

The urinary bladder meridian starts at the inner canthus of the eye and ascends parallel to the midline over the forehead to the neck. At the neck the meridian connects to DU 20, and then the meridian divides into two parallel lines (Fig. 4.8). The more important medial branch descends 1.5 cum lateral and parallel along the midline to the level of the fourth sacral foramen, where it turns back upward to the 1st sacral foramen, and then continues caudal to the dorsal side of the thigh to the popliteal fossa (UB 40). Here it connects with the lateral branch to descend along the dorsal side of the lower leg crossing over the lateral malleolus, to the lateral aspect of the foot, ending on the lateral corner of the nail of the small toe. The urinary bladder meridian is the longest meridian with 67 points.

Clinical Indications

Clinical indications include diseases of the neck, cervical spondylosis, back (including sciatica), and the lower extremities.

UB 1 (Jingming)

Location: 0.1 cun medial and superior to the inner canthus of the eye, near the medial border of the orbit.

UB 2 (Zanzhu)

Location: In the depression at the medial end of the eyebrow, directly above the inner canthus of the eye.
Indications: Frontal headache.
Recommended depth of needle penetration: 0.3 inch, horizontally.

UB 3 (Meichong)

Location: Directly above UB 2, 0.5 cun inside the hairline.
Indications: Headache.
Recommended depth of needle penetration: 0.3 inch, obliquely.

UB 4 (Quchai)

Location: 1.5 cun lateral to Du 24, 0.5 cun inside hairline.
Indications: Headache.
Recommended depth of needle penetration: 0.3 inch, obliquely.

UB 5 (Wuchu)

Location: 0.5 cun above UB 4.
Indications: Headache.
Recommended depth of needle penetration: 0.3 inch, obliquely.

UB 6 (Chengguang)

i*Location*: 1.5 cun posterior to UB 5.
Indications: Headache.
Recommended depth of needle penetration: 0.3 inch, obliquely.

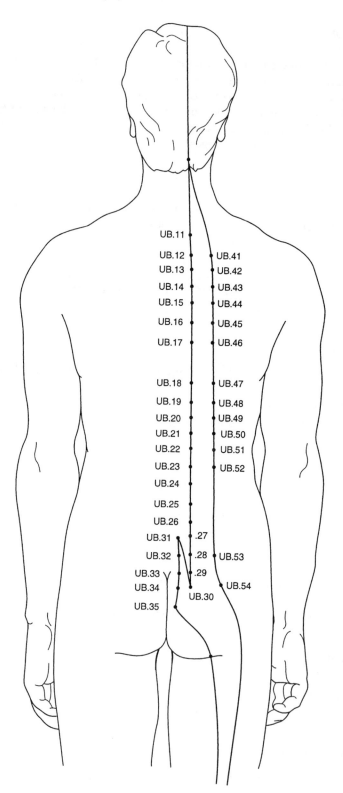

Figure 4.8. Urinary Bladder Meridian: Back Points

UB 7 (Tongtian)

Location: 1.5 cun posterior to UB 6.
Indications: Headache.
Recommended depth of needle penetration: 0.3 inch, obliquely.

UB 8 (Luoque)

Location: 1.5 cun posterior to UB 7.
Indications: Headache.
Recommended depth of needle penetration: 0.3 inch, obliquely.

UB 9 (Yuzhen)

Location: On the lateral side of the superior border of the external occipital protuberance, 1.3 cun lateral to Du 17.
Indications: Headache.
Recommended depth of needle penetration: 0.3 inch, obliquely.

UB 10 (Tianzhu)

Location: In the lower border of the occiput, between the transverse processes of cervical 1 and cervical 2 (Fig. 4.9a).
Indications: Cervical spondylosis, stiffness of the neck.
Recommended depth of needle penetration: 0.5 inch, perpendicularly.

UB 11 (Dashu)

Location: 1.5 cun lateral to the lower border of the spinous process of the first thoracic vertebrae.
Indications: Pain in the shoulder area, arthritis of the shoulder joints, rheumatoid arthritis, cervical spondylosis.
May be used in all joint, bone, and cartilage disorders.
Recommended depth of needle penetration: 0.3 inch, perpendicularly.

UB 12 (Fengmen)

Location: 1.5 cun lateral to the lower border of the spinous process of the second thoracic vertebrae.

UB 13 (Feishu)

Location: 1.5 cun lateral to the lower border of the spinous process of the third thoracic vertebrae.
Indications: Back pain.
Recommended depth of needle penetration: 0.3 inch, perpendicularly.

UB 14 (Jueyinshu)

Location: 1.5 cun lateral to the lower border of the spinous process of the fourth thoracic vertebrae.

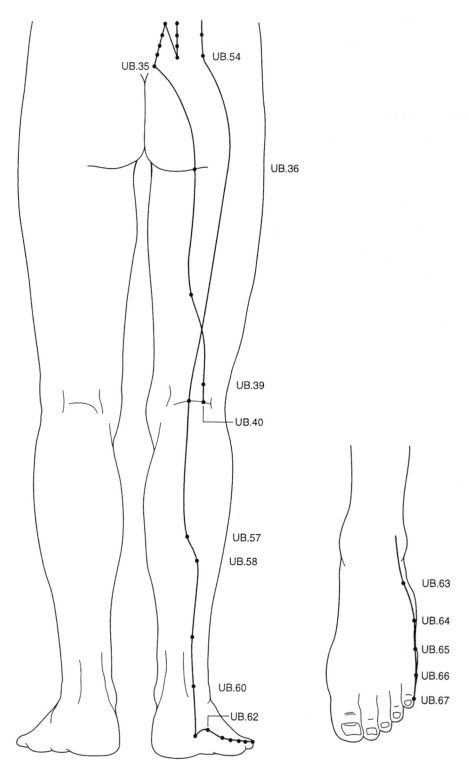

Figure 4.9a Urinary Bladder Meridian: Lower Extremity Points

Indications: Thoracic pain.
Recommended depth of needle penetration: 0.3 inch, perpendicularly.

UB 15 (Xinshu)

Location: 1.5 cun lateral to the lower border of the spinous process of the fifth thoracic vertebrae.
Indications: Neurasthenia.
Recommended depth of needle penetration: 0.3 inch, perpendicularly.

UB 16 (Dushu)

Location: 1.5 cun lateral to the lower border of the spinous process of the sixth thoracic vertebrae.

UB 17 (Geshu)

Location: 1.5 cun lateral to the lower border of the spinous process of the seventh thoracic vertebrae, at the level of the lower border of the scapula.
Indications: Back pain.
Recommended depth of needle penetration: 0.3 inch, perpendicularly.

UB 18 (Ganshu)

Location: 1.5 cun lateral to the lower border of the spinous process of the ninth thoracic vertebrae.
Indications: Muscle and tendon disorders, local disorders of the spine, back pain.
Recommended depth of needle penetration 0.3 inch, perpendicularly.

UB 19 (Danshu)

Location: 1.5 cun lateral to the lower border of the spinous process of the tenth thoracic vertebrae.
Indications: Local disorders of the spine.
Recommended depth of needle penetration: 0.3 inch, perpendicularly.

UB 20 (Pishu)

Location: 1.5 cun lateral to the lower border of the spinous process of the eleventh thoracic vertebrae.
Indications: Soft tissue pain in the back.
Recommended depth of needle penetration: 0.3 inch, perpendicularly.

UB 21 (Weishu)

Location: 1.5 cun lateral to the lower border of the spinous process of the twelfth thoracic vertebrae.

UB 22 (Sanjiaoshu)

Location: 1.5 cun lateral to the lower border of the spinous process of the first lumbar vertebrae.
Indications: Local disorders of the spine, back pain.
Recommended depth of needle penetration: 0.5 inch, perpendicularly.

UB 23 (Shenshu)

Location: 1.5 cun lateral to the lower border of the spinous process of the second lumbar vertebrae.
Indications: Bone disorders, local disorders of the spine, sciatica.
Recommended depth of needle penetration: 1 inch, perpendicularly.

UB 24 (Qihaishu)

Location: 1.5 cun lateral to the lower border of the spinous process of the third lumbar vertebrae.
Indications: Lumbago, sciatica.
Recommended depth of needle penetration: 1 inch, perpendicularly.

UB 25 (Dachangshu)

Location: 1.5 cun lateral to the lower border of the spinous process of the fourth lumbar vertebrae, at the level of the upper border of the iliac crest.
Indications: Low back pain, sciatica, paralysis of the lower extremities.
Recommended depth of needle penetration: 1 inch, perpendicularly.

UB 26 (Guanyuanshu)

Location: 1.5 cun lateral to the lower border of the spinous process of the fifth lumbar vertebrae.
Indications: Lumbago, sciatica.
Recommended depth of needle penetration: 1 inch, perpendicularly.

UB 27 (Xiaochangshu)

Location: 1.5 cun lateral to the midline, level with the first posterior sacral foramen, in the depression over the sacro-iliac joint.
Indications: Low back pain, sacro-iliac diseases, sciatica.
Recommended depth of needle penetration: 0.5 inch, perpendicularly.

UB 28 (Pangguangshu)

Location: 1.5 cun lateral to the midline, level with the second posterior sacral foramen, in the depression over the sacro-iliac joint.
Indications: Lumbosacral disorders, sciatica.
Recommended depth of needle penetration: 0.5 inch, perpendicularly.

UB 29 (Zhonglushu)

Location: At the level of the third posterior sacral foramen, 1.5 cun lateral to the midline of the back.
Indications: Lumbosacral pin, sciatica.
Recommended depth of needle penetration: 1 inch, perpendicularly.

UB 30 (Baihuanshu)

Location: At the level of the fourth posterior sacral foramen, 1.5 cun lateral to the midline of the back.
Indications: Sciatica.
Recommended depth of needle penetration: 0.5 inch, perpendicularly.

UB 31 (Shangliao)

Location: In the first posterior sacral foramen, about midway between the posterior superior iliac spine and the Du meridian.
Indications: Lumbago, sciatica.
Recommended depth of needle penetration: 1 inch, perpendicularly.

UB 32 (Ciliao)

Location: In the second posterior sacral foramen, about midway between the inferior aspect of the posterior superior iliac spine and the Du meridian.
Indications: Sciatica.
Recommended depth of needle penetration: 1 inch, perpendicularly.

UB 33 (Zhongliao)

Location: In the third posterior sacral foramen, about midway between UB 29 and the Du meridian.
Indications: Sciatica.
Recommended depth of needle penetration: 1 inch, perpendicularly.

UB 34 (Xialiao)

Location: In the fourth posterior sacral foramen, about midway between UB 30 and the Du meridian.
Indications: Sciatica.
Recommended depth of needle penetration: 1 inch, perpendicularly.

UB 35 (Huiyang)

Location: Lateral to the lower end of the coccyx, 0.5 cun lateral to the midline.
Indications: Back pain.
Recommended depth of needle penetration: 1 inch, perpendicularly.

UB 36 (Chengfu)

Location: In the middle of the gluteal fold.
Indications: Sciatica, paralysis of the lower limb.
Recommended depth of needle penetration: 1.5 inch, perpendicularly.

UB 37 (Yinmen)

Location: 6 cun distal to UB 36, on a line connecting the midpoints of the gluteal transverse crease and the popliteal transverse crease.
Indications: Sciatica, lumbo-sacral disorders, back pain, paralysis of the lower limb.
Recommended depth of needle penetration: 1 inch, perpendicularly.

UB 38 (Fuxi)

Location: 1 cun above UB 39.
Indications: Paralysis of the lateral aspect of the lower extremities.
Recommended depth of needle penetration: 1 inch, perpendicularly.

UB 39 (Weiyang)

Location: On the lateral end of the popliteal crease, lateral to UB 40, on the medial side of the biceps femoris tendon.
Indications: Spasm of the gastrocnemius, back pain.
Recommended depth of needle penetration: 0.5 inch, perpendicularly.

UB 40 (Weizhong)

Location: At the midpoint of the popliteal transverse crease.
Indications: Sciatica, lumbago, disorders of the knee joint, back pain.
Needle this point in severe acute back pain, as this point influences the lower area of the back. Pricking a small vein in the popliteal fossa and releasing a drop of blood should give acute relief of back pain.
Recommended depth of needle penetration: 0.8 inch, perpendicularly.
Anatomic precaution: Popliteal vessels (Fig. 4.9b-c)

UB 41 (Fufen)

Location: 3 cun lateral to the lower border of the spinous process of the second thoracic vertebrae.
Indications: Intercostal neuralgia, numbness of the elbow and arm.
Recommended depth of needle penetration: 0.3 inch, obliquely.

UB 42 (Pohu)

Location: 3 cun lateral to the lower border of the spinous process of the third thoracic vertebrae.
Indications: Shoulder pain.
Recommended depth of needle penetration: 0.3 inch, perpendicularly.

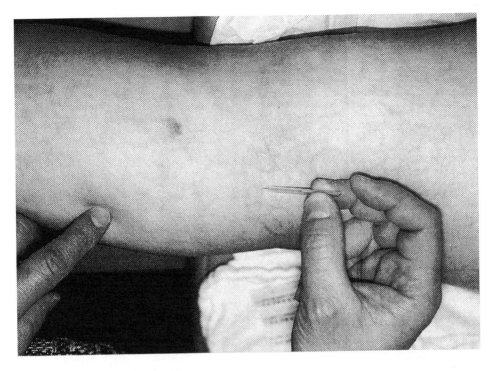

Figure 4.9b Urinary Bladder 40

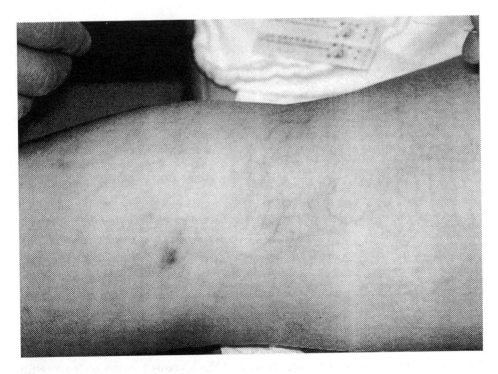

Figure 4.9c Urinary Bladder 40

UB 43 (Gaohuang)

Location: 3 cun lateral to the lower border of the spinous process of the fourth thoracic vertebrae.
Indications: General weakness.
Recommended depth of needle penetration: 0.3 inch, perpendicularly.

UB 44 (Shentang)

Location: 3 cun lateral to the lower border of the spinous process of the fifth thoracic vertebrae
Indications: Shoulder and back pain.
Recommended depth of needle penetration: 0.3 inch, perpendicularly.

UB 45 (Yixi)

Location: 3 cun lateral to the lower border of the spinous process of the sixth thoracic vertebrae.
Indications: Intercostal neuralgia.
Recommended depth of needle penetration: 0.3 inch, perpendicularly.

UB 46 (Genguan)

Location: 3 cun lateral to the lower border of the spinous process of the seventh thoracic vertebrae.
Indications: Spinal pain.
Recommended depth of needle penetration: 0.3 inch, perpendicularly.

UB 47 (Hunmen)

Location: 3 cun lateral to the lower border of the spinous process of the ninth thoracic vertebrae.

UB 48 (Yanggang)

Location: 3 cun lateral to the lower border of the spinous process of the tenth thoracic vertebrae.

UB 49 (Yishe)

Location: 3 cun lateral to the lower border of the spinous process of the eleventh thoracic vertebrae.
Indications: Back pain.
Recommended depth of needle penetration: 0.3 inch, perpendicularly.

UB 50 (Weicang)

Location: 3 cun lateral to the lower border of the spinous process of the twelfth thoracic vertebrae.

Indications: Spinal pain.
Recommended depth of needle penetration: 0.3 inch, perpendicularly.

UB 51 (Huangmen)

Location: 3 cun lateral to the lower border of the spinous process of the first lumbar vertebrae.

UB 52 (Zhishi)

Location: 3 cun lateral to the lower border of the spinous process of the second sacral vertebrae.
Indications: Stiffness and pain in back and lumbar region.
Recommended depth of needle penetration: 1 inch, perpendicularly.

UB 53 (Baohuang)

Location: 3 cun lateral to the Du channel, level to the second posterior sacral foramen.
Indications: Back pain.
Recommended depth of needle penetration: 1 inch, perpendicularly.

UB 54 (Zhibian)

Location: At the level of the fourth sacral foramen, 3 cun lateral to the midline (Du channel).
Indications: Sciatica, **hip disorders**, paralysis of the lower limb.
Recommended depth of needle penetration: 1.5 inch, perpendicularly.

UB 55 (Heyang)

Location: 2 cun below UB 40, on a line connecting UB 40 with UB 57.
Indications: Lumbago and leg pain.
Recommended depth of needle penetration: 1 inch, perpendicularly.

UB 56 (Chengjin)

Location: Midway between UB 55 and UB 57 in the center of the belly of the gastrocnemius muscle.
Indications: Leg pain, stiffness and pain in the back and lumbar region.
Recommended depth of needle penetration: 1 inch, perpendicularly.

UB 57 (Chengshan)

Location: At the level where the two bellies of the gastrocnemius unite to form the tendoachilles, 8 cun below UB 40; halfway between UB 40 and the ankle joint.
Indications: Sciatica, spasms of the calf muscles, plantar fasciitis.
Recommended depth of needle penetration: 1 inch, perpendicularly.

UB 58 (Feiyang)

Location: 7 cun proximal to UB 60, on the lateral aspect of the calf muscle, posterior to the lateral malleolus.
Indications: Leg pain, weakness in the legs, sciatica.
Recommended depth of needle penetration: 1 inch, perpendicularly.

UB 59 (Fuyang)

Location: 3 cun above UB 60, posterior to the lateral malleolus.
Indications: Pain and swelling in the ankle region, pain in the lumbosacral region, sciatica.
Recommended depth of needle penetration: 0.8 inch, perpendicularly.

UB 60 (Kunlun)

Location: Midway between the prominence of the lateral malleolus and the lateral border of the tendochilles.
Indications: **Painful disorders of the ankle (arthritis, achilles tendonitis)**, sciatica, lumbago, paralysis of the lower limb.
Recommended depth of needle penetration: 0.5 inch, perpendicularly.

UB 61 (Pushen)

Location: 1.5 cun inferior to the lateral malleolus, directly below UB 60, posterior to the calcaneus, at the junction of the "red and white" skin.
Indications: Heel pain, ankle joint pain, achilles tendonitis.
Recommended depth of needle penetration: 0.3 inch, perpendicularly.

UB 62 (Shenmai)

Location: 0.5 cun posterior to the tip (lower border) of the lateral malleolus.
Indications: Foot drop.
Recommended depth of needle penetration: 0.3 inch, perpendicularly.

UB 63 (Jinmen)

Location: Anterior and inferior to UB 62, in the depression posterior to the tuberosity of the fifth metatarsal bone.
Indications: Pain in the leg and ankle joint, lumbago.
Recommended depth of needle penetration: 0.3 inch, perpendicularly.

UB 64 (Jinggu)

Location: Below the tuberosity of the fifth metatarsal bone, at the junction of the "red and white" skin.
Indications: Leg pain.
Recommended depth of needle penetration: 0.3 inch, perpendicularly.

UB 65 (Shugu)

Location: Posterior and inferior to the head of the fifth metatarsal.
Indications: Leg pain.
Recommended depth of needle penetration: 0.3 inch, perpendicularly.

UB 66 (Tonggu)

Location: In the depression anterior and inferior to the fifth metatarsalphalangeal joint.

UB 67 (Zhiyin)

Location: 0.1 cun proximal to the lateral edge of the proximal nail fold of the small toe-nail.

KIDNEY MERIDIAN (K)

The kidney meridian is a Yin Meridian. The kidney meridian and the heart meridian make up the **Shao Yin** axis (Fig. 4.10).

General

The kidneys store kidney Shen. Shen is a term for spiritual energy. Body growth, development and reproductive functions depend on kidney Shen. The kidneys nourish bones and marrow, guide body fluids, assist inhalation and are responsible for the condition of the hair, ears, anus and urethra. The activities of the kidneys also encompass the functions of the central nervous, endocrine, and urogenital systems.

Superficial Course

The kidney meridian originates on the sole of the foot, it then courses along the medial side of the leg, to the abdomen, where it is located 0.5 cun lateral to the midline. In the thoracic region the meridian is 2 cun from the midline. The meridian ends in a depression just below the clavicle (K 27).

Clinical Indications

Points of the kidney meridian are useful in the treatment of rheumatoid disease, diseases of the lower extremities, and the urogenital system.

K 1 (Yongquan)

Location: In the sole of the foot, in the depression formed between the anterior one-third and posterior two-third parts of the sole when the toes are plantar flexed (Fig. 4.11).
Indications: Plantar fasciitis, plantar warts.
Recommended depth of needle penetration: 0.3 inch, perpendicularly.

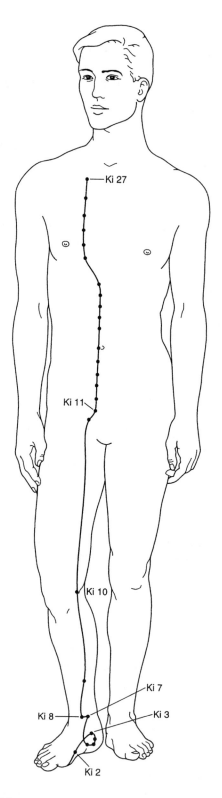

Figure 4.10 Kidney Meridian

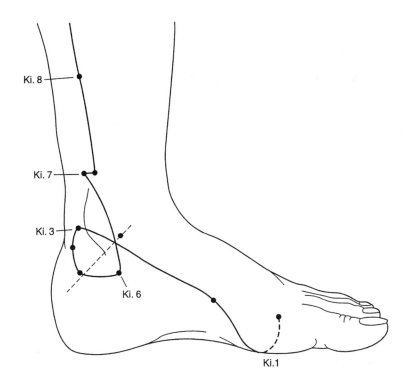

Figure 4.11 Ki Channel: Leg (Ki 1–10)

K 2 (Rangu)

Location: Anterior and inferior to the medial malleolus, in a depression at the anterior and inferior border of the navicular.

K 3 (Taixi)

Location: Midway between the prominence of the medial malleolus and the achilles tendon.
Indications: Low backache, disorders of the ankle joint.
Recommended depth of needle penetration: 0.5 inch, perpendicularly.
Anatomic precaution: Tibial artery.

K 4 (Dazhong)

Location: Anterior and inferior to the medial malleolus, in the depression medial malleolus to the attachment to the achilles tendon at the calcaneus, 0.5 cun below and slightly posterior to K 3.
Indications: Heel pain, pain in the ankle joint, lumbago.
Recommended depth of needle penetration: 0.3 inch, perpendicularly.

K 5 (Shuiquan)

Location: 1 cun below K. 3, in a depression on the medial surface of the calcaneous.

K 6 (Zhaohai)

Location: In the depression 1 cun directly below the prominence of the medial malleolus, or, 0.4 cun below the tip (lower border) of the medial malleolus.
Indications: Edema of the ankle, disorders of the ankle joint.
Recommended depth of needle penetration: 0.3 inch, perpendicularly.

K 7 (Fuliu)

Location: 2 cun proximal to K. 3 on the medial border of the tendo-achilles.
Indications: Lumbago.
Recommended depth of needle penetration: 0.5 inch, perpendicularly.

K 8 (Jiaoxin)

Location: 2 cun proximal to K.3, 0.5 cun anterior to K.7, posterior to the medial border tibia.

K 9 (Zhubin)

Location: 5 cun proximal to K.3, about 1 cun posterior to the medial border tibia.
Indications: Gastrocnemius spasm.
Recommended depth of needle penetration: 1 inch, perpendicularly.
Anatomic precaution: **Posterior tibial artery.**

K 10 (Yingu)

Location: At the medial end of the popliteal crease on the medial border of the semitendinosis.
Indications: Knee disorders, pain, swelling.
Recommended depth of needle penetration: 0.8 inch, perpendicularly.

K 11 (Henggu)

Location: In the lower abdomen, on the superior border of the pubic symphysis, 0.5 cun lateral to Ren 2.

K 12 (Dahe)

Location: 1 cun above K.11, 0.5 cun lateral to Ren 3.

K 13 (Qixue)

Location: 2 cun above K.11, 0.5 cun lateral to Ren 4.

K 14 (Siman)

Location: 3 cun above K.11, 0.5 cun lateral to Ren 5.

K 15 (Abdomen-Zhongzhu)

Location: 1 cun below the umbilicus, 0.5 cun lateral to Ren 7.

K 16 (Huangshu)

Location: 0.5 cun lateral to the umbilicus.

K 17 (Shangqu)

Location: 2 cun above K.16, 0.5 cun lateral to Ren 10.

K 18 (Shiguan)

Location: 3 cun above K.16, 0.5 cun lateral to Ren 11.

K 19 (Yindu)

Location: 4 cun above K.16, 0.5 cun lateral to Ren 12.

K 20 (Abdomen-Tonggu)

Location: 5 cun above K.16, 0.5 cun lateral to Ren 13.

K 21 (Youmen)

Location: 6 cun above K.16, 0.5 cun lateral to Ren 14.

K 22 (Bulang)

Location: In the fifth intercostal space, 2 cun lateral to the Ren channel.
Indications: Intercostal neuralgia, pleuritis.
Recommended depth of needle penetration: 0.3 inch, obliquely.

K 23 (Shenfeng)

Location: In the fourth intercostal space, 2 cun lateral to Ren 17.
Indications: Intercostal neuralgia, pleuritis.
Recommended depth of needle penetration: 0.3 inch, obliquely.

K 24 (Lingxu)

Location: In the third intercostal space, 2 cun lateral to the Ren channel, midway between the sternal and mammillary lines.
Indications: Chest and costal pain.
Recommended depth of needle penetration: 0.3 inch, obliquely.

K 25 (Shencang)

Location: In the second intercostal space, 2 cun lateral to the Ren channel, midway between the sternal and mammillary lines.
Indications: Intercostal neuralgia.
Recommended depth of needle penetration: 0.3 inch, obliquely.

K 26 (Yuzhong)

Location: In the first intercostal space, 2 cun lateral to the Ren channel, midway between the sternal and mammillary lines.
Indications: Chest pain.
Recommended depth of needle penetration: 0.3 inch, obliquely.

K 27 (Shufu)

Location: In the depression between the first rib and lower border of the clavicle, space, 2 cun lateral to the Ren channel.

PERICARDIUM MERIDIAN (P)

The Pericardium meridian is a Yin meridian. It can be thought of as a distant relative of the parasympathetic system. The pericardium meridian and the liver meridian together make up the **Jue Yin** axis (Fig. 4.12).

General

The pericardium is felt to represent a membrane or energy field surrounding the heart, protecting the heart from physical and emotional stress. Although there is a similarity between the functions of the heart and the pericardium, heart energy is the more powerful and essential of the two. In effect, the pericardium is auxiliary to the heart.

Superficial Course

The pericardium meridian starts in the middle of the anterior thorax 1 cun lateral to the nipple line in the fourth intercostal space. It then passes to the axilla, descending along the medial aspect of the arm to end in the palm on the palmer surface of the tip of the middle finger.

Clinical Applications

Clinical applications include diseases of the upper extremities, heart, chest, and stomach.

P 1 (Tianchi)

Location: 1 cun lateral to the nipple in the fourth intercostal space.
Indications: Pain in the hypochondriac region, intercostal neuralgia.
Recommended depth of needle penetration: 0.5 inch, obliquely.

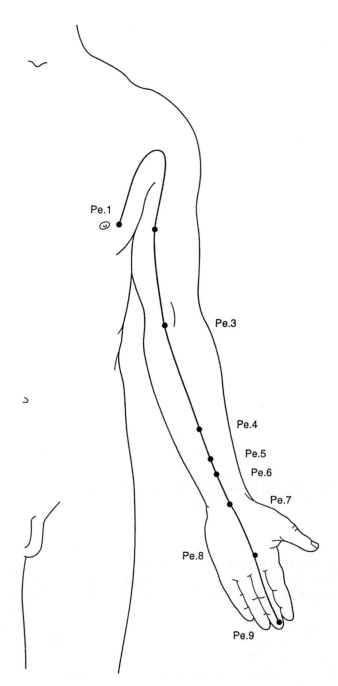

Figure 4.12 Pericardium Meridian

P 2 (Tianquan)

Location: 2 cun below the anterior axillary fold, between the two heads of the biceps muscle.

Indications: Pain in the back and medial aspect of the arm.
Recommended depth of needle penetration: 1 inch, perpendicularly.

P 3 (Quze)

Location: In the ante-cubital crease, on the medial (ulnar) border of the biceps tendon.
Indications: Arthritis of the elbow joint.
Recommended depth of needle penetration: 0.5 inch, perpendicularly.
Anatomic precaution: **Brachial artery, median nerve.**

P 4 (Ximen)

Location: 5 cun proximal to the midpoint of the wrist crease, between the tendons of the palmaris longus and the flexor carpi radialis muscles.
Indications: Neurasthenia.
Recommended depth of needle penetration: 0.5 inch, perpendicularly.

P 5 (Jianshi)

Location: 3 cun proximal to the midpoint of the wrist crease, between the tendons of the palmaris longus and the flexor carpi radialis muscles.

P 6 (Neiguan)

Location: 2 cun proximal to the midpoint of the wrist crease, between the tendons of the palmaris longus and the flexor carpi radialis muscles.
Indications: Numbness in the forearm and hands, Carpal Tunnel Syndrome, costal pain.
Recommended depth of needle penetration: 0.5 inch, perpendicularly.

P 7 (Daling)

Location: At the midpoint of the wrist crease, between the tendons of the palmaris longus and the flexor carpi radialis muscles.
Indications: Diseases of the wrist joint, Carpal Tunnel Syndrome.
Recommended depth of needle penetration: Subcutaneously, obliquely.
Anatomic precaution: Median nerve.

P 8 (Loagong)

Location: In the middle of the palm, between the tips of the middle and ring fingers—these touch the palm when making a fist.
Indications: Disorders of the palm and skin of the hand, rheumatoid arthritis of the hand and wrist, Dupuytren's contracture.
Recommended depth of needle penetration: 0.3 inch, perpendicularly.

P 9 (Zhongchong)

Location: At the midpoint of the tip of the middle finger

SANJIAO ("TRIPLE WARMER") MERIDIAN (SJ)

The Sanjiao meridian is a Yang meridian. The Sanjiao meridian can be thought of as related to the sympathetic system. The Sanjiao meridian and the gallbladder meridian together make up the **Shao Yang** axis (Fig. 4.13).

General

The exact function of the Sanjiao was an enigma to the ancient Chinese because it has no physical presence. It has an ill-defined effect on the biochemical metabolism of the body. The "triple warmer" has an effect ranging over three body regions: the thoracic cavity and the abdominal and pelvic regions. In the thoracic cavity, the heart, lungs, pericardium, and activities of the head occur in the upper heater. In the abdominal cavity, the middle heater controls the area of the stomach and spleen. The lower heater contains the remaining organs: the liver, kidneys, bladder, and the small and large intestines.

Superficial Course

The Sanjiao meridian starts on the ulnar side of the ring finger, at the ulnar corner of the nail; ascends along the dorsum of the hand, forearm, and arm to the shoulder; and circles around the auricle, to end on the lateral edge of the eyebrow.

Clinical Correlation

The *Huang Di Nei Jing* and other ancient literature describe the sanjiao as "burning, heating three cavities." There are no anatomic correlates, and therefore the sanjiao has been regarded as the three body cavities: the upper burner as the thorax, the middle burner as the abdominal cavity, and the lower burner as the pelvic region. The Sanjiao meridian is useful in chest and *shoulder pain* and headaches.

SJ 1 (Guanchong)

Location: On the ulnar side of the ring finger, 0.1 cun posterior to the corner of the nail.
Indications: Headache.
Recommended depth of needle penetration: 0.1 inch, obliquely.

SJ 2 (Yemen)

Location: 0.5 cun proximal to the margin of the web between the ring and small fingers
Indications: Pain in the hand and arm.
Recommended depth of needle penetration: 0.3 inch, perpendicularly.

SJ 3 (Zhongzhu)

Location: On the dorsum of the hand in the depression between the heads of the fourth and fifth metacarpals. This point is best located while making a fist.
Indications: Upper extremity edema, pain, polyneuropathy, and paralysis of the upper extremities or hands.
Recommended depth of needle penetration: 0.5 inch, perpendicularly.

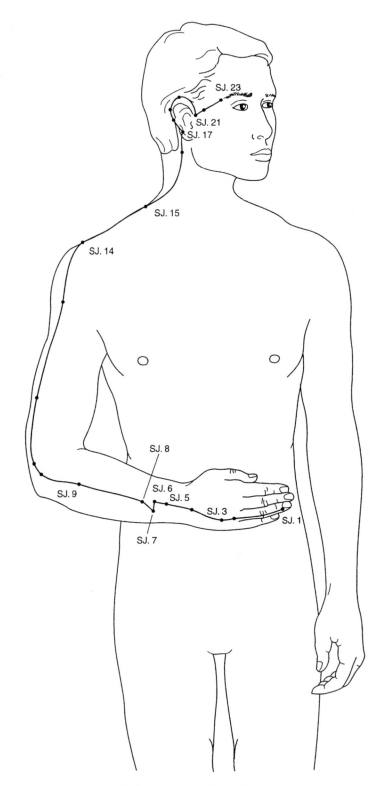

Figure 4.13 Anterior view of Triple Heater Meridian (SanJiao)

SJ 4 (Yangchi)

Location: In the depression of the transverse crease of the wrist, between the extensor digitorum communis and the extensor digiti quinti minimi.
Indications: Disorders of the wrist joint.
Recommended depth of needle penetration: 0.3 inch, perpendicularly.

SJ 5 (Waiguan)

Location: 2 cun proximal to the midpoint of the dorsal transverse crease of the wrist, between the radius and ulna.
Indications: Stiff neck, paralysis of the upper extremities, thoracocostal pain, **arthritis of the wrist and finger joints.**
Recommended depth of needle penetration: 0.5 inch, perpendicularly.

SJ 6 (Zhigou)

Location: 1 cun proximal to S.J.5, between the radius and ulna.
Indications: Shoulder and back pain, paralysis of the upper extremities, thoracocostal pain.
Recommended depth of needle penetration: 0.5 inch, perpendicularly.

SJ 7 (Huizong)

Location: 1 finger breadth ulnar to S.J.6, on the radial side of the ulna.
Indications: Pain in the upper extremities.
Recommended depth of needle penetration: 0.5 inch, perpendicularly.

SJ 8 (Sanyangluo)

Location: 1 cun proximal to S.J. 6.
Indications: Pain in the arm and costal region (herpes zoster).
Recommended depth of needle penetration: 0.5 inch, perpendicularly.

SJ 9 (Sidu)

Location: 5 cun below the olecranon, between the radius and ulna.
Indications: Pain in the forearm.
Recommended depth of needle penetration: 0.5 inch, perpendicularly.

SJ 10 (Tianjing)

Location: 1 cun posterior and superior to the olecranon, in the depression made by flexing the elbow.
Indications: Disorders of the elbow joint.
Recommended depth of needle penetration: 0.5 inch, perpendicularly.

SJ 11 (Qinglengyuan)

Location: 1 cun above S.J. 10, flex the elbow to locate this point.
Indications: Pain in the shoulder and arm.
Recommended depth of needle penetration: 0.5 inch, perpendicularly.

SJ 12 (Xiaoluo)

Location: Midway between S.J. 11 and S.J. 13.
Indications: Pain in the arm.
Recommended depth of needle penetration: 0.5 inch, perpendicularly.

SJ 13 (Naohui)

Location: 3 cun below S.J. 14, at the posterior border of the deltoid.
Indications: Pain in the shoulder and arm, swelling of the scapular joint.
Recommended depth of needle penetration: 0.5 inch, perpendicularly.

SJ 14 (Jianliao)

Location: With the arm abducted to a horizontal position, in the posterior depression of the origin of the deltoid muscle on the lateral border of the acromion. With the arm by the side, between the acromion and greater tuberosity of the humerus.
Indications: Frozen shoulder, arm pain, **painful disorders of the shoulder joint**.
Recommended depth of needle penetration: With the arm abducted, puncture perpendicularly 1 inch between the acromion and the greater tuberosity of the humerus.

SJ 15 (Tianliao)

Location: Midway between the tip of the acromion and Du 14, 1 cun posterior and inferior to GB 21.
Indications: Pain in the shoulder and arm, neck pain.
Recommended depth of needle penetration: 0.5 inch, perpendicularly.

SJ 16 (Tianyou)

Location: Posterior and inferior to the mastoid process, on the posterior border of the sternocleidomastoid, level with the angle of the mandible.
Indications: Rigidity of the neck.
Recommended depth of needle penetration: 1 inch, perpendicularly.

SJ 17 (Yifeng)

Location: In the highest point of the depression behind the earlobe, between the angle of the mandible and the mastoid process.
Indications: Facial paralysis.
Recommended depth of needle penetration: 0.5 inch, perpendicularly.

SJ 18 (Qimai)

Location: Behind the ear, in the center of the mastoid process.
Indications: Facial paralysis.
Recommended depth of needle penetration: 0.2 inch, perpendicularly.

SJ 19 (Luxi)

Location: 1 cun above SJ 18.

SJ 20 (Jiasun)

Location: On the scalp at the apex of the ear, when the ear is folded forwards.

SJ 21 (Ermen)

Location: In the depression in front of the supra tragic notch. It is easier to locate when the mouth is open.
Indications: Disorders of the temporomandibular joint.
Recommended depth of needle penetration: 0.5 inch, perpendicularly with the patient's mouth open.

SJ 22 (Ear-Heliao)

Location: On the hairline anterior and superior to SJ 21, anterior to, and level with, the root of the auricle, posterior to the superficial temporal artery.

SJ 23 (Sizhukong)

Location: In the depression at the lateral end of the eyebrow.
Indications: Temporal headache, migraine.
Recommended depth of needle penetration: 0.5 inch, horizontally and posteriorly.

GALLBLADDER MERIDIAN (GB)

The gallbladder meridian is a Yang meridian. The gallbladder meridian together with the sanjiao meridian make up the **Shao Yang** axis (Fig. 4.14).

General

The gallbladder stores bile, the only pure fluid stored (or formed) within the body. The purity of its energy gives the gallbladder the power to defend itself and the body, both emotionally and physically.

Superficial Course

The gallbladder meridian originates 0.5 cun lateral to the outer canthus of the eye and runs to the ear, encircling the ear and then curving downward to the occipital region. The meridian then runs back to the forehead and then returns backward

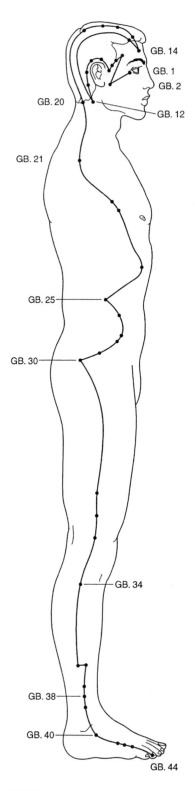

Figure 4.14 Gall Bladder Meridian

parallel to the midline of the neck, passing out over the shoulder to descend on the lateral side of the trunk, along the lateral side of the abdomen and along the lateral side of the leg and foot, ending on the lateral edge of the nail of the fourth toe.

Clinical Indications

The gallbladder meridian points are useful in the treatment of low back pain, sciatica, paralysis, and cervical spondylosis.

GB 1 (Tongziliao)

Location: 0.5 cun lateral to the outer canthus of the eye.
Indications: Headache, trigeminal neuralgia.
Recommended depth of needle penetration: 0.5 inch, obliquely.

GB 2 (Tinghui)

Location: In the depression immediately in front of the intertragic notch when the mouth is open.
Indications: Arthritis of the temporomandibular joint, trigeminal neuralgia.
Recommended depth of needle penetration: 0.8 inch, perpendicularly.
Anatomic precaution: Superficial temporal artery.

GB 3 (Shangguan)

Location: In front of the ear, on the upper border of the zygomatic arch, directly above St 7.
Indications: Toothache, facial paralysis.
Recommended depth of needle penetration: 0.5 inch, perpendicularly.

GB 4 (Hanyan)

Location: 1 cun below St 8 on the hairline of the temporal region.
Indications: Migraine.
Recommended depth of needle penetration: 0.3 inch, obliquely.

GB 5 (Xuanlu)

Location: On the line connecting GB 4 and GB 7, at the junction of the anterior and middle third on the line.
Indications: Migraine.
Recommended depth of needle penetration: 0.2 inch, obliquely.

GB 6 (Xuanli)

Location: On the line connecting GB 4 and GB 7, at the junction of the inferior and middle third on the line.
Indications: Migraine.
Recommended depth of needle penetration: 0.3 inch, obliquely.

GB 7 (Qubin)

Location: At the crossing point of the horizontal line of the auricle and the line that projects from the anterior auricle.
Indications: Stiff neck.
Recommended depth of needle penetration: 0.3 inch, obliquely.

GB 8 (Shuaigu)

Location: Directly above the apex of the ear, 1.5 cun above the hairline.
Indications: Migraine.
Recommended depth of needle penetration: 0.5 inch, horizontally.

GB 9 (Tainchong)

Location: 0.5 cun posterior to GB 8, superior and posterior to the auricle, 2 cun inside the hairline.
Indications: Headache.
Recommended depth of needle penetration: 0.5 inch, obliquely.

GB 10 (Fubai)

Location: 1 cun inferior to GB 9, at the upper border of the root of the auricle, 1 cun behind the hairline.

GB 11 (Head-Qiaoyin)

Location: Midpoint of the line connecting GB 10 with GB 12.
Indications: Headache.
Recommended depth of needle penetration: 0.5 inch, obliquely.

GB 12 (Head-Wangu)

Location: In the depression posterior and inferior to the mastoid process.

GB 13 (Benshen)

Location: 0.5 cun inside the hairline, directly above the outer canthus.
Indications: Stiff neck.
Recommended depth of needle penetration: 0.5 inch, obliquely.

GB 14 (Yangbai)

Location: 1 cun above the midpoint of the eyebrow.
Indications: Frontal headache.
Recommended depth of needle penetration: 0.3 inch, horizontally.

GB 15 (Head-Linqi)

Location: With the patient looking straight ahead, it is directly above the pupil, 0.5 cun inside the hairline.

GB 16 (Muchuang)

Location: 1 cun above GB 15.

GB 17 (Zhengying)

Location: 1 cun posterior to GB 16.
Indications: Headache
Recommended depth of needle penetration: 0.5 inch, obliquely.

GB 18 (Chengling)

Location: 1.5 cun posterior to GB 17.
Indications: Headache.
Recommended depth of needle penetration: 0.5 inch, obliquely.

GB 19 (Naokong)

Location: 1.5 cun above GB 20, on the lateral side of the occipital protuberance.
Indications: Stiff neck.
Recommended depth of needle penetration: 0.5 inch, obliquely.

GB 20 (Fengchi)

Location: In the depression medial to the mastoid process between the origins of the trapezius and sternocleidomastoid muscles.
Indications: Stiff neck, cervical spondylosis, occipital headache, **torticollis**.
Recommended depth of needle penetration: Superficially, subcutaneously, perpendicularly. It is not advisable to puncture too deeply.

GB 21 (Jianjing)

Location: Directly posterior to the midpoint of the clavicle, halfway between the clavicle and the superior border of the spine of the scapula.
Indications: Pain in the shoulder region, stiff neck, cervical spondylosis, ankylosing spondylitis, periarthritis of the shoulder.
Recommended depth of needle penetration: 0.5 inch, perpendicularly.

GB 22 (Yuanye)

Location: 3 cun below the anterior axillary fold, on the axillary fold, in the fourth intercostal space when the arm is raised.
Indications: Intercostal neuralgia.
Recommended depth of needle penetration: 0.5 inch, obliquely.

GB 23 (Zhejin)

Location: 1 cun anterior to GB 22, in the fourth intercostal space.

GB 24 (Riyue)

Location: On the nipple line in the seventh intercostal space.

GB 25 (Jingmen)

Location: At the free end of the twelfth rib.
Indications: Costal pain.
Recommended depth of needle penetration: 0.3 inch, perpendicularly.

GB 26 (Daimai)

Location: At the level of the umbilicus, on a vertical line drawn from the free end of the eleventh rib.
Indications: Costal pain, back pain.
Recommended depth of needle penetration: 1 inch, perpendicularly.

GB 27 (Wushu)

Location: 3 cun anterior and inferior to GB 26, level with Ren 4, in front of the anterior superior iliac spine.
Indications: Lumbago.
Recommended depth of needle penetration: 1 inch, perpendicularly.

GB 28 (Weidao)

Location: Anterior and inferior to the anterior superior iliac spine, 0.5 cun anterior and inferior to GB 27.

GB 29 (Femur-Juliao)

Location: Midway between the anterior superior iliac spine and the highest point of the greater trochanter of the femur. Best found with the patient recumbent.
Indications: Disorders of the hip joint, pain in the lower extremities.
Recommended depth of needle penetration: 1 inch, perpendicularly.

GB 30 (Huantiao)

Location: Draw a straight line between the highest point of the greater trochanter and the sacral hiatus: the point is located at the junction of the outer third with the medial two-thirds on this line. It is found more easily with the patient prone.
Indications: Sciatica, prolapsed lumbar disc, disorders of the hip joint
This is a very effective point for treating sciatica.
Recommended depth of needle penetration: 1.5 inch, perpendicularly.

GB 31 (Fengshi)

Location: On the lateral aspect of the thigh, 7 cun proximal to the transverse popliteal crease, between the vastus lateralis and biceps femoris muscles.
Indications: **Meralgia paresthetica** (paraesthesia in the distribution of the lateral cutaneous nerve of the thigh), pain in the lower extremities, pain in the lumbar region, sciatica, low back pain.
Recommended depth of needle penetration: 1.5 inch, perpendicularly.

GB 32 (Femur-Zhongdu)

Location: On the lateral aspect of the thigh, 2 cun below GB 31.
Indications: Sciatica, hemiplegia.
Recommended depth of needle penetration: 1.5 inch, perpendicularly.

GB 33 (Xiyangguan)

Location: In the depression superior to the lateral epicondyle of the femur, 3 cun above GB 34.
Indications: Pain in the knee joint.
Recommended depth of needle penetration: 0.5 inch, perpendicularly.

GB 34 (Yanglingquan)

Location: In the depression anterior and inferior to the head of the fibula.
Indications: Hemiplegia, pain and paralysis of the leg, **muscle and tendon disorders, tendonitis, rheumatoid arthritis**. GB 34 is an influential point for any muscle and tendon problems.
Recommended depth of needle penetration: 1 inch, perpendicularly.

GB 35 (Yangjiao)

Location: 7 cun above the tip of the lateral malleolus, in the anterior border of the fibula, on a line connecting the tip of the lateral malleolus with GB 34.
Indications: Pain in the lateral aspect of the leg, sciatica.
Recommended depth of needle penetration: 1 inch, perpendicularly.

GB 36 (Waiqiu)

Location: Level and 1 cun posterior to GB 35, and posterior to the border of the fibula.
Indications: Pain in the lateral aspect of the leg, spasm of the gastrocnemius, torticollis, cervical spondylosis.
Recommended depth of needle penetration: 1 inch, perpendicularly.

GB 37 (Guangming)

Location: 5 cun above the tip of the lateral malleolus, on the anterior border of the fibula.
Indications: Pain in the lower extremities.
Recommended depth of needle penetration: 0.5 inch, perpendicularly.

GB 38 (Yangfu)

Location: 4 cun above the tip of the lateral malleolus, on the anterior border of the fibula.
Indications: Arthritis of the knee joint.
Recommended depth of needle penetration: 1 inch, perpendicularly.

GB 39 (Xuanzhong)

Location: 3 cun above the tip of the lateral malleolus, on the posterior border of the fibula.
Indications: Stiff neck, disorders of the ankle joint, paralysis of the lower limbs. **Important distal point for torticollis.**
Recommended depth of needle penetration: 0.5 inch, perpendicularly.
Anatomic precaution: **Anterior tibial artery.**

GB 40 (Qioxu)

Location: At the meeting point of two lines; one drawn vertically on the anterior border of the lateral malleolus, the other drawn horizontally on its inferior border.
Indications: Arthritis, ankle joint pain, lower leg ulcers.
Recommended depth of needle penetration: 0.5 inch, perpendicularly.

GB 41 (Foot-Linqi)

Location: In the depression immediately distal to the junction of the base of the fourth and fifth metatarsals.
Indications: Foot pain and disorders.
Recommended depth of needle penetration: 0.5 inch, perpendicularly.

GB 42 (Diwuhui)

Location: On the cleft between the fourth and fifth metatarsals, 0.5 cun anterior to GB 41.
Indications: Axillary pain.
Recommended depth of needle penetration: 0.3 inch, perpendicularly.

GB 43 (Xiaxi)

Location: On the cleft between the fourth and fifth metatarsals, 0.5 cun proximal to the margin of the web.
Indications: Intercostal neuralgia.
Recommended depth of needle penetration: 0.3 inch, perpendicularly.

GB 44 (Foot-Qiaoyin)

Location: On the lateral side of the tip of the fourth toe, 0.1 cun posterior to the corner of the nail.
Indications: Headache.
Recommended depth of needle penetration: 0.1 inch, perpendicularly.

LIVER MERIDIAN (LIV)

The liver meridian is a Yin meridian. The liver meridian and the pericardium meridian together make up the **Jue Yin** axis (Fig. 4.15).

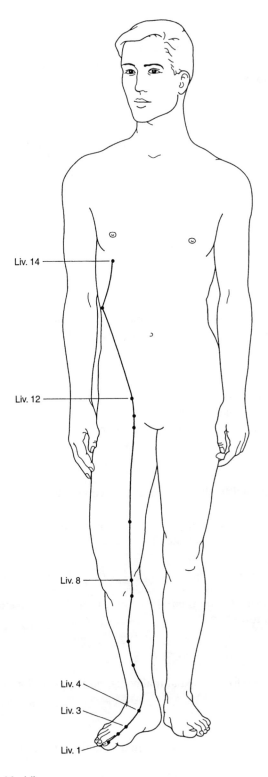

Figure 4.15 Liver Meridian

General

The liver regulates energy flow, stores and controls blood volume, nourishes the tendons, animates the eyes, directs the formation and secretion of bile, and governs the emotions.

Superficial Course

The liver meridian runs from the lateral aspect of the tip of the great toe along the medial side of the leg and thigh to the external genitalia, then ascending to the abdomen, to end at the lateral chest wall in the sixth intercostal space below the nipple.

Clinical Indications

Points of the liver meridian are useful in the treatment of headaches.

Liv 1 (Dadun)

Location: On the lateral aspect of the dorsum of the tip of the great toe, midway between the lateral corner of the nail and the interphalangeal joint.

Liv 2 (Xingjian)

Location: 0.5 cun proximal to the margin of the web of the first and second toes.
Indications: Costal pain, headache.
Recommended depth of needle penetration: 0.3 inch, obliquely.

Liv 3 (Taichong)

Location: 2 cun proximal to the margin of the web of the first and second toes.
Indications: Headaches.
Recommended depth of needle penetration: 0.5 inch, obliquely.
Anatomic precaution: **First dorsal metatarsal artery.**

Liv 4 (Zhongfeng)

Location: 1 cun anterior to the medial malleolus, in the depression medial to the anterior tibialis tendon.

Liv 5 (Ligou)

Location: 5 cun superior to the medial malleolus, on the posterior border of the tibia.

Liv 6 (Zhongdu)

Location: 7 cun superior to the tip of the medial malleolus on the medial border of the tibia.
Indications: Pain in the joints of the lower extremities.
Recommended depth of needle penetration: 0.5 inch, perpendicularly.

Liv 7 (Xiguan)

Location: In the posterior and inferior aspect of the medial condyle of the tibia, 1 cun posterior to Sp 9.
Indications: Pain in the knee joint.
Recommended depth of needle penetration: 1 inch, perpendicularly.

Liv 8 (Quanquan)

Location: In the transverse crease of the knee joint, at the medial border of the semimembranosis tendon.
Indications: Disorders of the knee joint.
Recommended depth of needle penetration: 1 inch, perpendicularly.

Liv 9 (Yinbao)

Location: 4 cun superior to the medial epicondyle of the femur, between the vastus medialis and sartorius.
Indications: Lumbago.
Recommended depth of needle penetration: 1 inch, perpendicularly.

Liv 10 (Femur-Wuli)

Location: 1 cun below Liv 11, on the medial aspect of the thigh.

Liv 11 (Yinlian)

Location: 1 cun inferior to the lateral aspect of the femoral artery in the inguinal groove. Locate the point with the patient supine.
Indications: Femoral neuralgia, leg pain.
Recommended depth of needle penetration: 1 inch, perpendicularly.

Liv 12 (Jimai)

Location: 2.5 cun lateral to the center of the pubic symphysis.
Indications: Pain in the medial aspect of the thigh.
Recommended depth of needle penetration: 0.5 inch, perpendicularly.

Liv 13 (Zhangmen)

Location: At the free end of the 11th rib.
Indications: Pain in the costal region.
Recommended depth of needle penetration: 0.5 inch, perpendicularly.

Liv 14 (Qimen)

Location: Vertically below the nipple, in the intercostal space between the sixth and secenth ribs.
Indications: Chest pain, intercostal neuralgia.
Recommended depth of needle penetration: 0.3 inch, obliquely.

DU MAI (GOVERNOR VESSEL) MERIDIAN (DU)

The governor vessel or "Du Mai" meridian is considered to be the "governor" of the six Yang meridians (Fig. 4.16).

General

The Du Mai (as well as the Ren) meridians are classified among the eight "extraordinary" channels. No internal organ is identified with the Du Mai meridian, but the Du Mai is considered to be closely related to, and have significant influence upon, the central nervous system.

Superficial Course

The Du Mai meridian starts at the os coccyx and travels upward along the dorsal midline to the neck, then runs along the midline of the head to the forehead and nose, to end below the upper lip.

Clinical Indications

These points are useful in the treatment of *lumbago, low back pain, cervical spondylosis, intercostal neuralgia,* and migraine.

Du 1 (Changqiang)

Location: Midway between the tip of the coccyx and the anus. This point is best located with the patient in the prone or lateral position.

Du 2 (Yaoshu)

Location: On the back, midline, at the sacral hiatus.
Indications: Pain in the sacrolumbar region. **In treatment of spastic paralysis, use with electrostimulation together with Du 6.**
Recommended depth of needle penetration: 0.5 inch, obliquely upward.

Du 3 (Yaoyangguan)

Location: On the back, midline, between the dorsal spines of the fourth and fifth lumbar vertebrae, at the level of the iliac crest.
Indications: Low back pain, sciatica.
Recommended depth of needle penetration: 1 inch, perpendicularly with the needle tilted upward.

Du 4 (Mingmen)

Location: On the back, midline, between the dorsal spines of the second and third lumbar vertebrae, at the level of the lower border of the ribcage.
Indications: Low back pain, sciatica.
Recommended depth of needle penetration: 1 inch, perpendicularly.

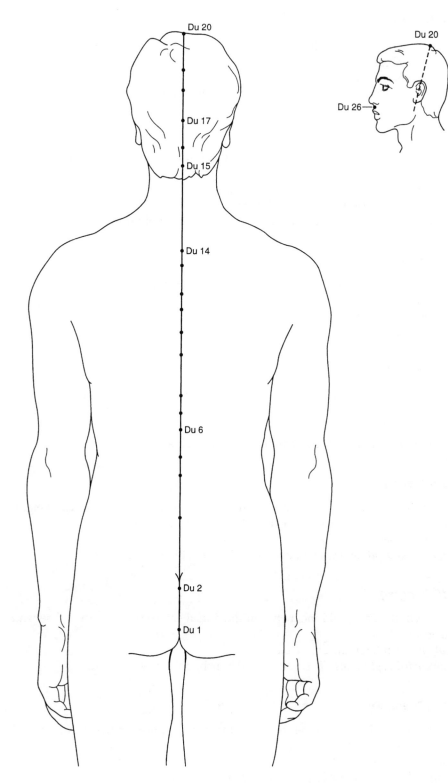

Figure 4.16 Du Mai Meridian

Du 5 (Xanshu)

Location: On the back, midline, between the dorsal spines of the first and second lumbar vertebrae.
Indications: Back pain.
Recommended depth of needle penetration: 0.5 inch, obliquely upward.

Du 6 (Jizhong)

Location: On the back, midline, between the dorsal spines of the eleventh and twelfth thoracic vertebrae.
Indications: Muscle spasticity, sciatica, lumbago. **In the treatment of spastic paralysis, electrostimulate this point with Du 2 or Ex. 20.**
Recommended depth of needle penetration: 0.5 inch, obliquely upward.

Du 7 (Zhongshu)

Location: On the back, midline, between the dorsal spines of the tenth and eleventh thoracic vertebrae.
Indications: Back pain.
Recommended depth of needle penetration: 0.5 inch, obliquely upward.

Du 8 (Jinsuo)

Location: On the back, midline, between the dorsal spines of the ninth and tenth thoracic vertebrae.
Indications: Back pain.
Recommended depth of needle penetration: 0.5 inch, obliquely upward.

Du 9 (Zhiyang)

Location: On the back, midline, between the dorsal spines of the seventh and eighth thoracic vertebrae, at the level of the inferior angle of the scapula.
Indications: Chest and back pain, stiffness of the spinal column.
Recommended depth of needle penetration: 0.5 inch, obliquely upward.

Du 10 (Lingtai)

Location: On the back, midline, between the dorsal spines of the sixth and seventh thoracic vertebrae.
Indications: Lumbago and back pain.
Recommended depth of needle penetration: 0.5 inch, obliquely upward.

Du 11 (Shendao)

Location: On the back, midline, between the dorsal spines of the fifth and sixth thoracic vertebrae.
Indications: Stiffness of the back.
Recommended depth of needle penetration: 0.5 inch, obliquely upward.

Du 12 (Shenzhu)

Location: On the back, midline, between the dorsal spines of the third and fourth thoracic vertebrae.
Indications: Stiffness and pain of the back.
Recommended depth of needle penetration: 0.5 inch, obliquely upward.

Du 13 (Taodao)

Location: On the back, midline, between the dorsal spines of the first and second thoracic vertebrae.
Indications: Stiffness of back, back pain, cervical spondylosis, neck pain.
Recommended depth of needle penetration: 0.5 inch, obliquely upward.

Du 14 (Dazhui)

Location: On the back, midline, between the dorsal spines of the seventh cervical and the first thoracic vertebrae.
Indications: Stiff neck, cervical spondylosis, torticollis, sprain of the cervical muscles, neck injuries, hypotonia of neck muscles, frozen shoulder with pain radiating to the back of the chest, paralysis of the upper limb, thoracic pain, ankylosing spondylitis, torticollis.
Recommended depth of needle penetration: 0.5 inch, perpendicularly.

Du 15 (Yamen)

Location: At the nape of the neck, on the midline, between the dorsal spines of the first and second cervical vertebra.
Indications: Stiff neck, torticollis.
Recommended depth of needle penetration: Superficially. Too dangerous to needle deeply.

Du 16 (Fengfu)

Location: At the nape of the neck, on the midline, in the depression directly below the occipital protuberance.
Indications: Headache.
Recommended depth of needle penetration: 0.5 inch, perpendicularly.

Du 17 (Naohu)

Location: 1.5 cun above Du 16, superior to the occipital protuberance.
Indications: Stiffness and pain in the neck.
Recommended depth of needle penetration: 0.5 inch, obliquely.

Du 18 (Qiangjian)

Location: 1.5 cun above Du 17, midway between Du 16 and Du 20.
Indications: Headache.
Recommended depth of needle penetration: 0.5 inch, obliquely.

Du 19 (Houding)

Location: 1.5 cun anterior to Du 18.
Indications: Headache.
Recommended depth of needle penetration: 0.5 inch, obliquely.

Du 20 (Baihui)

Location: Draw a line from the tip of the earlobe to the apex of the auricle and extend this line upwards on the scalp until it intersects the midline; the point lies at this intersection. Alternatively, on the vertex of the skull, 5 cun behind the anterior hairline and 7 cun above the posterior hairline, midline.
Indications: Headache, parkinsonism. **The point Du 20 is located on the vertex of the skull, and is the most important governing and harmonizing point. It is therefore indicated for every acupuncture treatment**.
Recommended depth of needle penetration: 0.3 inch, horizontally, posteriorly.

Du 21 (Qianding)

Location: 1.5 cun anterior to Du 20.
Indications: Headache.
Recommended depth of needle penetration: 0.5 inch, obliquely.

Du 22 (Xinhui)

Location: 3 cun anterior to Du 20.
Indications: Headache.
Recommended depth of needle penetration: 0.5 inch, obliquely.

Du 23 (Shangxing)

Location: 1 cun above the midpoint of the anterior hairline, 4 cun anterior to Du 20.
Indications: Headache.
Recommended depth of needle penetration: 0.5 inch, obliquely.

Du 24 (Shenting)

Location: 0.5 cun above the midpoint of the anterior hairline.
Indications: Headache.
Recommended depth of needle penetration: 0.5 inch, obliquely.

Du 25 (Suliao)

Location: At the tip of the nose.
Indications: Epistaxis, shock.
Recommended depth of needle penetration: 0.2 inch, perpendicularly.

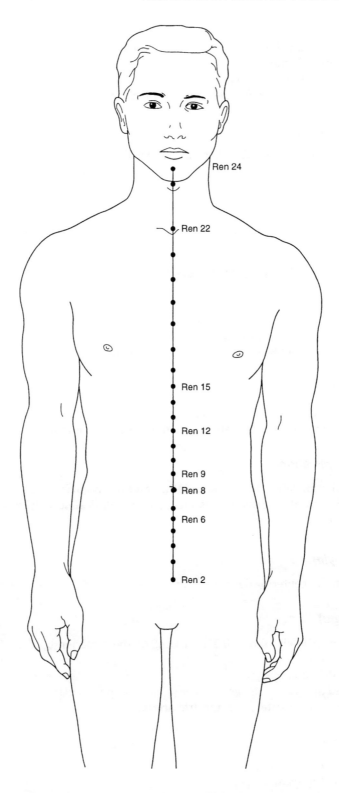

Figure 4.17 Ren Mai Meridian

Du 26 (Renzhong)

Location: At the junction of the upper third and lower two thirds of the philtrum of the upper lip, midline.
Indications: Shock, heat stroke, lumbago.
Recommended depth of needle penetration: 0.3 inch, needle point tilted upward.

Du 27 (Duiduan)

Location: On the medial tubercle of the upper lip, at the junction of the philtrum and upper lip.

Du 28 (Yinjiao)

Location: Between the gum and upper gum in the labial frenulum.

REN MAI MERIDIAN (ALSO CALLED JENN MO AND CONCEPTION VESSEL) (REN)

The Ren Mai meridian does not correspond to an internal organ. The Ren mai controls the six Yin meridians and the alarm points. The Ren Mai is called the "Conception Vessel" because it has an influence over the genital organs (Fig. 4.17)

Superficial Course

The Ren meridian starts in the center of the perineum, ascending anteriorly, midline, over the thorax and abdomen to end below the mouth.

Clinical Application

The Clinical application has a coordinating and harmonizing effect on all regions of the body and all organs. Points are used for cervical spondylosis, intercostal neuralgia, and neurologic disorders.

Ren 1 (Huiyin)

Location: In the center of the perineum.

Ren 2 (Qugu)

Location: Immediately above the midpoint of the superior border of the pubic symphysis.
Indications: Pelvic pain.
Recommended depth of needle penetration: 1 inch, perpendicularly.
Anatomic precaution: **Inferior epigastric artery**.

Ren 3 (Zhongji)

Location: In the front, midline, 4 cun below the umbilicus, 1 cun above Ren 2.
Indications: Pelvic pain.
Recommended depth of needle penetration: 1 inch, perpendicularly.

Ren 4 (Guanyuan)

Location: In the front, midline, 3 cun below the umbilicus, 2 cun above Ren 2.
Indications: Pelvic pain.
Recommended depth of needle penetration: 1 inch, perpendicularly.

Ren 5 (Shimen)

Location: In the front, midline, 2 cun below the umbilicus.
Indications: Arm swelling, edema.
Recommended depth of needle penetration: 1 inch, perpendicularly.

Ren 6 (Qihai)

Location: In the front, midline, 1.5 cun below the umbilicus.

Ren 7 (Abdomen-Yinjiao)

Location: In the front, midline, 1 cun below the umbilicus.

Ren 8 (Shenjue)

Location: In the center of the umbilicus.
Anatomic precaution: **It is forbidden to needle this point!**

Ren 9 (Shuifen)

Location: In the front, midline, 1 cun above the umbilicus.
Indications: Edema.
Recommended depth of needle penetration: 1 inch, perpendicularly.

Ren 10 (Xiawan)

Location: In the front, midline, 2 cun above the umbilicus.

Ren 11 (Jianli)

Location: In the front, midline, 3 cun above the umbilicus.

Ren 12 (Zhongwan)

Location: In the front, midline, midway between the xiphoid process and the umbilicus, or 4 cun above the umbilicus.

Ren 13 (Shangwan)

Location: In the front, midline, 5 cun above the umbilicus.

Ren 14 (Jujue)

Location: In the front, midline, 6 cun above the umbilicus.

Ren 15 (Jiuwei)

Location: In the front, midline, 7 cun above the umbilicus.

Ren 16 (Zhongting)

Location: In the midline of the sternum, at the level of the fifth intercostal space, 1.6 cun below Ren 17.

Ren 17 (Shanzhong)

Location: On the sternum, midway between the two nipples (at the level of the fourth intercostal space).
Indications: Thoracic rib pain.
Recommended depth of needle penetration: 0.5 inch, horizontally, with the needle tilted.

Ren 18 (Yutang)

Location: On the midline of the abdomen, 1.6 cun above Ren 17, at the level of the third intercostal space.

Ren 19 (Chest-Zigong)

Location: On the midline of the sternum, 3.2 cun above Ren 17, at the level of the second intercostal space.

Ren 20 (Huagai)

Location: On the midline of the sternum, at the junction of the sternal manubrium and the body of the sternum.
Indications: Thoracic chest pain.
Recommended depth of needle penetration: 0.3 inch, obliquely.

Ren 21 (Xuanji)

Location: On the midline of the sternum, 1 cun below Ren 22.
Indications: Thoracic chest pain.
Recommended depth of needle penetration: 0.3 inch, obliquely.

Ren 22 (Tiantu)

Location: At the center of the suprasternal fossa, 0.5 cun above the sternal notch.

Ren 23 (Lianquan)

Location: On the midline of the neck, midway between the adam's apple and the lower border of the mandible.

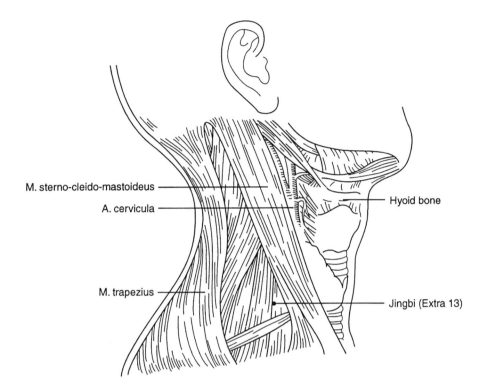

Figure 4.18 Extra 13

Ren 24 (Chengjiang)

Location: In the middle of the mental labial groove, in the depression between the point of the chin and midpoint of the lower lip.
Indications: Trigeminal neuralgia, toothache.
Recommended depth of needle penetration: 0.2 inch, perpendicularly.

EXTRAORDINARY POINTS

Extra 13 (Jingbi) (Fig. 4.18)

Location: With the head turned sideways, the point is at the junction of the medial one-third and lateral two-thirds of the clavicle, at the lateral head of the sternocleidomastoid muscle.
Indications: Numbness and pain of the hand and arm, paralysis of upper extremities.
Recommended depth of needle penetration: 0.5 inch, perpendicularly.
Anatomic precaution: Avoid aiming needle downward, as it may injure apex of lung.

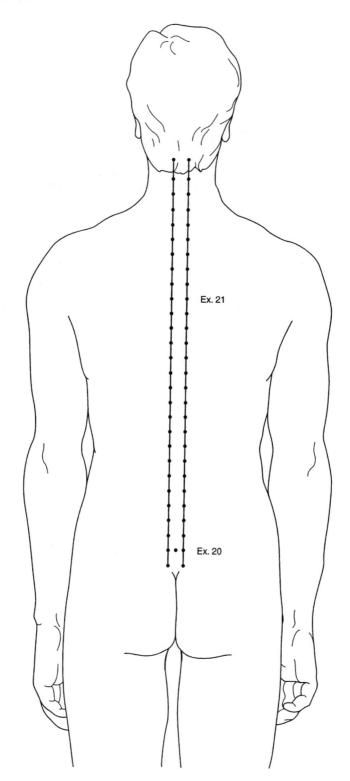

Figure 4.19 Extra 20, Extra 21

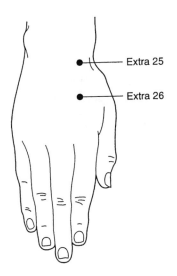

Figure 4.20 Extra 25 and Extra 26 (with addition)

Extra 28

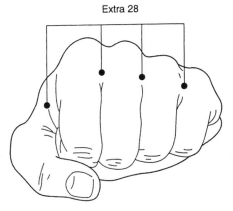

Figure 4.21 Extra 28

Extra 20 (Yaoqi)

Location: On the dorsal midline 2 cun above the os coccyx.
Indications: Muscle relaxation in spastic paralysis.
Recommended depth of needle penetration: 1 inch upward, horizontally along the skin.

Extra 21 (Huatuojiaji) (Fig. 4.19)

Location: This is a series of 28 point pairs, located 0.5 cun lateral to the lower border of the spinous processes between the first cervical and the fourth sacral vertebrae.
Indications: Pain along the spine, segmental pain radiation.
Three to five Huatuo points are used together in each treatment session.
Recommended depth of needle penetration: 1–1.5 inches, slightly obliquely, towards the spinal column along the lumbar vertebrae. At the level of the thoracic and cervical vertebrae, needle depth is less (0.5–1 inch).

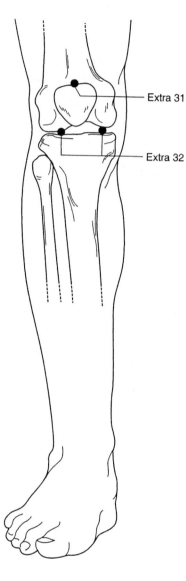

Figure 4.22 Extra 31, Extra 32

Extra 25 (Zhongquan)

Location: On the wrist, in a depression on the radial aspect of the tendon of the extensor digitorum communis.
Indications: Disorders of the wrist joint.
Recommended depth of needle penetration: 0.5 inch, perpendicularly.

Extra 26 (Luozhen) (Fig. 4.20)

Location: On the dorsum of the hand, between the second and third metacarpals, 0.5 cun proximal to the metacarpalphalangeal joint.

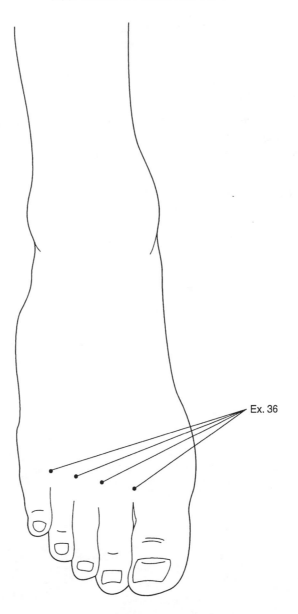

Ex. 36

Figure 4.23 Extra 36

Indications: Neck stiffness and rigidity.
Recommended depth of needle penetration: 0.5 inch, perpendicularly.

Extra 28 (Baxie) (Fig. 4.21)

Location: On the dorsum of the hand, in the webs between the five fingers; four points in each hand, totaling eight points (ba means eight in Chinese). These points are best located having the patient form a fist.

Indications: Swelling of the hand and wrist, disorders of the fingers, rheumatoid arthritis, numbness of the fingers, polyneuropathy, neck pain.
Recommended depth of needle penetration: 0.5 inch, perpendicularly.

Extra 31 (Heding)

Location: On the midpoint of the upper border of the patella.
Indications: Disorders of the knee joint.
Recommended depth of needle penetration: 0.5 inch, perpendicularly.

Extra 32 (Xiyan) (Fig. 4.22)

Location: In a depression on the medial side of the patellar tendon.
Indications: Disorders of the knee joint.
Recommended depth of needle penetration: 1 inch, perpendicularly.

Extra 36 (Bafeng) (Fig. 4.23)

Location: On the dorsum of the foot, 0.5 cun proximal to the borders of the webs between the five toes; four points in each hand, totaling eight points.
Indications: Swelling of the foot and ankle, disorders of the toes, rheumatoid arthritis, numbness of the foot and toes, polyneuropathy, arthritis of the toes.
Recommended depth of needle penetration: 0.5 inch, obliquely upward.

PART II

ACUPUNCTURE TREATMENT OF THE MUSCULOSKELETAL SYSTEM

5

EVALUATION AND TREATMENT OF THE PAIN PATIENT: AUTHOR'S PREFERRED TECHNIQUE

Harris Gellman, M.D.

Initially I try to determine the type and etiology of the pain. Is it chronic or acute, traumatic or non-traumatic? Is the pain sympathetically mediated, or is it structural? In the Chinese system, pain is usually due either to an excess of energy (requiring "dispersion" treatment to decrease or eliminate the "stored" or "blocked" energy), or to a deficiency in energy (requiring "tonification" to increase the energy in the system. "Tonification" is accomplished by manipulating the needle or the use of electrical stimulation).

I also try to determine if there is an emotional or stress related component to the pain (e.g., chronic tension headaches, fibromyalgia, myofascial disorders), as these often respond well to trigger point treatment or the techniques described in the chapters by Drs. Gunn and Seem. Trigger point needling is a very interesting phenomenon in Chinese medicine. While many acupuncture texts do not specifically discuss the treatment of trigger points, almost all texts recommend the needling of tender points known as "ah shi" points. There may be a significant relationship between trigger points and acupuncture points. In fact, Melzak et al.[103] reported finding a high correlation (71%) between tender trigger points and the corresponding acupuncture points.

A stepwise approach to evaluation and treatment as follows helps to simplify treatment options.

EVALUATION: STAGE ONE

For acute musculoskeletal injuries (sprains, bruises, tendonitis, fractures) within a few weeks of injury, I use the crossed method of point selection described previously. This method usually provides rapid relief of pain. Often only a few treatments over a one to two week period of time are all that are necessary.

121

For traumatic, or post surgical pain, treatment of the principle meridian along which the pain is located may result in cure. Needles placed distally into the hand or foot are usually placed at one of the three most distal points along the meridian. Additional needles are placed proximal to the area of pain. The needles are stimulated electrically, connecting the negative (black) electrode distally, and the positive (red) electrode proximally. Current is run along the meridian at 2–4 hz at the threshold of sensation for twenty minutes.

If there is an area of bruising, surround the area with needles, pointing towards the painful bruise or hematoma. These are passive needles and are not stimulated.

For painful scars, either acute or chronic, needles are placed alternately along the length of the scar on both sides. A needle is also threaded into each end of the scar towards the midline, and current is passed along the scar for twenty minutes (Fig. 5.1).

EVALUATION: STAGE TWO

If fibromyalgia-like symptoms are present, especially with symptoms of nerve compression (i.e., carpal or cubital tunnel syndrome), I usually start the treatment by dry needling the tender trigger points. This is done by locating tight knots or tender points along the splenius capitus muscles and the trapezius and rhomboids (bilaterally) for the upper extremity. For the back the paraspinal muscles are usually involved, and for the lower extremity, trigger points are usually found in the lumbosacral paraspinal muscles as well as the gluteals and piriformis. Needles are placed into the trigger points, rotated

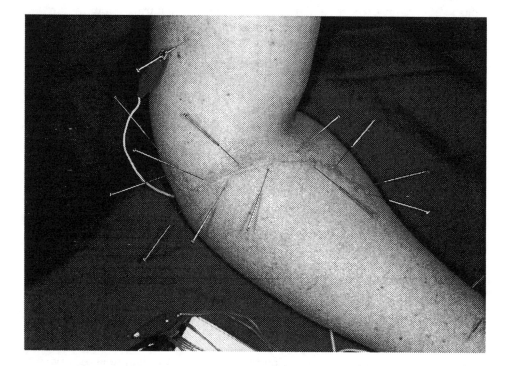

Figure 5.1 Photo of Scar Needling

rapidly once or twice, and then the lift and thrust technique is used. Needles are left in place for five minutes.

Most patients will experience a dull aching sensation when the trigger points are needled as the muscle spasm releases. The physical placement of the needle in the muscle causes an electrical depolarization of the area resulting in a change in the muscle physiology locally where the needles have been placed. Most trigger points tend to be over the motor end-plates of the muscle. Dry needling of the trigger points has been found to be superior to injecting the trigger points with an anaesthetic agent such as lidocaine, and is longer lasting. The use of acupuncture needles causes less trauma and tearing of the muscle than the hollow, cutting needles used for injection. Treatments are usually done once or twice weekly until symptoms improve.

Interestingly, many patients with complaints of Carpal or Cubital Tunnel Syndrome have normal sensibility testing and electrodiagnostic studies. Many of these patients will respond very well to this method of treatment. This is also an effective modality for patients with chronic headaches, and is the initial treatment I use for patients with Reflex Sympathetic Dystrophy symptoms in the upper extremity.

EVALUATION: STAGE THREE

For patients with acute or chronic pain localized to a specific anatomic region (e.g., shoulder, knee, back), points are selected from the treatment protocols listed in the section *Acupuncture Treatment by Anatomic Location*.

EVALUATION: STAGE FOUR

For upper or lower extremity chronic pain syndromes (e.g., reflex sympathetic dystrophy, chronic back pain), a treatment technique that I initially learned from Joseph Helms, M.D. (as developed by William Craig, M.D. [see Chapter Twelve]) seems to work well. The nice thing about this technique is that it seems to work well with a minimum of accuracy in needle placement.

Upper Extremities

Two parallel rows of needles are placed lateral to the Cervical spine at C4, C6, C7, and T1. The needles are connected to an electroacupuncture stimulator at 2 to 4 hz. and the amplitude is increased until threshold level (when the patient just begins to feel the tingle of the electric current). Treatment is continued for twenty minutes (Fig. 5.2).

Lower Extremities

Two parallel rows of needles are placed lateral to the Lumbo-Sacral spines at L3, L4, L5, S1/2. These locations correspond approximately to the acupuncture points: **UB 47, UB 25, UB 26,** and **GB 30**. As above, the needles are connected to the stimulator at 2 to 4 hz., amplitude is increased until threshold level, and treatment is continued for twenty minutes (Fig. 5.3).

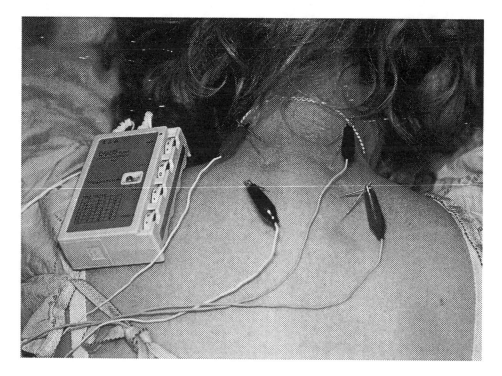

Figure 5.2 Photo of "Craig" upper treatment

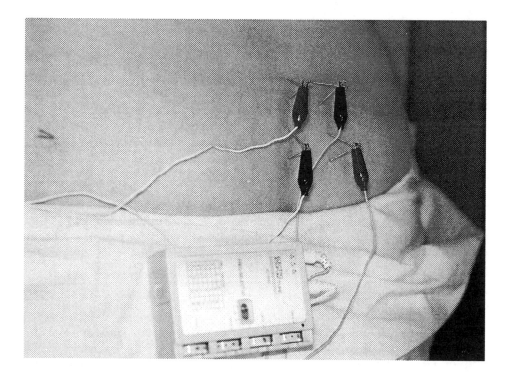

Figure 5.3 Photo of "Craig" lower treatment

Using the needles and stimulator as described stimulates sympathetic activity resulting in increased bloodflow and warmth in the extremity. Pain usually improves significantly after one to two treatments. A typical treatment series starts by treating twice a week for the first three to four weeks, followed by once a week for four weeks, and finally every other week for four treatments.

For patients with chronic low back pain, Macdonald et al.[104] reported 77% improvement in pain after each treatment with the use of superficial (subcutaneous) acupuncture treatments. Acupuncture needles are inserted to an approximate depth of 4 mm into the skin and subcutaneous tissues immediately overlying trigger points. When using this method, care should be taken to avoid penetrating the muscles or their fascia. Initial treatments are 5 minutes in length, getting progressively longer in 5 minute increments, up to 20 minutes. Electroacupuncture stimulators may be connected to the needles at 2 hz for 5 to 20 minutes. A satisfactory response to treatment includes vasodilatation of the skin surrounding the needles accompanied by a feeling of warmth. Additionally, palpation should reveal improvement or absence of the pain in the trigger points.

The above treatment methods seem to work well regardless of the etiology of the pain. If these treatments are unsuccessful, more detailed and sophisticated approaches are taken to identify the involved meridian systems.

EVALUATION: STAGE FIVE

Often, when patients have had a longstanding problem, an underlying imbalance exists in the meridian energies and systems. The initial patient interview should help identify which meridians the symptoms involve using the description of systemic systems by acupuncture meridians (see page 00). Treating meridian subcircuits (paired meridians) is often more effective than treating single meridians. Initially, have the patient describe the type and character of the pain. The area of the pain is often a good place to start when trying to determine which meridian(s) will need treatment. Look for key non-pain related symptoms or groups of symptoms, which can help to identify the meridian subcircuits involved. The subcircuits serve as an access route by which the acupuncturist can modify the energetic activity of the subcircuit territory of influence and address abnormal functioning, whether the dysfunction is expressed as a slight exaggeration of normal functioning, a pain from trauma and a concomitant obstructed flow in the channel, or a dense and fixed histopathologic process.[105] Once a meridian pair (subcircuit) has been identified as a source of a problem, due to either an excess or a deficiency, these meridians should be treated in an effort to balance the body's energies.

MERIDIAN SUBCIRCUITS

1. Tai Yang—Shao Yin

The Tai Yang meridian includes the small intestine and the bladder meridians. Musculoskeletal symptoms of Tai Yang imbalance include headaches (particularly in the temples), back pain, stiff neck, and migrating pains. Non-musculoskeletal symptoms include headaches, frequent urination, cystitis, digestive symptoms, and rhinitis (Fig. 5.4).

The Shao Yin meridian includes the heart and kidney meridians. Symptoms of Shao Yin imbalance include lumbar pain, arm pain, arthritis, motor impairment, and muscular atrophy of the lower extremities. Non-musculoskeletal symptoms include night sweats, insomnia, thirst, asthma, irregular menstruation, dryness of the tongue, ear infection, congestion, and soreness of throat.

A simple treatment plan for patients with these symptoms would be to place needles at Ki 3, UB 60, and SI 3 bilaterally. Adding Ki 10 will allow the use of electroacupuncture between Ki 3 (negative-black electrode) and Ki 10 (red-positive electrode) at 2–4 hz for twenty minutes. Stimulation is done at the threshold of sensation.

2. Yang Ming—Tai Yin

The Yang Ming meridian includes the large intestine and the stomach meridians. **Stimulation of LI 4 and St 36 bilaterally is a often good starting point when dealing with almost any type of pain.** Symptoms of Yang Ming imbalance include neck pain, and lower limb pain. Non-musculoskeletal symptoms include post prandial migraines, epistaxis, abdominal pain and distension, colitis, diarrhea, edema, epigastric pain, vomiting, congested and sore throat, acne, depression, and mental disturbances (Fig. 5.5).

The Tai Yin meridian includes the lung and spleen meridians. Symptoms of Tai Yin imbalance include shoulder pain, back pain, pain in the lateral border of the anterior arm, thigh, and knee pain. Non-musculoskeletal symptoms of Tai Yin

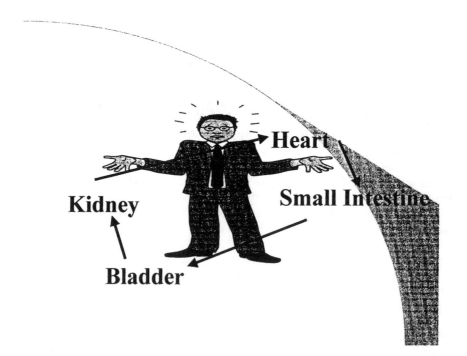

Figure 5.4 Sub-circuit diagram: Tai Yang—Shao Yin

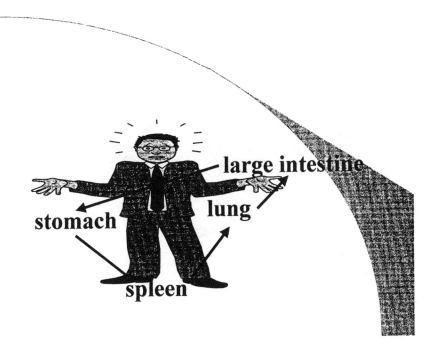

Figure 5.5 Sub-circuit diagram: Yang Ming—Tai Yin

imbalance include skin disorders and respiratory problems, cough, asthma, canker sores, allergies, blood dyscrasias, hemoptysis, belching, sluggishness and general malaise, and sensation of fullness in the chest.

A good treatment protocol for patients with imbalance of Yang Ming—Tai Yin is to place needles at LI 4, St 36, and Sp 6, bilaterally.

Tennis elbow can be treated by electrostimulation along the Large Intestine meridian. Place the negative (black) electrode at LI 4, and the positive (red) electrode at LI 11.

3. Shao Yang—Jue Yin

The Shao Yang meridian includes the Triple Heater and Gallbladder meridians. Musculoskeletal symptoms of Shao Yang imbalance include generalized musculoskeletal muscle and joint pain, headache (radiating from the neck to forehead), myalgias, muscle aches and cramps, and lumbosacral pain radiating to the hips. Non-musculoskeletal symptoms include hypertension, abdominal distension, edema, tinnitus, headache, blurring of vision, immune system problems, bitter taste in the mouth, and jaw pain (Fig. 5.6).

The Jue Yin meridian includes the Liver and Pericardium meridians. Musculoskeletal symptoms of Jue Yin imbalance include low back pain, and Carpal Tunnel Syndrome. Non-musculoskeletal symptoms include Hernia, fullness in the chest, pain in the lower abdomen, mental disturbances, palpitations, insomnia, allergies, visual problems, nail problems, anxiety, facial flushing, and emotional outbursts.

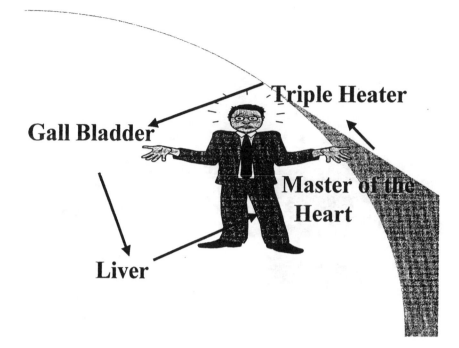

Figure 5.6 Sub-circuit diagram: Shao Yang—Jue Yin

A good treatment protocol for patients with an imbalance or the Shao Yang-Jue Yin subcircuit is Liv 3, Liv 8, and GB 34.

For patients with *Carpal Tunnel Syndrome* a treatment which has been found to work well is PC 6, PC 7, SJ 5, and SJ 8 bilaterally. The treatment may be used unilaterally if the symptoms are predominately on one side.

Adding the Bauxie "extra" points (located between the metacarpal heads with the metacarpalphalangeal joints flexed) helps if there is edema present in the extremity. This is also a good treatment for edema and limitation of motion seen after distal radius fracture. This treatment is particularly helpful to decrease edema and stiffness while the patient is in an external fixator after wrist fracture.

6

ACUPUNCTURE TREATMENT PROTOCOLS BY ANATOMIC LOCATION

Harris Gellman, M.D.

Based on the musculoskeletal diagnosis, treatment protocols can be used as described below. Points chosen from those listed should include points along the involved principal meridian.

ACUTE INJURY BY ANATOMIC LOCATION AND DIAGNOSIS (SPRAIN, MUSCULO-TENDINOUS INJURY, FRACTURE)

General Treatment Principles

Sprains

1. Acute: Use the equivalent ipsilateral, contralateral, or reverse-mirror point as described in the section on point selection, with strong sedating technique.
2. Sub-acute: a. ear points
    b. local point (if swelling has gone down)
    c. intermediate point (if swelling has not gone down)
    d. distal points
3. Chronic: Ah shi, local, and distal points. When using local points insert the needle obliquely across the direction of the fibers involved.

UPPER EXTREMITY

Shoulder: Important Points

The local points are LI 14, LI 15, Ren 14, Ren 15, SJ 10, SJ 14, SJ 15, SI 9, and SI 10 (extra points around the shoulder). The distal points are LI 4, Lu 5, Ren 10, SI 6, St 38, and UB 62.

The hand-shoulder point is on radial side of the index finger, over the MCP joint, at the junction of the red and white skin.

Shoulder Pain

Painful shoulder often occurs as a symptom due to sprain or strain of the soft tissues surrounding the shoulder joint, which may cause perifocal inflammation of the shoulder joint, supraspinatous tendonitis, sub-acromial bursitis, rotator cuff tendonitis, bicipital tendonitis. First use the lower extremity points on the diseased side using the points St 38 and GB 34. While manipulating the needle, ask the patient to exercise the affected shoulder. Treat once a day or once every other day. *Shoulder Pain* points include GB 34, LI 11, LI 15, LI 16, SJ 14, SI 10, SI 11, St 38, UB 57.

Perifocal Inflammation of the Shoulder Joint: SI 11

This is due to chronic degeneration and inflammation of the bursae and soft tissues surrounding the shoulder joint. It may be due to overuse or occur spontaneously. The pain usually covers a large area around the shoulder and may radiate into the neck and arm. Pain that intensifies during quiescence is accompanied by limited range of motion of the shoulder, especially when abducting the arm or with extension and external rotation of the shoulder. A notable feature of this disease is that pain is the main early complaint, while in the later stages limitation of motion is the chief complaint.

Supraspinatous Tendonitis, Sub-Acromial Bursitis, and Impingement Syndrome: LI 16, SJ 14

Supraspinatous tendonitis is usually due to a chronic inflammatory or a degenerative change of the tendon often seen in laborers over 40 years of age. Pain usually occurs on the lateral aspect of the shoulder, and there is tenderness at the tendon attachment of the supraspinatous to the greater tuberosity of the humerus. With impingement syndrome, pain and limited motion occurs when the arm is moved anteriorly and posteriorly or horizontally compressing the supraspinatous tendon under the acromial arch.

Bicipital Tendonitis: H1, Ren 6, Ren 10, Ren 15, SJ 14, Ah Shi Points, Local Points

Chief symptoms are pain, swelling, and tenderness in the region of the long head of the biceps brachii anterior to the shoulder. Flexing the elbow with voluntary contraction of the biceps against resistance causes intense pain. Pronounced pain is encountered when the arm is abducted raised or stretched posteriorly. Patients often complain of inability to lie on the affected shoulder.

Rotator Cuff Tear/Tendonitis

Treatment points include

1. Local points: Ren 15, SJ 14, SJ 15, and LI 14
2. Distal points: SJ 5, Ren 4, Ren 5, Ren 11, and St 38
3. Ah Shi points
4. Ear Point for the Shoulder

Adhesive Capsulitis (Frozen Shoulder)

For the initial treatment, manually stimulate St 38 while the patient mobilizes the shoulder joint to obtain an increased range of movement. A significant improvement in range of motion may be obtained with this treatment in up to 75% of cases. Treat every other day.

- As indicated add these points: GB 20, LI 16, UB 57.
- Local points are also selected according to the location of the most severe pain: Du 20, GB 34,LI 4, LI 11, LI 15, SJ 14, SI 9, SI 10, and SI 11.

Treatment of Frozen Shoulder Based on Meridian Area of Maximal Pain

a. **Front of Shoulder**: (**Yang Ming meridian**): Du 20, LI 4, LI 11, LI 14, LI 15, LI 16, and St 38
b. **Lateral Shoulder**: (**Shao Yang meridian**): Du 20, LI 4, SJ 14, SJ 13, SJ 5, and St 38
c. **Posterior Shoulder** (**Tai Yang meridian**): Du 14, Du 20, SI 3, SI 6, SI 9, SI 10, and SI 11

Elbow

Elbow Pain

The most frequent types of elbow pain seen (other than arthritis) are (1) inflammation of the lateral epicondyle of the humerus (lateral epicondylitis). Chief symptoms are pain and tenderness around the lateral epicondyle of the humerus and radio-capitellar joint, intensified when the forearm is rotated with the wrist held in resisted extension; and (2) acute lesion of the soft tissues of the elbow. There is a history of acute trauma with local swelling, congestion, or bleeding. Clinically, the patient must be evaluated thoroughly for fracture or dislocation.

Important Elbow Points for Injury and Sprains are LI 11, LI 12, GB 34, and Ah Shi points.

Tennis Elbow/Lateral Epicondylitis

Try treatment of GB 34, with electroacupuncture of LI 4 (negative) to LI 10 and LI 11 (positive) first. Then add Du 20, GB 34, H 3, LI 4, LI 10, LI 11, Lu 5, P 3, SJ 5, and Ah Shi points.

Acupuncture treatment for tennis elbow has been reported to be more effective than steroid injections by Bratterg.[106] Junnila found acupuncture superior to treatment with non-steroidal anti-inflammatory drug piroxicam in osteoarthritis in a study of 32 patients.[107]

Molsberger and Hille,[108] performed a single treatment, placebo-controlled, study of 48 patients. Using only the single point GB 34, (based on the contralateral/ipsilateral point selection theory), most patients reported pain relief of 70%. The mean reduction in pain score was 56%, with an average duration of pain relief of 20 hours, in the treatment group compared to only 15% in the control group.

Wrist

Most problems around the wrist are the result of either trauma, tendonitis, or fractures. Treatment after fracture will help both swelling and stiffness as well as aid in fracture healing.

Wrist Sprain

Treatment points include H 7, LI 4, P 7, Lu 9, LI 5, LI 6, LI 11, SJ 2, SJ 3, SJ 4, SJ 5, SI 2, SI 4, SI 6, Bauxie (Extra 28), and any local points over tender areas of the wrist.

DeQuervain's Tendonitis

Tendonitis of the tendons passing through the first dorsal compartment as it passes over the radial styloid is a common occupational disorder as a result of friction of the abductor pollicis longus and extensor pollicis brevis tendons as they pass through the tendon sheath. Treatment points for *DeQuervain's tendonitis* include Ah Shi points, GB 34, LI 4, LI 5, and Lu 7.

Wrist Fractures

If there is edema present in the extremity after fracture, add the Bauxie "extra" points located between the metacarpal heads with the metacarpalphalangeal joints flexed. This is also a good treatment for edema and limitation of motion seen after distal radius fracture. This treatment is particularly helpful to decrease edema and stiffness while the patient is in an external fixator after wrist fracture.

Carpal Tunnel Syndrome

An excellent first treatment for *Carpal Tunnel Syndrome* is PC 6, PC 7,SJ 5, and SJ 8 bilaterally. The treatment may be used unilaterally if the symptoms are predominately on one side. If symptoms persist add Du 20, GB 34, LI 4, LI 5, SI 4, LI 9, LI 11, Lu 8, SJ 6, SJ 10, Sp 9, and St 36.

Hand

Commonly encountered problems of the hand include trigger finger and thumb, tendonitis, Dupuytren's contracture and Carpal Tunnel Syndrome. For **tendonitis and trigger finger and thumb use** Lu 7. Add P7 for **index and long trigger finger.** For **ring and small trigger finger** use H 7 and H 8. For **Dupuytren's contracture** use Du 20, H 8, LI 4, Lu 10, P 8, St 44, and Bauxie (Ex 28).

LOWER EXTREMITY

Hip

Treatment points for **Trochanteric Bursitis, Sprain** include GB 29, GB 30, GB 34, LI 4, Liv 5, Liv 11, St 31, St 36, St 44, UB 32, and UB 54.

Knee

Important points around the knee are as follows:

Knee Injuries, Ligament Sprain: Extra 31, Extra 32, GB 32, GB 35, Ki 10, Liv 1, Liv 8, Liv 11, P 5, Sp 10, St 34, St 35, UB 54, UB 56, UB 67, and Ah Shi points.

Sports Injuries and Tendonitis: Extra 31, Extra 32, GB 29, GB 30, GB 34, GB 35, GB 39, GB 43, Liv 2, Liv 3, Liv 4, Liv 7, Liv 8, Sp 9, St 35, St 36, St 44. UB 40, UB 60.

Ankle

Points used for treatment of ankle sprains include GB 39, GB 40, LI 4, Liv 6, Sp 5, SP 6, SP 9, St 41, St 43, St 44, UB 60, and Ah Shi points. For achilles tendonitis use Du 20, GB 40, Ki 3, Ki 6, LI 4, Liv 3, Sp 5, St 41, UB 60, and UB 62.

Foot

Treatment points for sprain include GB 3, GB 4, GB 31, GB 32, GB 34, GB 35, GB 39, GB 43, Ki 5, Liv 3, Liv 8, Liv 9, SJ 34, SJ 4, St 43, UB 55, UB 60, and UB 67. For swelling after foot or ankle injury use GB 31, Ki 2, LI 8, St 36, UB 40, UB 57, and UB 60. For plantar fasciitis use Du 20, K 3, UB 57, UB 60, and Ah Shi points. Du 20, LI 4, St 44, Extra 36, and Ah Shi points are used to treat metatarsalgia. For pain in the toes use Du 20, GB 34, Ki 1, LI 4, St 44, Ex 36, and Ah Shi points.

POST-OPERATIVE CARE

Pain (see section entitled *Acute Injury by Anatomic Location*)
The following points are used for the treatment of swelling and edema:

Shoulder: SJ 11, St 22, St 36, UB 38, UB 58
Swelling of the Arm, Wrist and Hand: H 3, H 7, LI 2, LI 4, LI 5, LI 8, LI 10, LI 11, LI 15, Lu 5, Lu 6, Lu 9, P 2, P 3, P 7, Ren 17, SJ 2, SJ 3, SJ 4, SJ 5, SI 2, SI 4, SI 5, SI 10, St 36, UB 38, UB 58
Wrist: Ki 8, Ren 17, Sp 4, St 36, UB 38, UB 58.
Hand: Bauxie points (Extra 28)
Knee: Ki 10, GB 34, UB 38, UB 58
Swelling of the Foot or Ankle: GB 31, Ki 2, Ki 6, LI 8, Ren 17, SJ 6, St 2, St 36, UB 57, UB 60, UB 38, UB 40

7

ARTHRITIS AND CHRONIC JOINT PAIN

Harris Gellman, M.D.

INITIAL TREATMENT FOR EXTREMITY ARTHRITIS

As a first treatment use GB 34, Sp 9, St 36, Ren 1, Ren 5, Ren 6, Ren 13, Ren 17, UB 38, and UB 58. **This combination of points may act for weeks to months after a series of treatments are given.**
For *early* arthritis add LI 4, and LI 11. For *chronic* arthritis add GB 3, GB 4, LI 3, SJ 5, SI 3, SI 10, Sp 4, and Sp 6.

General treatment points for symptomatic patients with Rheumatoid arthritis are Du 4, Du 13, Du 14, H 8, Ki 7, LI 10, LI 11, Ren 6, Ren 8, Ren 12, Sp 6, St 36, UB 20, UB 22, and UB 23.

ARTHRITIS TREATMENT BY ANATOMIC LOCATION

During an acute exacerbation treat once every other day. For chronic conditions treat once every other day, retaining needles for 15–20 minutes. Use local points and distal points along the course of the meridians involved by pain. Then add the following points:

Shoulder: GB 20, GB 22, GB 34, LI 15, LI 11, LI 6, P 3, P 6, SJ 8, SJ 11, SJ 12, SJ 13, SJ 14, SJ 15, SJ 16, SI 10, St 13, St 38, UB 41, and UB 57
Arm: LI 6, LI 7, LI 11, LI 12, LI 17, Lu 6, P 4, SI 6, SI 10, and SI 12
Elbow: GB 34, LI 11, LI 12, Lu 5, and Ah Shi points
Wrist: H 8, Lu 7, Lu 8, and Lu 9
Hand: Du 20, Ex 28, H 8, LI 4, Lu 10, P 8, and St 44
Fingers: Liv 3, P 4, Sp 4, and UB 3
Hip arthritis: Du 20, GB 30, GB 34, LI 4, St 44, UB 32, UB 36, UB 40, UB 54, UB 60, and Ah Shi points
Knee Arthritis: Acupuncture treatment is very effective in the relief of pain of the knee joint. Even in severe joint deformities some pain relief can be expected.

Basic knee arthritis protocol: Ex 31, Ex 32, St 35 (These three points are also called the *three eyes* and are essential to the treatment.) Additional points to treat include Du 20, GB 33, GB 34, GB 35, LI 4, Liv 8, Sp 9, St 36, St 44, UB 11, UB 40, UB 60,and Ah Shi points.

In a control group of ten **Rheumatoid** arthritis patients with arthritis of their knees, Man and Baragar[109] achieved a 90% moderate decrease in pain after only one treatment using only the points GB 34, SP 9, and St 43. The needles were placed and stimulated for a period of 15 minutes. Reduced pain, in the order of two grades or more, was still evident in seven patients at the end of one month, and in four patients at the end of two months. By contrast, the control group of ten patients treated with placebo acupuncture achieved only a 10% improvement in their pain which lasted less than 10 hours.

For **osteoarthritic** knees, Christensen et al.[110] reported an 80% subjective improvement, and a significantly improved range of knee motion in a group of 29 patients waiting for total knee arthroplasty (42 osteoarthritic knees) followed for an average of 49 weeks. In each affected knee the following points were used: **St 34, St 35, St 36, Sp 10,** and **Ex 32.** Needles were inserted to a depth of 10–15 mm. The ipsilateral hand point **LI 4** was also used. If the patient had bilateral osteoarthritis, the needles were placed bilaterally, otherwise only the affected knee was treated. Needles were left in place for 20 minutes and manually stimulated. (I would recommend electrostimulation rather than manual stimulation for consistency). Seven patients in the study responded so well to treatment that they declined knee arthroplasty.

Foot and Ankle Arthritis: Useful Points

Ankle: Du 20, GB 39, GB 40, Ki 3, Ki 6, LI 4, St 41, St 43, St 44, UB 60, UB 11, Ah Shi points.
Foot: GB 30, GB 31, GB 34, Ki 2, Ki 7, Liv 2, Liv 4, Liv 8, Sp 1, Sp 2, St 36, St 41, UB 40, UB 60.

8

NECK, CERVICAL SPINE, AND BACK: ACUTE AND CHRONIC

Harris Gellman, M.D.

NECK: STRAINS AND SPRAINS

First start by dry needling trigger points; then add local points as follows:

1. B 20, GB 29, SI 6, and Ah shi points for *neck strain/overuse*
2. Du 14, Du 15, Du 16, Du 17, Du 20, GB 12, GB 20, GB 39, H 3, Ren 24, SI 3, SI 6, UB 7, UB 10, UB 11, and Ah Shi points for *stiff neck*
Treat once daily, with the patient rotating the head slowly during treatment.
3. Du 14, LI 17, SI 3, and SI 6 for a *cute onset neck pain*

It may be possible to cure muscle pain in the neck using a single point. Dengqi[111] reported that the use of **SI 6** alone produced a 97% total effective cure rate in a group of 75 patients, with a 66% rate of cure after only one session in the treatment group compared to 8% in the control group.

In a separate series of 50 patients with acute stiff neck, 48 were cured with on treatment alone using only **LI 17**.[112]

Chronic Neck Pain and Cervical Spondylitis

Treatment is based on location of pain. **Midline Pain** is usually over the small intestine meridian. Needle the local and distal points corresponding to the painful area on the small intestine and urinary bladder meridians (Tai Yang): Du 14, Du 20, EX 21, LI 4, Lu 7, SI 3, SI 6, UB 10, UB 11, and UB 60. **Lateral Pain** occurring along the side of the neck usually involves the San-Jiao and Gallbladder meridians (shao yang): Du 14, Du 20, GB 20, GB 21, GB 34, GB 39, LI 4, SJ 5, Ah Shi points.

UPPER (THORACIC) SPINE

Treatment points include LI 10, LI 16, Lu 7, SJ 15, SI 6, SI 11, UB 10, and UB 11.

LOWER (LUMBAR) SPINE

Strains and Sprains

Acute back pain due to strain is often the result of overstretching the muscles, tendons, and ligaments of the back during lifting.

Lumbar Sprain

Treatment points for lumbar sprain include Du 26, Extra 21, GB 30, GB 31, GB 34, GB 38, Ki 7, Liv 2, Lu 5, SI 3, SI 6, UB 23, UB 34, UB 40, UB 51, UB 52, UB 60, and Ah Shi points. Treat every other day, retaining needles 15–20 min.

Sciatica

Ancient Chinese experience has shown that many cases of sciatica can be cured using **GB 30** alone. Initial treatment should always include **GB 30, GB 34** and **GB 39, UB 40**, and **UB 54**. If pain persists after the initial treatment the following points may be added: **Du 3, Du 14, Extra-21, GB 30, GB 34, GB 39, H 3, UB 23, UB 25, UB 34, UB 37, UB 52, UB 54**, UB 57, UB 59.

Sciatica pain usually localizes to either the lateral side of the leg running along the gallbladder meridian, or posteriorly along the Urinary Bladder channel. If there is pain along the urinary bladder meridian, use points Du 3, Du 4, Du 20, HAND POINT 1, LI 4, UB 23, UB 25, UB 26, UB 27, UB 32, UB 36, UB 37, UB 40, UB 54, UB 57, UB 58, and UB 60. If there is pain along the gallbladder meridian, use Du 3, Du 4, Du 20, GB 30, GB 31, GB 34, GB 39, and LI 4.

A course of treatment usually starts with daily treatments for 10 days. If there is not adequate relief of symptoms a 3–4 day rest period is allowed and the treatment course is repeated.

When Radicular Symptoms are present,[113] use GB 30 and add the following:

> **L4:** St 33, St 35, St 36
> **L5:** GB 31, GB 34, GB 36, GB 37, GB 39, LV 3, St 41, bafeng
> **S1:** UB 35, UB 37, UB 40, UB 57, UB 39, UB 60, GB 41
> **S2:** UB 36, UB 37, UB 57, K 10

Chronic Lower Back Pain: *Du 10, Du 15, Liv 3, Liv 9, Sp 2, Sp 5, UB 51.*

Another method for the treatment of low back pain involves the use of superficial acupuncture.[104] Patients are first examined to localize areas of "trigger points". These are areas where severe pain is elicited when firm pressure is applied to any abnormally tender muscle region, particularly during any maneuver that increases the isometric tension in the muscle. Painful regions are typically found in the erector spinae, multifidus, iliocostalis and quadratus lumborum, iliopsoas, obliqus externus and internus abdominus, and rectus abdominus muscles.

Sterile 30 gauge acupuncture needles are inserted to a depth of 4 mm into the skin and subcutaneous layers immediately overlying the trigger points. Care is taken to avoid penetrating the muscles or their fascia. The needles are left in place from 5 to 20 minutes. Electroacupuncture stimulus of 2 hz. at the threshold can be added to the treatment for increased effectiveness. The usual findings of a satisfactory response include vasodilatation of the skin surrounding the needles, accompanied by a feeling of warmth. After successful treatment, palpation should reveal that the tender trigger points in the muscles are improved or resolved. [104]

9

SPECIAL PAIN PROBLEMS

Harris Gellman, M.D.

FIBROMYALGIA

In addition to the techniques described by Drs. Gunn and Seem, the following points may be used for Fibromyalgia: GB 38, LI 4, LI 8, LI 17, LI 18, LI 19, LI 10, Liv 13, Lu 5, Ren 5, Ren 13, Ren 17, St 25, UB 58, UB 60, UB 62, and UB 67.

MYOFASCIAL PAIN SYNDROMES

Dry needling has been found very effective in patients with chronic low-back pain of a myofascial nature and without a mechanical etiology for their symptoms. In addition to the techniques described by Drs. Gunn and Seem, the following points may be used when pain crosses or lies on their respective meridians: UB 10, SJ 15, and St 36.

REFLEX SYMPATHETIC DYSTROPHY

I usually start the treatment by dry needling any tender trigger points. This is done by locating tight knots or tender points along the splenius capitus muscles and the trapezius and rhomboids (bilaterally). Needles are placed into the trigger points, twirled once or twice, and then the lift and thrust technique is used. Needles are left in place for five minutes. Most patients will experience a dull aching sensation when the trigger points are needled as the muscle spasm releases. The needle causes an electrical depolarization of the area causing a change in the muscle locally where the needles are placed. Most trigger points tend to be over motor end-plates. Dry needling of the trigger points has been found to be superior to injecting the trigger points with an anaesthetic agent such as lidocaine, and is longer lasting. Treatments are usually done once or twice weekly until symptoms improve.

If patients do not respond to the above treatment, or have only temporary relief, I use a technique I initially learned from Joseph Helms, M.D. (as mentioned in Chapter Five).

The above treatment methods seem to work well regardless of the etiology of the pain. If these treatments are unsuccessful, more detailed and sophisticated approaches are taken to identify the involved meridian systems.

GENERALIZED PAIN OF UNKNOWN ETIOLOGY

If no musculoskeletal diagnosis has been made the following point combinations may be helpful for pain relief:

Upper Extremities: Du 20, LI 4, LI 11, LI 15, SJ 5, St 36, and Bauxie (extra 28)
Shoulder: GB 20, GB 22, LI 6, P 3, P 6, SJ 8, SJ 11, SJ 12, SJ 13, SJ 14, SJ 15, SJ 16, St 13, and UB 41
Arm: GB 38, LI 6, LI 7, LI 11, LI 12, LI 17, Lu 6, P 4, SI 6, SI 10, SI 12, St 36, UB 38, and UB 67
Elbow: Lu 5, GB 38, LI 12, LI 15, LI 16, SJ 1, St 36, UB 38, and UB 67
Wrist Pain: Du 20, H 7, LI 4, Lu 9, LI 5, P 7, SJ 4, St 44, and Ah Shi points
Hand Pain: LI 4, SI 3, SI 7, St 36, Ren 13, UB 38, and UB 58
Finger Pain: SI 7, St 36, UB 38, UB 58, and Ren 13
Lower Extremities: GB 30, GB 34, GB 39, GB 40, St 36, St 35, St 41, and extra 36
Hip: Du 20, GB 29, GB 30, GB 34, LI 4, St 44, UB 32, UB 36, UB 37, UB 40, UB 54, and UB 60
Knee: GB 32, GB 33, GB 34, GB 35, P 5, Sp 9, St 34, St 35, Extra 31, Extra 32, UB 56, and UB 67
Ankle: GB 38, Liv 6, St 36, UB 38, and UB 67
Foot: Du 20, Extra 36, GB 31, GB 34, GB 38, GB 39, Ki 3, LI 4, LI 8, Sp 5, St 36, St 44, Sp 4, UB 40, UB 57, UB 60, UB 65, and Ah shi points
Stiff Neck: Du 18, Ki 18, LI 1, LI 3, LI 14, LI 17, SI 6, Sp 3, Sp 4, Sp 7, Sp 15, Sp 16, Sp 18, St 36, UB 2, UB 10, UB 60, and UB 64
Neck Pain with Shoulder Pain: GB 12, GB 13, GB 21, GB 38, GB 39, GB 40, LI 12, LI 14, LI 15, LI 16, LI 17, SJ 4, SJ 10, SI 3, SI 9, SI 11, SI 13, St 4, and St 36
Back Pain: Du 10, GB 20, GB 23, GB 38, LI 14, Liv 3, Liv 9, SJ 3, SJ 13, Sp 2, Sp 3, Sp 5, Sp 8, Sp 9, St 30, St 31, St 32, St 36, UB 18, UB 33, UB 38, UB 40, UB 44, UB 45, UB 47, UB 51, UB 58, and UB 67
Upper Back Ache: Du 26, GB 21, LI 10, LI 11, LI 15, SJ 10, SI 5, and UB 43
Back Pain Radiating into Shoulder Area: GB 21, GB 27, GB 39, UB 12, and UB 60
Stiff Back: Du 16, Du 26, and UB 13
Back Tension: Lu 8
Low Back Pain: UB 23
Back Pain Radiating into Waist: Du 26, GB 30, and UB 40
Intercostal Neuralgia: extra-21, GB 34, Liv 14, and Liv 3
TMJ Pain: Du 20, GB 2, H 7, LI 4, SJ 5, SJ 21, SI 18, SI 19, St 7, and St 44

PART III

SPECIAL TECHNIQUES

10

INTRAMUSCULAR STIMULATION (IMS)— A NEUROANATOMIC DRYNEEDLING TECHNIQUE FOR MYOFASCIAL PAIN SYNDROMES AFFECTING THE MUSCULOSKELETAL SYSTEM

C. Chan Gunn, M.D.

INTRODUCTION

Chronic myofascial pain—or chronic pain that occurs in the musculoskeletal system when there is no obvious injury or inflammation—often defies diagnosis and treatment. Medications and commonly available physical therapies typically only give temporary relief. Many patients, therefore, wander from therapist to therapist in a vain quest for relief. This is a deplorable circumstance, as myofascial pain (unquestionably the largest category of chronic pain) can be diagnosed and helpful treatment given.

In this section:

- A peripheral neuropathy model which explains myofascial pain in a new way is presented.[6,7] Instead of presuming myofascial pain to be the consequence of signals of tissue injury, the model blames pain on subtle dysfunction in the nervous system, notably, peripheral neuropathy. In peripheral neuropathy, pain receptors and pathways can become excessively sensitive (or supersensitive), causing benign signals to be exaggerated and misinterpreted as painful ones. For example, in photophobia, it is not the light that is too bright, but the eye that is too sensitive.

- Because there are no satisfactory laboratory or imaging tests for early neuropathy—the diagnosis of neuropathic pain is necessarily by examination for signs of peripheral neuropathy. These are described.[114]

- Neuropathic pain does not respond to medication but requires some form of physical therapy. Most commonly used physical therapies are, however, ineffective, and a needling technique is ultimately necessary. The rationales of three needling techniques are compared: (1) traditional acupuncture.[115,116,117,118] (2) injection of trigger points and (3) Intramuscular Stimulation,[119] or IMS, which is an alternative, neuroanatomic system of diagnosis and dryneedling. IMS is taught at many pain centers, including the Multidisciplinary Pain Center, University of Washington, and the Institute for the Study and Treatment of Pain (ISTOP) in Vancouver.

- A fundamental but little known physiologic law—Cannon and Rosenblueth's Law of Denervation[120]—is cited to explain the abnormal physiology and supersensitivity that occurs in neuropathic and denervated structures.

- The most crucial ingredient of myofascial pain—muscle shortening from contracture (or "spasm") is highlighted. In fact, myofascial pain does not exist without muscle shortening. Prolonged shortening not only causes pain in muscle but also physically pulls on tendons, thereby straining them and distressing the bone and joints they insert into and act upon.[121] Chronic traction increases wear and tear and expedites degenerative changes such as "osteoarthritis." A primary goal of treatment, therefore, is to release early muscle shortening before degenerative changes develop.

- The radiculopathy model is notably significant because it is able to account for pain that occurs and persists without any evidence of injury or inflammation. Also, by regarding pain as an epiphenomenon of neural dysfunction (just as fever is a manifestation of infection), it explains many apparently different and unrelated pain syndromes, and places them all into one classification (Table 10.1). There may be hundreds of "conditions," but only one underlying mechanism: radiculopathy.[122]

THE NATURE OF NEUROPATHIC AND RADICULOPATHIC PAIN

Medical diagnosis traditionally presumes pain to be a signal of tissue injury conveyed to the central nervous system via a healthy nervous system. The definition of pain, as given by the International Association for the Study of Pain, underscores this—"an unpleasant sensory and emotional experience associated with actual or potential tissue damage, or described by the patient in terms of such damage." But, although pain may be linked causally to tissue injury, it need not be so. Injury does not always generate pain, nor does pain always signal injury. Pain perception can arise from non-noxious input, and spurious pain can arise from within the body when there is some functional disturbance in the nervous system: this category of pain is referred to as "neurogenic pain."

Pain can become persistent or "chronic" if any of the following occurs:

(1) *Ongoing nociception or inflammation.* Chronic pain can be caused by ongoing noxious or inflammatory input, but nociception is not a common cause of

Table 10.1. Common myofascial pain syndromes caused by the Shortened Muscle Syndrome

(Reproduced with permission from C. *Chan Gunn, The Gunn Approach to the Treatment of Chronic Pain—Intramuscular Stimulation (IMS) for Myofascial Pain of Radiculopathic Origin.* Churchill Livingstone, 1996.)

Muscles shorten on neuropathy, compressing supersensitive nociceptors to generate pain within the muscle. Shortening also causes pain by physically pulling on tendons and distressing the joints they activate. Shortening increases war and tear, eventually leading to degenerative changes in many structures. Myofascial pain syndromes are, therefore, of great diversity.

In radiculopathy, muscles of both primary rami are involved and symptoms can appear in peripheral as well as in paraspinal muscles of the same segment. When paraspinal muscles shorten, they can press upon nerve roots to perpetuate radiculophatic pain (see Figure 3). It is important to note that radiculopathy also involves the automatic nervous system.

Some common syndromes are listed below.

Syndrome	Shortened muscle
Achilles tendonitis	gastrocnemii, soleus
Bicipital tendonitis	biceps brachii
Bursitis, pre-patellar	quadriceps femoris
Capsulitis, frozen shoulder	All muscles acting on the shoulder: deltroid, trapezius, levator scapulae, rhomboidei, pectoralis major, supra- and infraspinati, teres major & minor, subscapularis
Carpal tunnel syndrome	The median nerve can be entrapped by the pronator teres and the tendinous arch connecting the humero-ulnar and radical heads of the flexor digitorum superficialis (the sublimis bridge). Trophedema can also compromise the nerve in the forearm and carpal tunnel.
Cervical fibrositis	cervical paraspinal muscles
Chondromalacia patellae	quadriceps femoris
De Quervain's tenosynovitis	abductor policis longus, extensor pollicis brevis
Facet syndrome	muscles acting across the facet joint, e.g., rotatores, multifidi, semispinalis
Finromyalgia	multisegmental radiculopathy (diffuse myofascial pain syndrome)
Hallux valgus	Extensor hallucis longus and brevis
Headaches: frontal	upper trapezius, semispinalis capitis, occipitofrontalis
Temporal	temporalis, trapezius
Vertex	splenius capitis & cervices, upper trapezius, semispinalis capitis, occipitofrontalis
Occipital	sub-occipital muscles
Infrapatellar tendonitis	quadriceps femoris
Intervertebral disc	muscles acting across the disc space, e.g., rotatores, multifidi, semispinalis.

Table 10.1. (*continued*)

Juvenile kyphosis and	unbalanced paraspinal scoliosis muscles (e.g., iliocostalis thoracis and lumborum)
"Low back sprain"	paraspinal muscles: e.g., iliocostalis lumborum and thoracis, multifidi; also see "Intervertebral disc".
Plantar fascitis	flexor digitorum brevis, lumbricals
Piriformis syndrome	piriformis muscle
Rotator cuff syndrome	supra- and infraspinati, teres minor, subscapular.
"Shin splints"	tibialis anterior
Temporomandibular joint (TMJ)	masseter, temporalis, pterygoids
Tennis elbow	brachioradialis, extensor carpi ulnaris, extensor carpi radialis brevis and longus, ext. digitorum, anconeus, triceps.
Torticollis (acute)	splenius capitis & cervicis.

chronic pain, and inflammation is easily recognized (redness, increased local temperature, swelling and inflammation), and it is usually self-limiting (unless there is some abnormal immunologic response as in rheumatoid arthritis).

(2) *Psychologic factors* such as a somatization disorder, depression, or operant learning processes.

(3) *Abnormal function in the nervous system.* Neurogenic pain can arise in the CNS or PNS.[123] "Neuropathic" pain refers to pain that arises when there is peripheral neuropathy (i.e., altered or abnormal function in the peripheral nervous system with or without structural change).[124,125] "Myofascial" pain describes neuropathic pain that presents predominately in the musculoskeletal system.

Myofascial pain syndromes often appear puzzling because they arise and persist in the absence of any detectable injury or inflammation—a response occurs and is sustained without a discernible stimulus. Such syndromes are mundane and can affect muscles and their connective tissue attachments in all parts of the body. Although they are considered as distinct and unrelated local conditions and customarily labelled according to the location of the painful part, e.g., "headache," "lateral epicondylitis," "bicipital tendonitis," "low back pain," "whiplash," and so on, the neuropathic findings in all these conditions, regardless of location, are the same. Wherever the condition may be situated, the underlying mechanism is the same: neuropathic dysfunction,[126] regularly accompanied by the physical consequences of muscle shortening (see Table 10.1).

Although we had first described this category of pain as "pain following neuropathy"[122] (now generally abbreviated to "neuropathic pain"), our subsequent experience has been that signs of neuropathy are almost always found in the distribution of both dorsal and ventral rami of the segmental nerve. This marks the site of neuropathy to be at the nerve root—"radiculopathic" pain is therefore a more accurate descriptive term.[119]

Not all physicians are familiar with the condition of peripheral neuropathy.[125] It may be defined as a disease that causes disordered function in the peripheral nerve. Although sometimes associated with structural changes in the nerve, a neuropathic nerve can, deceptively, appear normal: it still conducts nerve impulses, synthesizes and releases transmitted substances and evokes action potentials and muscle contraction.

CANNON AND ROSENBLUETH'S LAW OF DENERVATION

The normal physiology and integrity of innervated structures are contingent on the flow of nerve impulses in the intact nerve to provide a regulatory or "trophic" effect. When this flow (a combination of axoplasmic flow and electrical input) is blocked, innervated structures are deprived of the trophic factor which is necessary for the regulation and maintenance of cellular function. "A-trophic" structures become highly irritable and develop abnormal sensitivity or supersensitivity according to Cannon and Rosenblueth's Law of Denervation:[120]

> When a unit is destroyed in a series of efferent neurons, an increased irritability to chemical agents develops in the isolated structure or structures, the effect being maximal in the part directly denervated.

All denervated structures develop supersensitivity (including skeletal muscle, smooth muscle, spinal neurones, sympathetic ganglia, adrenal glands, sweat glands, and brain cells). Cannon and Rosenblueth's original work was based on total denervation and decentralization for supersensitivity to develop, accordingly, they named the phenomenon *denervation* supersensitivity. But it is now known that physical interruption and total denervation are not necessary—any circumstance that impedes the flow of motor impulses for a period of time can rob the effector organ of its excitatory input and cause *disuse* supersensitivity in that organ and in associated spinal reflexes.[127]

The importance of disuse supersensitivity cannot be overemphasized. When a nerve malfunctions, the structures it supplies become supersensitive and will behave abnormally. These structures over-react to many forms of input, not only chemical, but physical inputs as well, including stretch and pressure. Supersensitive muscle cells can generate spontaneous electrical impulses that trigger false pain signals or provoke involuntary muscle activity,[123] and supersensitive nerve fibres can become receptive to chemical transmitters at every point along their length instead of at their terminals only. Sprouting may occur, and denervated nerves are prone to accept contacts from other types of nerves, including autonomic and sensory nerve fibres. Short circuits are possible between sensory and autonomic (vasomotor) nerves and may contribute to "reflex sympathetic dystrophy" or the "complex regional pain syndrome."

Disuse supersensitivity is basic and universal, yet not at all well known or credited. The important role of supersensitive structures following neuropathy or denervation has been, until recently, neglected. Many diverse pain syndromes of apparently unknown causation can be attributed to the development of hypersensitive receptor organs and supersensitivity in pain sensory pathways.

RADICULOPATHY—ITS RELATIONSHIP TO SPONDYLOSIS

It is not at all unusual for the flow of nerve impulses to be obstructed. Peripheral neuropathy, often accompanied by partial denervation, is not exceptional in adults. Of the innumerable causes of nerve damage, such as trauma, metabolic, degenerative, toxic, and other conditions, chronic attrition from spondylosis (the structural disintegration and morphologic alterations that occur in the intervertebral disc, with pathoanatomic changes in surrounding structures) is by far the most common.[122] The spinal nerve root, because of its vulnerable position, is notably prone to injury from pressure, stretch, angulation, and friction. (Other causes of radiculopathy, such as arachnoiditis, neuroma, and intraspinal tumors are much less common). Spondylosis increases with age, therefore, spondylotic pain is more common in middle-aged individuals who have accumulated an "injury pool"—an accumulation of repeated major and minor injuries to a segment leading to unresolved clinical residuals which may or may not produce pain.

Collagen degenration. Ironically, neuropathy itself contributes to degenerative conditions (including spondylosis). Neuropathy degrades the quality of collagen, causing it to have fewer cross-links; it is therefore markedly frailer than normal collagen.[128] The amount of collagen in soft and skeletal tissues is also reduced. Because collagen lends strength to ligament, tendon, cartilage, and bone, neuropathy can expedite degeneration in weight-bearing and activity-stressed parts of the body, including the spine and joints. Degenerative conditions, generally regarded as primary diseases, are actually secondary to radiculopathy. Radiculopathic pain syndromes therefore deserve prompt treatment to prevent degeneration.

Ordinarily, spondylosis follows a gradual, relapsing, and remitting course that is silent, unless and until symptoms are precipitated by an incident often so minor that it passes unnoticed by the patient. All gradations of spondylosis can exist, but prespondylosis or early, incipient spondylotic changes, even when unsuspected, can nevertheless irritate and upset function in the segmental nerve.[122]

Another reason for the emphasis on neuropathy is that an acute structural deformation of a healthy nerve is usually not painful or only briefly so. For example, peroneal nerve palsy or radial nerve "Saturday night palsy" are without pain, and animal experiments have shown that an acute mechanical injury to a healthy dorsal nerve root does not produce a sustained discharge unless there has been pre-existing minor chronic injury to the nerve.[129] In other words, for pain to become a persistent symptom, the affected fibers must have been primed with previous damage. This would explain why some people develop severe pain after an apparently minor injury, and why that pain can persist beyond a "reasonable" period.

PHYSICAL SIGNS ASSOCIATED WITH NEUROPATHY

The signs of neuropathy are subtle and differ from those of outright denervation (such as loss of sensation and reflexes). The effects of neuropathy vary according to the type (sensory, motor, autonomic, or mixed) and distribution of the nerve fibres involved. In radiculopathy, symptoms and signs are projected to dermatomal, myotomal, and sclerotomal target structures supplied by the affected neural structures.[114] A careful search for signs of autonomic, motor and sensory dysfunction in the skin and affected muscles is critical for diagnosis and treatment. Signs of autonomic dysfunction are the first to be discussed, as they are often the ones first seen by the examiner.

Pilomotor Reflex

The autonomic system is a division of the peripheral nervous system and is by definition entirely motor (except for vascular and visceral afferents). Although "automatic" in the sense that most of its functions are carried below the conscious level, it is highly integrated in structure and function with the rest of the nervous system. Autonomic efferent fibers supply the piloerector muscles, smooth muscles of the blood vessels, and sweat glands. When autonomic ganglia and effector muscles are affected, denervation supersensitivity develops. For example, as the patient undresses and as cool air plays on exposed skin, there may be seen a pilomotor effect or cutis anserina ("goose flesh") in the dermatomes of affected segmental levels. It is important to be aware of this reflex as it may be present for only a brief moment. The pilomotor reflex may be induced by firm digital pressure over any tender motor point within the affected segment. (The North American practice of providing a female patient with a gown for modesty conceals this sign.) There can be interaction between pain and autonomic phenomena. A stimulus such as chilling, which arouses the pilomotor response can precipitate pain; vice versa, pressure upon a tender motor point can provoke the pilomotor and sudomotor reflexes.

Vasomotor Disturbances

In complete division of a peripheral nerve, the denervated region of the skin has a pink or rosy appearance because of vasodilatation brought about by interruption of sympathetic fibers to that part. In partial denervation, vasoconstrictor disturbance caused by denervation supersensitivity consists of mottling of the skin, i.e., combined pallor and cyanosis. Rarely, a reticular pigmentation may occur, resembling erythema ab igne even when the patient has not applied local heat. In neuropathy, affected parts are perceptibly colder. Vasoconstriction differentiates neuropathic pain from inflammatory pain: in neuropathic pain, the skin has a lower temperature which only become discernible to touch after sufficient exposure to cool air (from 10 to 15 minutes).

Sudomotor Reflex

Complete denervation results in anhidrosis or absence of sweating; however, in partial nerve palsies, there is an increased tendency to sweat. The sudorific reflex may occur either spontaneously, under the duress of emotion, or during examination when painful movements are performed. Sweating usually extends beyond the anatomic confines of the nerve concerned, covering an extensive area which includes the axillae, palms of hands, and soles of feet. (Autonomic postganglionic outnumber preganglionic neurons by a ratio of at least 32:1.) Sweating can be so profuse that droplets of sweat run down from the axillae. A quick inspection of the examination couch sheet soon confirms the distribution of hyperhidrosis.

Cutaneous Hyperesthesia

Hyperpathia in skin can be demonstrated by drawing the point of a pin across skin, it is felt more sharply over affected dermatomes.

Trophic Disturbances

Nuritional or trophic changes form an important part of any neurologic disorder and may occur in the skin, nails, subcataneous tissues, muscles, bones, and joints. Trophic changes such as dermatomal hair loss may also accompany neuropathy. In addition to a neurologic basis, factors such as activity, blood supply, and lymph drainage are involved in the causation of trophic changes. When a peripheral nerve is completely interrupted, the skin loses it delicate indentation, becomes inelastic, smooth, and shiny; but when interruption is partial, neurogenic edema or trophedema occurs. There is gradual fibrosis of the subcutaneous tissue and overlying skin tends to be fissured and prone to heavy folds. This alteration in the quality of skin produces a "peau d'orange" effect similar to that described for malignant lumps of the female breast. The effect is accentuated when the skin is gently squeezed together, or when the back is fully extended. Trophedematous subcutaneous tissue has a boggy, inelastice texture when rolled between thumb and finger, easily distinguishable from subcutaneous fat. When a patch of skin and subcutaneous tissue of a few centimeters in diameter is gently squeezed together, instead of immediately forming a fold of flesh, trophedematous tissue does not budge, or it finally yields altogether with a sudden distending or swelling movement similar to that of inflating a rubber dinghy or air mattress.

Trophedema is non-pitting to digital pressure, but when a blunt instrument, e.g., the end of a matchstick is used, the indentation produced is clear-cut and persists for several minutes, distinctly longer than that over normal skin. This "matchstick test" may be positive, yielding deep indentations over an extensive area (commonly over the low back and hamstrings), or in mild cases may only give slight indentation of skin overlying a tender motor point or the neurovascular hilus. This simple test for neuropathy is more sensitive than electromyography.

Enthesopathy

In neuropathy, tendinous attachments to bone are often thickened or enthesopathic. Some common sites for enthesopathy are:

- origin of extensor muscles at lateral epicondyle of elbow
- origin of the tibialis anterior muscle
- origin of erector spinae muscles
- insertion of semispinalis capitis muscle at the occiput
- insertion of longissimus capitis muscle at the mastoid process
- insertion of the deltoid muscle.

Signs Associated with Dysfunction of the Muscle Nerve

Signs in muscle are the most relevant and abundant. The musculoskeletal system is the most massive system of the body and therefore receives the largest efferent outflow from the central nervous system. Likewise, the predominant input to the central nervous system is the sensory input from the musculoskeletal system. Sensory fibers arise from nerve endings in a variety of somatic structures in myofascial and articular tissues, entering the cord via the dorsal root to be routed to various centers of the nervous system including the cerebral cortex and the autonomic nervous system. The sensory input from the musculoskeletal system is so extensive, intensive and unceasing as to be the dominant influence on the central nervous system and therefore the person as a whole.

Each skeletal muscle receives one or more nerve supplies. In the limbs, the supply is usually single, but where a nerve more obviously retains its segmental arrangement, e.g., the muscles of the abdominal wall, its nerve supply is multiple. After dividing into several small branches, the nerve together with the principal blood vessels of the muscle enter the deep surface of the muscle nearer to its origin at a small, elongated, oval area—the neurovascular hilus. Its terminals are not distributed to the entire muscle but are confined to a fairly narrow transverse motor band near the center of the muscle. The skin region overlying this motor band is known as the "motor point" and is the site where an innervated muscle is most accessible to percutaneous electrical excitation at the lowest intensity.

Myalgic hyperalgesia, or muscle pain, is mediated by bare nerve endings in fascia and pressure-pain nociceptors around blood vessels. These may become supersensitive secondary to altered autonomic activity or to loss of selective inhibitory input from nonnociceptive mechanoreceptors. Noiciceptor afferents are abundant around blood vessels and tenderness is therefore greatest at the neurovascular hilus deep to the motor point. Motor points are fixed anatomic sites and easily found. (Charts showing their distribution are generally available: The earliest chart was prepared by the neurologist Wilhelm Erb in 1882.) Motor points are not tender in the normal individual, but mild and transient points may occasionally be found in asymptomatic subjects after unusual activities such as jogging. Moderately tender points are usually present in individuals who give a history of a vulnerable back or who have had lesser degrees of trauma. Acutely tender motor points are almost constantly found in patients having radiculopathy with the degree of tenderness and the number of points paralleling the patient's condition.[114]

To be aware of tenderness at motor points may help with the diagnosis of pain and tenderness around a joint. For example, a tender gluteus medius motor point over the upper lateral quadrant of the buttock is commonly attributed to "gluteal bursitis"; a tensor fascia lata motor point to trochanteric bursitis, and tenderness at the gluteus maximus motor points (focal) has been mistaken for a tender sciatic nerve (linear). The motor fibers of the muscle nerve comprise the large myelinated alpha-efferents of the anterior horn cells which supply extrafusal muscle fibers and the smaller myelinated gamma-efferents which supply the muscle spindles. The motor unit is defined as the anterior horn cell, its branched axon, and the muscle fibers which it innervates. In disorders of the alpha motoneuron there is atrophy of some muscle fibers and reinnervation of others by surviving motoneurons (territorial invasion). Supersensitivity of single denervated fibers to circulating acetycholine is seen in electromyography as fibrillation potentials, but clinical assessment of early weakness in muscle is unreliable and not usually detectable unless atrophy has involved a great number of muscle fibers. (An analysis of the density of the electromyographic interference pattern during maximum effort is a valuable procedure but not accurate quantitatively.)

Muscle shortening is a fundamental feature of musculoskeletal pain syndromes and of all the structures that develop supersensitivity the most widespread and significant is striated muscle. Supersensitivity can affect the muscle, and Cannon described four types of increased sensitivity:

1. Increased susceptibility, where lessened stimuli that do not have to exceed a threshold produce responses of normal amplitude.
2. Hyperexcitability, where the threshold for the stimulating agent is lower than normal.
3. Super-reactivity, where the ability of the tissue to respond is augmented.
4. Superduration of response, where the amplitude of responses is unchanged, but their course is prolonged.

Supersensitivity can also affect the muscle spindle. The spindle, about 3 millimeters in length, is enclosed in connective tissue. Its intrafusal muscle fibers are innervated by the gamma motoneurons, and its afferent neurons are from the primary endings or annulospiral endings wound around the intrafusal fibers and the secondary flower-spray endings on both sides of the annulospiral endings. These endings are sensitive to stretch of the central portion of the spindle and form part of the essential feedback mechanism by which skeletal muscle and resting muscle tonus are controlled. The afferent discharge of the spindle via the dorsal root on the motor neurons of the same muscle is excitatory. Thus, when a muscle is stretched, e.g., the hamstrings as in the straight leg-raising test, the spindles reflexedly stimulate it to contract and resist stretching. The spindle is, in effect, the sensory component of the muscle-stretch or myotatic reflex, commonly misnamed the "tendon reflex" test. Super-sensitivity of the gamma-alpha loop may lead to hyperexcitation of muscle and contribute toward muscle shortening and contracture seen in neuropathy. Conversely, shortening of the muscle favors relaxation. Through interneurons and collaterals, spindle activity also determines the activity of antagonists and synergists. (This is discussed in a later paragraph).

Muscle shortening is therefore an early irritative sign indicative of neuropathy and occurs before depression or interruption of the deep myotatic reflex from denervation.

Muscle shortening mechanically causes a large variety of pain syndromes by its relentless pull on various structures (Fig. 10.1 and Table 10.1). Even when symptoms appear in joints or tendons, most often it is not pain in muscle that predominates[130] but pain caused by the physical pull of muscle shortening on tendons, ligaments, and joints.

Shortening in muscle is easily overlooked unless a deliberate scan of all major muscles is undertaken. During examination, each and every constituent muscle must be palpated and its condition noted. Palpation requires detailed knowledge of anatomy, and the skill to palpate comes only with practice. Normal resting muscle is soft, yet has a certain resilience, but its shape and boundaries are not easily discernible to palpation. Shortened muscle fasciculi can be palpated as ropey bands. Focal areas of tenderness and pain in contractures are often referred to as "trigger points" (see Fig. 10.2). Tender points can be found throughout the myotome and in paraspinal muscles. Because many paraspinal muscles are compound (e.g., the longissimus) and extend throughout most of the length of the vertebral column, the entire spine must be examined even when symptoms are localized to one region.

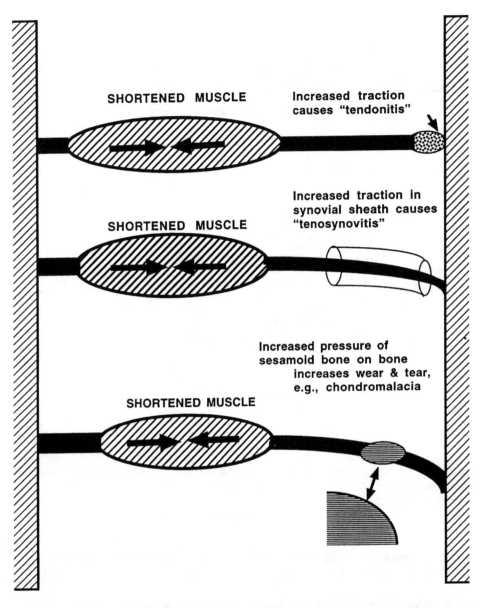

SHORTENED MUSCLE   **Increased traction causes "tendonitis"**

Increased traction in synovial sheath causes "tenosynovitis"

SHORTENED MUSCLE

Increased pressure of sesamoid bone on bone increases wear & tear, e.g., chondromalacia

SHORTENED MUSCLE

Figure 10.1 Shortening creates tension in tendons and their attachments and can cause such syndromes as epicondylitis, tendonitis, tenosynovitis, or chondromalacia patellae. (Reproduced with permission from the Gunn Approach to the Treatment of Chronic Pain: Intramuscular Stimulation for Myofascial pain of Radiculopathic Origin, by C. Chan Gunn, 2nd Edition. Published by Churchill Livingstone, September 1996.)

CHALLENGES IN DIAGNOSIS

Diagnosing pain and dysfunction caused by radiculopathy depends almost entirely on the examiner's clinical experience and acumen. The history gives little assistance. Pain often arises spontaneously with no history of trauma, or else the

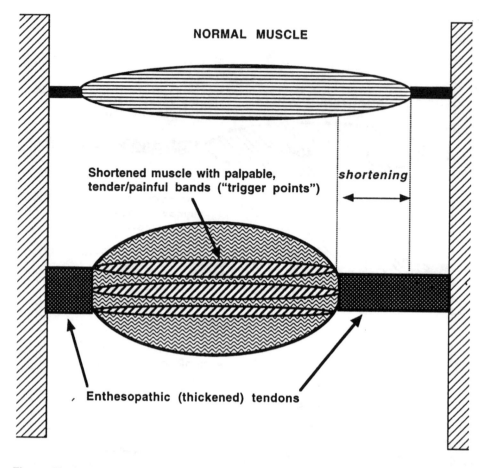

Figure 10.2 Neuropathy can cause muscle contracture with concurrent muscle shortening. (Reproduced with permission from The Gunn Approach to the Treatment of Chronic Pain: Intramuscular Stimulation (IMS) for Myofascial Pain of Radiculopathic Origin, by C. Chan Gunn, 2nd Edition. Published by Churchill Livingstone, September 1996.)

degree of reported pain far exceeds that consistent with the injury. Some features that indicate neuropathic pain are:

- Pain when there is no ongoing tissue-damaging process.
- Delay in onset after precipitating injury. (It generally takes 5 days for supersensitivity to develop.)
- "Deep, aching" and/or brief "sharp or stabbing" neuralgic pain.
- A mild stimulus can cause extreme pain.
- Pronounced summation and after-reaction with repetitive stimuli.
- Loss of joint range or pain caused by the mechanical effects of muscle shortening;
- Abnormal bowel function (e.g., "irritable bowel syndrome");
- Increased vasoconstriction and hyperhidrosis;
- "Causalgic pain"; "reflex sympathetic dystrophy" or "complex regional pain syndrome".
- Local conditions are rare. Although most musculoskeletal pain syndromes appear confined to one region, e.g., "lateral epicondylitis" or "frozen shoulder,"

careful examination will always reveal signs of neuropathy, especially muscle tenderness and shortening in muscles belonging to the same segment. Often, signs are found in several segments on the same side of the body, and to a lesser extent, on the contralateral side.

LABORATORY AND RADIOLOGIC FINDINGS

These are generally not helpful. Thermography reveals decreased skin temperature in affected dermatomes—this can be an indication of neuropathy but does not necessarily signify pain nor identify individual painful muscles. Radiculopathies are difficult to document with routine nerve conduction studies which measure only the few fastest-conducting and largest fibres and take no account of the majority of smaller fibres. In focal neuropathy, nerve conduction velocities remain within the wide range of normal values, but F-wave latency may be prolonged. Electromyography is not specific either.

PHYSICAL THERAPY—TREATMENT PRINCIPLES

The goal in treatment is to desensitize supersensitivity by restoring the flow of impulses in a peripheral nerve. When the flow of impulses is briefly blocked, any supersensitivity that develops will also be transient. But when contractures and shortened muscles are present, their release is usually necessary to restore joint range and relieve pain: typically, when the several most painful contracture bands in a muscle are released, relaxation of the entire muscle follows.

A contracture does not release with medication—its freeing requires a physical stimulus. A physical stimulus is sensed by receptors in skin and muscle and it stimulates the target contracture *reflexively*. All forms of stimuli have their specific receptors—massage and focal pressure excites tactile and pressure receptors; heat (including ultrasound) and cold activate thermal receptors; traction, exercise, or manipulation stimulate muscle proprioceptors, such as a muscle spindles and Golgi organs, and so on. These stimuli are sensed by their specific receptors, transduced intro electrical signals and relayed to the spinal cord. As with the patellar reflex, stimulation reaches the affected part via a reflex. All physical and counter-irritational therapies achieve their effect by reflex-stimulation. They are effective only if the nerve to the painful part is intact. Of all the physical stimuli used for therapy, that produced by a needle is the most efficacious, as it is particularly capable of releasing contractures.

DRYNEEDLING TECHNIQUES

This section a describes Intramuscular Stimulation, a dryneedling technique based on neurophysiologic concepts.

Varieties of acupuncture. Classical or Traditional Acupuncture, which forms part of the total entity of traditional Chinese medicine (TCM),[118] is widely employed in China. Western medical doctors, or medical acupuncturists, who practice acupuncture in North America and Europe usually have had some training in classical acupuncture, but many of them do not apply TCM techniques, such as pulse diagnosis, or prescribe Chinese herbs, even though they continue to use TCM nomenclature and terminology.[117] Most medical acupuncturists restrict their practice to pain management. They generally assume chronic pain to be ongoing signals of tissue damage (nociception or inflammation) and are preoccupied with analgesia and the suppression of nociception. Thus, when endogenous opioids were discovered, they were quick to explain acupuncture as a neuro-modulating technique capable of stimulating the endogenous pain suppression system to release neurotransmitters and endogenous opioids.[131] However, these neuro-chemicals are also released under other stressful conditions (including drug and smoking withdrawal) which do not necessarily produce pain. Their role may be to modulate various homeostatic mechanisms and act as an endocrine-endorphin stress system that complements the neuronal regulatory system. In application, acupuncture's capability to suppress nociception is limited. Acupuncture cannot be relied on to block the perception of a noxious input—even in China it is not a popular choice for surgery.

Some medical acupuncturists call electrical stimulation with surface electrodes applied over acupuncture points "acupuncture", but this is incorrect as a needle is central to the procedure. Other medical acupuncturists use acupuncture, in effect, as a form of trigger point therapy or as a means for electric stimulation.

INTRAMUSCULAR STIMULATION (IMS)

IMS is a system of dryneedling based on our radiculopathy model for chronic pain. Unlike acupuncture, IMS requires a medical examination and diagnosis, and it treats specific anatomic entities selected according to physical signs.[120] Examination, diagnosis, rationale for the selection of points for treatment, as well as progress of therapy are all determined according to physical signs of radiculopathy. The IMS therapist, with a sound background in anatomy and neurophysiology and guided by physical signs, is much more effective than the traditional acupuncturist.

Some observations that led to the radiculopathy model:

- Points found to be effective for treatment are nearly always situated close to known neuroanatomic entities, such as muscle motor points or musculotendinous junctions; these points often coincide with acupuncture points.
- Effective treatment points generally belong to the same segmental level(s) as presenting symptoms or the injury.
- These points generally coincide with palpable muscle bands that are tender to digital pressure and are generally referred to as trigger points.
- Tender points are distributed in a segmental or myotomal fashion, in muscles of both anterior and posterior primary rami, which is indicative of radiculopathy. Radiculopathic pain is especially common in "prespondylosis," the early stage of spondylosis when neuropathy is already present, though unsuspected.[6]
- Muscles with tender points are shortened from contracture (Fig. 10.2).
- Virtually every condition that responds to needling demonstrates signs of peripheral neuropathy, but because these signs are not well known, they are usually missed.
- Symptoms and signs typically disappear when tender and shortened muscle bands are needled and contractures released.

IMS practitioners purposely seek out tender and tight muscle bands in affected segments for needling. Following needling, physical signs of peripheral neuropathy, such as muscle contracture ("spasm"), vasoconstriction and tenderness can disappear within seconds or minutes. (It is extremely satisfying to see these signs disappear before one's eyes.) Other signs, like trophedema, may diminish more gradually, sometimes even taking days to disappear, but all signs ultimately vanish following successful treatment.

The needle as a powerful diagnostic and treatment tool. The fine, flexible, solid needle is more than a therapeutic tool, it is also a unique and powerful diagnostic instrument. Contracture is invisible to X-rays, CT scans or MRI. Contractures in deep muscles are beyond the finger's reach and can only be discovered by probing with a needle: the fine, flexible needle transmits feedback on the nature and consistency of the tissues that it is penetrating. When the needle penetrates normal muscle, it meets with little hindrance; when it penetrates a contracture, there is firm resistance, and the needle is grasped by the muscle (causing the patient to feel a peculiar, cramping or grabbing sensation described by acupuncturists as the "Deqi response"). When the needle enters fibrotic tissue, there is a grating sensation (like cutting through a pear). Sometimes, the resistance of a fibrotic muscle is so intense that its hardness is mistaken for bone, and increased pressure on the needle may be required to force it in.

The needle grasp. When the needle penetrates a shortened muscle, it often provokes the muscle to fasciculate and release quickly—in seconds or minutes. A shortened muscle that is not quickly released, however, will invariably grasp the needle. The needle-grasp can be detected by the therapist when an attempt is made to withdraw the needle—the grasp resists withdrawal. Leaving the grasped needle in situ for a further period (typically 10 to 30 minutes) can lead to the release of a persistent contracture. Failure of a correctly placed needle to induce needle-grasp signifies that spasm is not present and therefore not the cause of pain, in which case, the condition will not respond to this type of treatment.

When there are many muscles, each with many muscle bands or fasciculi requiring treatment, it is convenient to hasten contracture-release by augmenting the intensity of stimulation. The traditional method is to twirl the grasped needle, a motion that specifically stimulates proprioceptors. As an alternative to twirling the needle, heat (moxibustion) or electrical stimulation is sometimes used.

How does twirling the needle stimulate proprioceptors? When a muscle is in spasm, muscle fibres cling to the needle, and twisting causes these fibres to wind around its shaft. This coiling of muscle fibres shortens their length, converting the twisting force into a linear force. Unlike traction or manipulation, stimulation is very exact and intense because the needle is precisely placed within a taut muscle band. The needle-twirling manoeuvre vigorously stimulates muscle proprioceptors and gives rise to a peculiar, subjective sensation known in TCM as the Deqi (formerly written as Teh Ch'i) phenomenon. This distinctive sensation is an extreme version of the muscle-ache felt in myofascial pain. Patients have variously described the sensation as "cramping", or "grabbing", or a "dull, heavy ache". Deqi is outside any normal experience of pain and need experiencing in person (especially by the therapist) in order to fully comprehend the unmistakable quality of myofascial pain. The muscle's grasp on the needle and the sensation the patient feels are both intensified as the needle is twirled to increase stimulation, until some moments later, the shortened muscle is released with coincident disappearance of pain.

Twirling the grasped needle elicits the *stretch* or *myotatic* reflex (seen clinically in the knee-jerk). The reflex is activated by the muscle stretch and causes a contraction in that same muscle. Twirling the grasped needle is like stretching the muscle: it stretches muscle spindles, causing Group-Ia fibers from the annulospiral endings to monosynaptically excite skeletomotor neurons that supply homonymous and synergist muscles. The same afferent volley disynaptically inhibits skeletomotor neurons that supply antagonist muscles. Group-Ia and group-Ib fibers work together in close association; whereas the muscle spindle signals the velocity of muscle stretch and muscle length, the Golgi tendon organ (GTO) signals the velocity of muscle tension development as well as steady tension. Group-Ib fibers from the GTO make disynaptic inhibitory connections with both homonymous and synergist skeletomotor neurons. By identifying the needle-grasp and the Deqi phenomenon as essential requirements for diagnosis and treatment, (inserting a needle into normal muscle does not produce needle grasp or Deqi), TCM has perceptively recognized the central role of muscle proprioceptors in chronic neuropathic pain. A-delta and C-fibers, carriers of injury signals, are not primarily involved in chronic neuropathic pain; their stimulation produces nociception, *which elicits a different reflex—the flexion or withdrawal reflex*. It is important to note that the end-product of any single spinal reflex, such as a muscle contraction, will itself initiate other reflexes.

A knowledge of the segmental nerve supply to muscles is the best guide to segmental identification. The examiner, guided by the needle-grasp and the Deqi response, is able to identify a distressed segment quickly and with greater accuracy than with X-rays, scans, or MRIs. Indeed, radiological findings can be misleading, as they are not capable of distinguishing old, non-active lesions from an ongoing, irritable one.

In recurrent or chronic pain, fibrosis eventually becomes a major feature of the contracture; the response to dryneedle treatment is then much less dramatic and less effective. The extent of fibrosis present is not necessarily correlated with chronologic age: scarring can occur after injury or surgery, and many older individuals have sustained less wear and tear than younger ones who have subjected their musculature to repeated physical stress. The treatment of extensive fibrotic contractures necessitates more frequent and extensive needling because release of the contracture is usually limited to the individual muscle bands needled. To relieve pain in such a muscle, it is necessary to needle all tender bands. It is rare to encounter a muscle that is totally fibrotic and cannot be released by accurate, vigorous needling.

The important observation is this: when shortened muscles are released, all associated epiphenomena of peripheral neuropathy (including pain, tenderness, vasoconstriction) vanish from the treated area, not infrequently from the entire segment. Simultaneous resolution of the different epiphenomena of radiculopathy by reflex stimulation may be explained by the overlap of neuronal circuits in the periphery (where two reflexes may share the same afferent receptor population), and in the spinal cord where the same interneuronal circuit and/or motor neuron may serve more than one reflex.

Contractures in paraspinal muscles For long-lasting pain relief, it is imperative to release contractures in paraspinal muscle that is compressing a disc (see Fig. 10.3). IMS is a valuable therapeutic tool, as it is notably effective in releasing contractures and dispersing the dense, fibrotic tissue that usually entraps a nerve root. Surgical intervention is rarely necessary, as the needle can reach deeply located contractures.

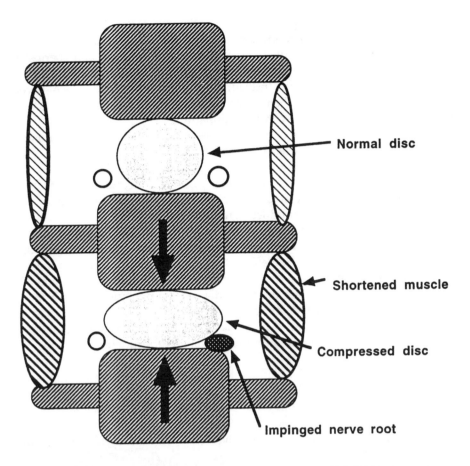

Figure 10.3 Shortened paraspinal muscles across an intervertebral disc space can compress the disc and impinge on the nerve root. (Reproduced with permission from The Gunn Approach to the Treatment of Chronic Pain: Intramuscular Stimulation (IMS) for Myofascial Pain of Radiculopathic Origin, by C. Chan Gunn, 2nd Edition. Published by Churchill Livingstone, September 1996.)

IMS differs from Traditional Acupuncture in that it:

- requires a medical examination searching for early signs of radiculopathy;
- requires a knowledge of anatomy;
- requires a medical diagnosis that usually implicates spondylosis;
- uses neuroanatomic points that are found in a segmental pattern, instead of using traditional acupuncture points;
- determines the points to be treated according to physical signs. The effects of IMS appear very quickly, even during needling, and can be used to monitor treatment and progress.

INJECTION OF "TRIGGER-POINTS"

In recent years, the injection of "trigger points" has become widely used. IMS and trigger point injection may appear to have features in common, but in fact they differ considerably in concept and therapeutic objectives. The trigger point approach regards painful points primarily as localized phenomena—foci of hyper-irritable tissue (myofascial, cutaneous, fascial, ligamentous and periosteal) occurring as the result of compensatory overload, shortened range, or response to activity in other trigger points. Instead, IMS views pain as only one of several possible supersensitivity epiphenomena or manifestations (motor, sensory, autonomic, trophic) that occur with radiculopathy.

In trigger point therapy, saline or local anaesthetic, with or without steroids, is injected into the painful muscle. The local anaesthetic can numb the noxious source temporarily, but does not eliminate it. All too frequently, pain resurfaces when the effect of the local anesthetic has worn out. Because it is the reflex response conveyed in efferent fibers to the affected structure that stimulates the therapeutic target, it is counterproductive to block the reflex with local anaesthetic.

The needle used for injecting trigger points is a hollow needle with a beveled, cutting edge that can cause harm to soft tissues. Injected material, especially steroids can caused serious side-effects such as infection, impaired healing, weakened tissue elements, local atrophy of fatty tissue, "dimpling" of skin, skin pigmentation, inflammation due to crystal deposits, suppression of the hypotha-lamic-pituitary axis, localized bleeding, and joint destruction by avascular necrosis. The needle used in IMS is pointed and virtually atraumatic; no medications are injected, and the needle is employed for different purposes:

- The needle produces local inflammation which is the necessary prelude to healing, and generates the "current of injury" (which is discussed later).
- The needle reflexively activates other components of the segmental nerve that may be situated some distance from the needle. For example, treating the cervical spine can relieve pain in the head or hand and also produce vasodilatation in the entire arm.
- A fundamental purpose of IMS is to relieve shortening in paraspinal muscle that is entrapping the nerve root and perpetuating pain (Fig. 10.3). The needle is utilized to break down fibrotic tissue surrounding the nerve.

DISCUSSION AND IMPLICATIONS

The mechanism of neuropathic pain is different from nociception and inflamma-tion. Its diagnosis and treatment therefore call for different approaches. Diagnosis is mainly by clinical examination because laboratory and radiological tests are unhelpful in early neuropathy. Signs of neuropathy are different from the well-known ones of outright denervation (such as absent reflexes and loss of sensation). Neuropathic signs are subtle, but they can be found if the examiner knows where to look, and what to look for.

Treatment of neuropathic pain is also different—supersensitivity needs to be soothed by the alleviation of neuropathy.

Lomo has shown that supersensitivity and all the other features of denervation in muscle can be reversed by stimulating the muscle with electricity.[133] Continuous electrical stimulation is able to counteract "disuse" supersensitivity and substitute for the trophic factor that is diminished or absent in neuropathy. Unfortunately, all external forms of physical stimulation have a critical drawback. They are passive and when application is halted, stimulation ceases. Ideally, stimulation should use the body's own bio-energy, which can be recruited in the form of the "current of injury".[134] First described by Galvani in 1797, this current is generated when tissue is injured, for example, following injection or dryneedling techniques including acupuncture. When the needle pierces muscle, it disrupts the cell membrane of individual muscle fibers, mechanically discharging a brief outburst of injury potentials referred to as "insertional activity". Injury potentials delivered on needle insertion are able to relax a shortened muscle instantly or within minutes.

Needling also induces a sympatholytic effect that spreads throughout the body segment, releasing vasoconstriction. Pain in muscles, tendons and joints caused by excessive muscle tension is eased when the shortened muscles are relaxed. Subjective improvement (which can astonishingly occur within minutes) is easily confirmed objectively. For example, a decrease in muscle tenderness is confirmed with a pressure algometer; a painful, resticted joint regains its normal range; a joint effusion disappears or a juvenile scoliosis straightens. Endogenous opiates, presently used to explain the effects of needling, cannot account for all the observed effects.

Unlike external forms of stimulation, stimulation from a needle lasts for several days until the miniature wounds heal. Needling has another unique benefit unavailable to other forms of local therapy: It delivers to the injured area the platelet-derived growth factor (PDGF) which induces deoxyribonucleic acid (DNA) synthesis and stimulates collagen formation.[135] Body cells are normally exposed to a filtrate of plasmas (interstitial fluid) and would only see the platelet factor in the presence of injury, hemorrhage and blood coagulation.

CONCLUSION

Chronic myofascial pain syndromes represent a far greater problem than is generally recognized. They generally defy proper diagnosis and treatment because they belong to a category of chronic pain that is poorly understood. When chronic pain persists in the absence of detectable injury or inflammation, radiculopathy must be suspected. Many clinicians rely on laboratory tests and imaging procedures for diagnosis, but myofascial pain is diagnosed primarily by clinical examination that searches for specific neuropathic signs. Our radiculo-pathy model explains these syndromes, not as signals of injury, but as epiphenomena of radiculopathy. Treatment must be directed, not only to the pain, but to the cause of the neuropathy. The model is important because it allows many apparently dissimilar syndromes to be grouped under one etiologic classification (radiculopathy).

Intramuscular Stimulation is an alternative system of diagnosis and dryneedling directed at general practitioners, orthopedic and sports medicine physicians and others who seek an effective therapy for chronic myofascial pain. IMS is based on neuroanatomy, but its dryneedling technique is enhanced from traditional acupuncture. The efficacy of IMS therapy for chronic low back pain has been demonstrated by a randomized clinical trial involving a large group of patients in the British Columbia Workers' Compensation Board. At their seven-month follow-up, the treated group was clearly and significantly better than the control group.[136]

11

ACUPUNCTURE PHYSICAL MEDICINE

By Mark D. Seem, Ph.D., L.Ac.

AN ACUPUNCTURE POINT OF VIEW

Acupuncture pain management should be a major part of any acupuncture student's training. In classical acupuncture textbooks up through the sixteenth century, it was taught that energy (qi) and blood congestion caused by trauma, repetitive strain, climactic influences or emotional turmoil causes pain and dysfunction that can best be adjusted by inactivation of reactive tender points known as "a shi" points. In fact, these reactive points, similar in most respects to Travell and Simons' "subcutaneous and myofascial trigger points"[138] are, as Japanese acupuncturists today repeatedly stress, the site of the patient's complaint and in fact often identical to the complaint itself: the tight tender points, which I shall henceforth refer to as TTPs, are the problem. In acupuncture, as it was taught in the People's Republic of China until recently, very little importance is given to TTPs in diagnosis or treatment. This is because the traditional Chinese Medicine curriculum, known as TCM, developed during the communist regime reframed acupuncture, previously taught as an "exterior," physical medicine, as internal medicine. This stemmed from the dominant tradition of Chinese herbal training developed from the seventeenth century on, where focus was placed on the internal visceral functions and their regulation. Such a focus aims at a "root" treatment of visceral dysfunction in chronic complaints, such that local, tender "a shi" points only have a major role to play in acute pain, where every style of acupuncturist will insert a needle into the local painful area. In chronic pain and dysfunction, however, from a TCM point of view, the main focus will be on internal regulation, say, of constrained Liver energy or deficient Spleen energy.

This is altogether different from the classical acupuncture point of view, still taught in several European styles of acupuncture and in Japan, often known as meridian acupuncture. Here the focus is on evaluation and treatment of the meridian system itself, diagnosed by palpation of the musculature of the abdomen and ventral aspect of the torso (looking for TTPs collectively known as "Mu" points), palpation of the dorsal paraspinal musculature (looking for TTPs collectively known as "Shu" points) and palpation of three different locations on the radial artery as well as palpation for TTPs along the meridian pathways that comprise the dorsal, lateral and ventral myofascial and musculo-skeletal regions of the body. In the Japanese acupuncture point of view, as in classical acupuncture, points palpated as tight, tender or otherwise reactive (hotter, colder, discolored, lacking elasticity, congested or stuck such as scar tissue or fibrositic nodules or subcutaneous fatty thickening or constriction) signify local constriction and often correspond with the patient's presenting complaint, especially in chronic conditions where the nature of the constriction has become solidified. I refer to these chronic patterns of constriction as **holding patterns**, which is why I coined the term "acupuncture osteopathy" to stress the similarity between this view of acupuncture and classical osteopathy. I believe that what acupuncture has to offer to modern orthopedics and physical medicine and rehabilitation is an understanding of these holding patterns even more comprehensive, but utterly consistent with Travell and Simons descriptions of myofascial pain and dysfunction patterns. In fact, as I argued elsewhere (ibid), Travell's discoveries of trigger point referred pain pathways are consistent with the acupuncture meridian pathways, and ischemic compression and dry-needling techniques discussed by Travell and Simons are similar to the acupuncture and acupressure techniques already practiced for many centuries in China and Japan and the rest of the far East and for the last century in Europe.

The problem with Travell and Simon's approach is that it focuses on acute pain and single muscle problems (and their corresponding myototic unit) but it neglects the complexities of chronic pain and dysfunction where there is often compensation causing a multiplicity of myofascial TTPs—a veritable myofascial conspiracy wrought by past injuries and insults to the body overlain with repetitive strains and stresses; constrictions brought on by emotional tension with tightness always being held in a certain group of muscles and the effects of ageing causing more and more compression on the musculature and discs of the spine. The other problem with their approach is the focus on injections with hypodermic needles. These needles are not suited well for the fanning needling technique discussed by Travell and Simons, whereas fine filiform solid needles, as used in acupuncture, are perfectly suited (as are EMG needles). This is why Chan Gunn, a physician specializing in dry-needle treatment with acupuncture needles, which he terms "intramuscular stimulation"[139] only uses acupuncture needles. The benefit of acupuncture needles is that they are solid and cause far less trauma to the subcutaneous and myofascial tissues contacted, and many sites can be needled easily at the same time with far less distress for the patient. Also, as I will discuss later, dry-needling with acupuncture needles often leads to myofascial release while just stimulating the superficial fascia over, but superficial to Travell and Simons' trigger points. In my own technique, I often needle superficially all along the area of referred pain that Travell sprays in her spray-and-stretch or ice-and-stretch technique, with muscular fasciculations and myofascial release the length of the area treated.

In brief, then, acupuncture practiced from a meridian as opposed to an internal medicine, visceral point of view, is physical medicine. I concur with Dr. Gunn when he states that "dry-needling is the most effective form of physical therapy for recurrent and chronic pain and dysfunction. Dry-needling stimulation "lasts longer than other forms of physical therapies, probably through the generation of a current-of-injury which can continue for days and may also provide a unique therapeutic benefit: it can promote healing by releasing a growth factor" (Ibid, p. 112).

ACUPUNCTURE HOLDING PATTERNS AND MYOFASCIAL CHAINS

In the theory of acupuncture there are twelve main pathways or "meridians" and over fifty secondary ones with acupuncture points the length of each pathway. These acupuncture points are often chosen, in the classical Chinese or Modern Japanese acupuncture approaches, based on reactivity. This is also how points are usually selected for stimulation in Oriental bodywork therapies like shiatsu, amma and tuina. Such reactivity might include tightness on palpation, such as a taught band in or overlying muscles, tenderness to palpation ("pressure points) or the fact that other tight or sensitive points might be inactivated once the spot in question is appropriately stimulated and inactivated itself. This conceptualization is strikingly similar to the description of "trigger point regions" by Dr. Chang-Zern Hong, a physiatrist from the University of California-Irvine.[140] Dr Hong cites his own and his colleagues' research with EMG testing of twitch responses elicited in trigger points demonstrating that within one trigger point, there may be "multiple sensitive loci" and that needle stimulation of each locus elicits a "local twitch response". As Travell and Simmons showed in their epic two volume **Myofascial Pain and Dysfunction: The Trigger Point Manual,**[138] elicitation of the local twitch response, mediated through local mechanical reactions and Central Nervous System reflexes most likely, lengthens taut muscle fibers and releases the myofascial constrictions due to trigger points in a muscle or myototic unit of interacting muscles.

While Travell and Simons argue for locating the active trigger point or points and needling only these, Hong argues, especially in the case of recalcitrant chronic pain and dysfunction, that rapid stimulation of every sensitive locus within what he prefers to term a "trigger point region" elicits far more local twitch responses and greater subsequent myofascial release.

In Japanese acupuncture one of the main goals of treatment is the elimination of tight or tender points, defined as palpable taut bands or nodules or indurations in subcutaneous tissue and muscles. Their descriptions of these reactive points are essentially identical to that of "trigger points" as expanded upon by Hong, (differentiating in great detail among subcutaneous trigger points and muscular ones). The difference between the trigger point conceptualization and that of acupuncture is that, in acupuncture, these points are thought to occur in a series or chain, each point on the chain being somehow connected to all the others. While ancient Chinese philosophical concepts such as yin and yang and the flow of Qi (energy) are used to describe these chains, it might be that they can be just as effectively described from a myofascial perspective, as "reactive point series" or "constellations of trigger points" or, as Headley (in EMG and Myofascial Pain) suggests, "myofascial chains".[141]

In her research on nineteen back patients, Headley identified a myofascial chain extending from the piriformis and anterior pectineus, through the tensor fascia lata and biceps femoris and down through the gastrocnemius and soleus muscles. Myofascial release of the local area of back pain proved helpful, as did stimulation of just the distal reactive areas on the thigh and calves, but the most significant relief from back pain came from stimulating the entire chain of muscles involved.

And this is what acupuncture has to offer to physical medicine's treatment of acute and chronic pain: not only local myofascial release, but release of the entire myofascial chain involved. After eighteen years of practicing and almost as many years of teaching acupuncture in my own practice in New York City and at the Tri-State Institute of Traditional Chinese Acupuncture there, I have come to the conclusion that the meridian system is just such a theory, or map of those myofascial chains most predisposed to dysfunction which I refer to as holding patterns.

At a seminar she gave at the Tri-State Institute which I founded and direct, Dr. Janet Travell was asked by someone in the audience if she was familiar with the relatively "new" disorder called "repetitive strain injury." With a twinkle in her eye she replied that, for someone of her advanced years who has been treating pain sufferers for half a century, it was clear that "life is a repetitive strain injury!" What Travell meant by this is that chronic pain develops as a result of a repetitive series of insults to the body, both from injuries sustained and reactions to internal turmoil and external factors (including poor posture, structural imbalances, repetitive strain at work or playing an instrument or in sports, metabolic imbalances and nutritional deficiencies). While all of these precipitating factors must also be addressed, great relief from pain and its associated dysfunctions can occur by releasing the myofascial chains that make up the patient's particular holding pattern.

Looking at acupuncture from this myofascial perspective, and reformulating acupuncture theory accordingly, I have come to view acupuncture as a system for identifying and releasing these holding patterns or myofascial chains based on a few simple principles.

Firstly, while acupuncture textbooks show exact locations for each acupuncture point, many classical and modern practitioners of acupuncture believe that points should only be needled if reactive (tight or sensitive to pressure) and that these reactive loci, like Hong's "multiple sensitive loci" above, are different in each person. In other words, just as with Travell and Simon's description of trigger points, the depicted locations in the texts are just approximations of the most common sites for trigger points in a given muscle or acupuncture points in a given region: the place where palpation for the actual reactive points is to be initiated.

One of the main goals of acupuncture therapy in Japan is the elimination of these tight or tender points. In acupuncture there is a principle for releasing these points known as the eight conditions: inside/outside; upper/lower; right/left; front/back.

"Inside/outside" refers to the fact that visceral disorders can manifest on the body surface as myofascial constrictions, usually in the musculature of the ventral and dorsal aspects of the body directly over the viscera in question (known as Mu and Shu points in acupuncture) just as myofascial constrictions on the surface, such as tightness in the rectus abduminus muscle, can lead not only to local discomfort but also to visceral symptoms—in this case, flatulence, bloating, disrupted stools, etcetera. Travell and Simons discuss the exact same concept in the last chapter of volume one of their work, when they describe "somato-visceral" disorders starting in the musculature. They state that in disorders starting on the surface, such as the rectus abdominis trigger points mentioned above, inactivation of these trigger points eliminates the visceral symptoms as well. Likewise, in viscero-somatic disorders, inactivation of the trigger points on the surface often leads to significant relief of symptoms, but not, of course, cure of the underlying disease or lesion. For example, elimination of trigger points in the pectoralis muscle in a patient with asthma might well lead to a lessening of chest constriction, dyspnea and freer breathing, but the asthma remains. Thus, a major principle of Japanese acupuncture is the regulation of the ventral and dorsal aspects of the body through elimination of the reactive points there, in order to bring about viscero-somatic/somato-visceral regulation.

"Upper/lower" refers to the fact that there are reactive points in distal aspects of the meridian (read: myofascial chain), say on the gastrocnemius, plantaris and hamstring muscles, that when inactivated help to also inactivate local areas of the chain where the pain or dysfunction originates, say in the piriformis and gluteal muscles. As in Headley's findings, acupuncturists who work this way believe distal as well as local points, when inactivated, provide greater relief than with only local or only distal points.

"Right/left" refers to reactive points on one side of the body being inactivated to treat pain or dysfunction on the opposite side. The most notable example is using points on the sound side that match the exact site: treating the tibialis anterior where tender and reactive to pressure on the right to relieve phantom limb pain in that location on the amputated side.

"Front/back" refers to treating points directly in front or in back of the symptomatic area: for example, inactivating trigger points in the right infraspinatus muscle for pain in the right subclavius and pectoralis muscles.

In the sequel to my last book **A New American Acupuncture: Acupuncture Osteopathy**, I will describe in detail the Japanese and classical acupuncture concepts of Tight/Tender Points and the principles for their release not only for acupuncturists unfamiliar with these myofascial concepts and techniques, but also for physicians, osteopaths, Asian body workers and physical therapists interested in the myofascial release of holding patterns based on these concepts. In this way I hope to "acupuncturize" orthodox physical medicine and rehabilitation, infusing it with acupuncture approaches that will render myofascial release far more effective and also lead to viscero-somatic/somato-visceral regulation. It is my hope that this approach will lead to collaboration among Asian medical and physical medical practitioners for the improved qualify of life and relief from suffering for our patients. For it is my belief that the inclusion of acupuncture, practiced from this myofascial perspective, in physical therapy and rehabilitation regimens for chronic and recalcitrant conditions will greatly improve health care for these difficult patients.

This may be done by mainstreaming the concepts of acupuncture into physical medicine and rehabilitation as well as by referral networks from practitioners in physical medicine and rehabilitation to acupuncturists and oriental medical body workers. This may also be accomplished by training orthopaedists and rehabilitation specialists in aspects of acupuncture and dry needling where appropriate.

HISTORICAL PERSPECTIVE ON ACUPUNCTURE IN AMERICA

The main style of acupuncture in the United States and in the west as a whole is acupuncture practiced according to the principles of traditional Chinese medicine (abbreviated as TCM in most textbooks). It must be understood that this style of acupuncture is developed based on internal, herbal, medical perspectives. There is a long tradition in the People's Republic of China that stems from the seventeenth century at least, whereby acupuncture is understood more and more in terms of herbal medical principles. This has led to the development, in the People's Republic of China, of indications given for every acupuncture point, so that description of a point might indicate its use for headaches, pain in the frontal aspects of the head and neck, or sinus congestion, for example. These types of indications for points are based on the way in which herbal and pharmacological materia medica are organized with indications for each herb within a formula. Most acupuncturists, trained in the TCM style of acupuncture, therefore develop a formula of points just as they would develop a formula of herbs or pharmacological substances to treat a specific condition or complaint. These conditions or complaints are usually framed in terms of the organs and bowels of traditional Chinese medicine, known collectively as the ZangFu. While the ZangFu are not identical to western organs and bowels, they do include the functions of the organs and bowels as well as functions specific to oriental medical understandings of the body. In TCM textbooks, disorders of the ZangFu, or functional disorders, are described in terms of patterns of disharmony or syndromes for each of the ZangFu. There are, for example, disorders such as constrained Liver Qi, deficient yang of the spleen or kidney, deficient liver blood, or dampness distressing the spleen. It is these patterns of disharmony that are treated by an herbalist after the herbalist carefully palpates the radial artery taking the Chinese pulses into account, looks at the coating and body and shape of the tongue to gather information there, and does what is known as the four examinations which include a history, palpation of the pulse, palpation of sensitive points on the front of the body known as Mu points, and sensitive points on the back of the body known as Shu points as well as information pertaining to odors and sounds, such as odors of stools and urine and the breath, and sounds of an asthmatic patient, etc. The results of the four examinations including pulse and tongue evaluation, are analyzed in terms of what are known as the eight principles, an analytical system for differentiating signs and symptoms as to their nature, hot or cold, as to whether they are more internal and chronic or external and acute, as to whether they are more deficient and in need of tonification and support, or excess conditions that need to be calmed or drained.

The eight principle evaluation of information gleaned from the four examinations focuses heavily on the information on the tongue and in the pulse, as well as basic information about stools, urine and a few other characteristic signs and symptoms for every specific condition. Herbal formula are developed based on these evaluations and have been utilized for thousands of years in China. Acupuncture, classically, was not practiced based on the same principles but rather based on an evaluation of the meridian system itself, which relies heavily on different styles of pulse evaluation, palpation of reactive and sensitive points on the front and back of the body as above, but also palpations of the meridians themselves, which is to say of the musculature of the extremities, the torso, the back of the body, the head, and the face and neck. This palpation of the body as a whole, is what characterizes what is now known as meridian acupuncture in Japan, the main form of acupuncture practiced there, as well acupuncture in many places in Europe, and especially in France. In the UCLA program for training physicians in acupuncture, Dr. Joseph Helms has been teaching the French meridian perspective to acupuncture to physicians for the past twenty years, consistent with what we are discussing here. The acupuncture perspective espoused in traditional Chinese medicine has been very useful for students who want to learn herbal medicine.

Dr. Yitian Ni, O.M.D., in her new text **Navigating the Channels of Traditional Chinese Medicine**,[142] clarifies this perspective when she states "While teaching in American schools of oriental medicine I observed that, in an effort to provide students with sound diagnostic and treatment principles, there is a tendency to emphasize ZangFu. This satisfactorily addresses the needs of the herbalists, but it subordinates those of the acupuncturists." Throughout her text Dr. Ni articulates the theories of the channels and collaterals of classical and modern acupuncture and shows how a meridian acupuncture approach is also part of traditional Chinese medicine understood in a larger sense not only as the approach to acupuncture practiced in the People's Republic of China but more importantly, as an approach to acupuncture from the beginning on. In fact, acupuncture is always a meridian perspective, that is to say, a myofascial or physical medicine perspective since acupuncture is a medicine that has to do with treating from the outside in, from the exterior to the interior and from the surface to the internal organ function. And as an external, outside, surface medicine acupuncture is a physical medicine.

DRY NEEDLING AND MYOFASCIAL RELEASE

Acupuncture understood as dry needling consists of the insertion of thin filiform needles usually from 32 to 40 gauge and from 1 to 3 inches in length into the subcutaneous tissue or into the muscle. Classically, disorders were differentiated as to disorders of the surface where there is pain and discomfort resulting in tight tender points or TTPs that can be needled subcutaneously much like in Dr. Huang's understanding of multiple tender loci and these superficial insertions often create major reactions in the musculature with fasciculations and myofascial release almost instantaneously. There are also disorders of what is known as the nourishing energy level or the level of the principal meridian that pertain to the organ and bowel functions or ZangZu, and needling here was done into the muscles themselves as the regular meridians pertaining to the organs and bowels of oriental medicine are thought to flow within the muscles. This is the form of needling most prominent in the People's Republic of China where points are needled deeply in the musculature until a dull aching sensation is created by lifting and thrusting and twirling the needle is known as "De Qi" which means the arrival of Energy. Finally, in disorders that are thought to be genetic or acquired early in life, needling is done as deep as the bone, which is understood either as periosteal acupuncture by some practitioners, or as the needling of points for meridians known as the extraordinary vessels, which open the territory governed by these vessels, and these opening points are always located directly over bones in areas where there is very little musculature.

Therefore, classically, needling was differentiated based on the depth of a disorder with acute and myofascial conditions being treated superficially with surface subcutaneous needling; organ and bowel disorders and internal disharmonies treated in the musculature; and genetic or early acquired disorders treated at the depth of the bones or by special points right over boney areas to treat the extraordinary vessels. In TCM acupuncture, needling is always done at the depth of the musculature because TCM is an internal medical perspective and therefore disorders are always framed as internal disorders of the ZangFu. Since needling of the meridians associated with the ZangFu is directed at the muscles, TCM acupuncture needling technique is musculature needling in many ways very similar to trigger point injections. In meridian acupuncture, on the other hand, in disorders not only having to do with pain, but also in disorders of the viscera themselves, a main focus of treatment is directed toward symptomatic relief and therefore directed toward the surface where these symptoms manifest. In chronic pain, this is easily understood, when one needles local points in the area of pain and its referred pathways, with shallow needling techniques consistent with Japanese and classical acupuncture practices in China and also consistent with Dr. Huang's trigger point needling to release the multiple tender loci according to his understanding of manifestations on the surface. When treating symptomatic areas in a visceral problem, the case is somewhat more complex. In the case of dysmenorrhea, for example, while distal points may be selected according to acupuncture principles of imbalances of the organs and bowels (these points being situated either in the extremities or points on the front known as Mu points or in the back known as Shu points directly over the organs or bowels indicated), in addressing the symptomatic aspects of such a disorder, meridian acupuncturists will palpate the area of discomfort, in the case of dysmenorrhea, in the pelvic region of the front, and the gluteal region of the back over the sacral foramen, for tight tender points throughout these regions. This will yield many tight tender points never found by practitioners of traditional Chinese medicine because these points are not necessarily the front Mu or back Shu points in TCM textbooks. The meridian perspective on needling, therefore, has to do essentially with looking for reactive points in extremities as well as in local areas of discomfort or dysfunction, treating local and distal points on this chain in order to relieve not only the symptoms in a particular condition or complaint but also to free up the chain itself: myofascial release.

In my own dry needling techniques, developed based on Travell and Simon's trigger point concepts as well as on concepts derived from Chan Gunn and Dr. Huang, I needle shallowly, usually subcutaneously, into the area of tight tender points compressing the tissue with my left index and middle finger which straddle the needle. By compressing the tissue in this fashion, I believe that this compression with the left hand causes a strain in the superficial fascia directly over the tight tender points which are usually located in the musculature akin to Travell's trigger points. This strain makes the tissue even more reactive to the needle sensation and in fact in Japanese acupuncture the deepest tissue in the adipose tissue itself, that is to say the superficial fascia directly over the musculature, is known as "Yang reactive tissue." This can be seen in EMG needling where needling of this superficial fascia before penetrating the muscle creates strong reactions on the monitoring devices. This reactivity means, according to Japanese acupuncture, that one can make major myofascial changes with minor needle techniques. I have found, for example, that needling over the piriformis muscle, after locating trigger points within the muscle, while compressing the tissue with the left hand, can be done to depths of only one-half to one inch, causing major fasciculation and release of the piriformis that is obvious to the patient and practitioner alike. This type of shallow needling must always be accomplished with an uneven pecking motion, and the pecking must be directed in the direction of the trigger point uncovered during palpation. This technique is much safer for many difficult muscular areas, such as the sternocleidomastoid, scalenes, subclavius, and deep cervical muscles. One can also needle all tight and tender points involved in a particular patient, in the same sitting, which could never be accomplished with trigger point injections with

Lidocaine or other substances. For example, in a patient with a thoracic outlet like syndrome and repetitive strain leading to neuropathy down the dorsal aspect of the upper arm and forearm to the thumb and index finger, in this acupuncture dry needling technique, one would needle reactive points over the first dorsal interosseous muscle, the flexor hallucis longus, the brachioradialis, the brachialis, the anterior deltoid, the coracobrachialis, the subclavius, the sternocleidomastoid, the masseter and platysma, the scalenes, the supraspinatus, and the upper trapezius muscles. Often in such conditions, one would also needle the upper aspect of the pectoralis major muscle, and the pectoralis minor, and may also needle the subscapularis muscle, the serratus anterior muscle, and even the upper latissimus dorsi muscle. Needled together these points represent the lung and large intestine pathways of acupuncture known as Hand Tai-yin and Yang-ming.

If one takes this acupuncture perspective, and applies it to a physical medicine perspective, one could speak of needling distal muscles or muscle groups, for problems in local areas. That is to say local and distal dry needling of points on a myofascial chain.

THE TERRITORIES OF CHRONIC PAIN AND DYSFUNCTION

If we take the meridian system of acupuncture in the broader sense, as I explained in part II of **A New American Acupuncture** (footnote ibid), and if one includes the muscles in the portrayal of the meridian systems of acupuncture, then one could speak of the musculature of the ventral aspect of the body which is know as the Yangming zone, the lateral aspect of the body or zone known as the Shaoyang zone, or the dorsal aspect of the body, the Taiyang zone.

Below are images of the meridian system in this broader, myofascial sense, as well as trigger points laid onto each of the three zones. I have included a list of the most important muscles in each zone (Fig. 11.1).

Note that these images and lists are derived from part II of **A New American Acupuncture**.

MAIN POINTS OF THE DORSAL ZONE

The main distal acupuncture points of the dorsal zone are Bl. 67, 64, 62, 60, 59, 58, 57, and 40. S.I. 3, 4, 6, 7, and 8.
The main local points are
    Bl. 53–54 and Bl. 31–34 for the buttocks
    Bl. 11–25 and Bl. 41–54 for the paraspinal muscles and local TTP points for the multifidi and also for the rotatores muscles
    Bl. 10 for the occipital region
    Bl. 9 through Bl. 3 for the occipitofrontalis muscle
    Bl. 1–2 for the orbicularis oculi muscle
    S.I. 9–14 for the infraspinatus muscle
    S.I. 16 for the scalenus muscles
    S.I. 17 for the posterior digastric muscle
    S.I. 18 for the zygomaticus major muscle
It should be noted that distal acupuncture points from elbows and knees down, are also local points for problems of the extremities.

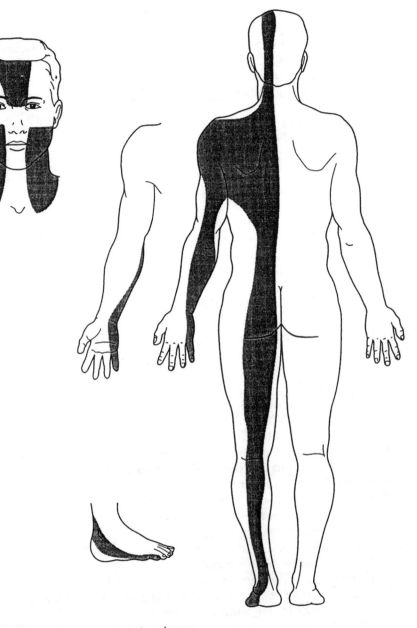

Figure 11.1 Dorsal zone acupuncture image

MAIN MUSCLES OF THE DORSAL ZONE

Head & Neck: Middle and lower trapezius, posterior digastric, orbicularis oculi, occipitofrontalis, splenius capitis, splenius cervicus, multifidi of the neck, semispinalis cervicis, semispinalis capitis, and suboccipital muscles

Upper Back, Shoulder, & Upper arm: Levator scapulae, supraspinatus, infraspinatus, teres minor, teres major, subscapularis, and rhomboideus muscles

Torso: Serratus posterior superior, serratus posterior inferior, superficial paraspinal muscles (erector spinae muscles, namely iliocostalis thoracis and lumborum and longissimus thoracis), and deep paraspinal muscles, namely multifidi and rotatores

Lower Arm & Hand: Extensor carpi ulnaris, abductor digiti minimi, and flexor carpi ulnaris muscles

Lower Torso: Latissimus dorsi, quadratus lumborum, pelvic floor muscles, gluteus maximus and medius, gluteus minimus, piriformis, and obturator externus muscles

Hip, Thigh, & Knee: Hamstring muscles (biceps femoris, semi-tendinosus, semi-membranosus) and popliteus muscles

Leg, Ankle, & Foot: Plantaris, soleus, gastrocnemius, tibialis posterior, flexor digitorum longus, flexor hallucis longus, adductor digiti minimi, and quadratus plantae

The interested reader should consult Travell & Simons for details of the most common locations of the main trigger points in these muscles of the *tai yang* dorsal zone (Figs. 11–2, 11–3, 11–4).

MAIN POINTS OF THE LATERAL ZONE

The main distal points of the lateral zone are
G.B. 44, 41, 40, 39, 38, and 34.
T.H. 3, 4, 5, 8, and 10

The main local points are
G.B. 31 for the iliotibial tract
G.B. 29 for the tensor fasciae latae
G.B. 24, 27, and 28 for the external oblique
G.B. 26 for the internal and external obliques
G.B. 22 for the serratus anterior and latissimus dorsi
G.B. 21 and 20 for the upper trapezius
G.B. 19 and 14 for the occipitofrontalis muscle
G.B. 8, 6, 5, 4, and 3 for the temporalis muscle
G.B. 1 for the orbicularis oculi muscle
T.H. 9 for the finger extensor muscles
T.H. 14 for the supraspinatus tendon
T.H. 15 for the supraspinatus muscle
G.B. 16 for the upper sternocleidomastoid and scalenus medius muscles
T.H. 20, 21, and 22 for the temporalis muscle
T.H. 23 for the orbicularis oculi muscle

MUSCLES OF THE LATERAL ZONE

Head and Neck: Upper trapezius, temporalis, suboccipital, occipitofrontalis, orbicularis oculi, sternocleidomastoid, and scalenus medius muscles

Upper Back, Shoulder, & Upper Arm: Supraspinatus, latissimus dorsi, posterior deltoid, and triceps brachii muscles

Torso: Serratus anterior, external oblique, internal oblique, and latissimus dorsi muscles

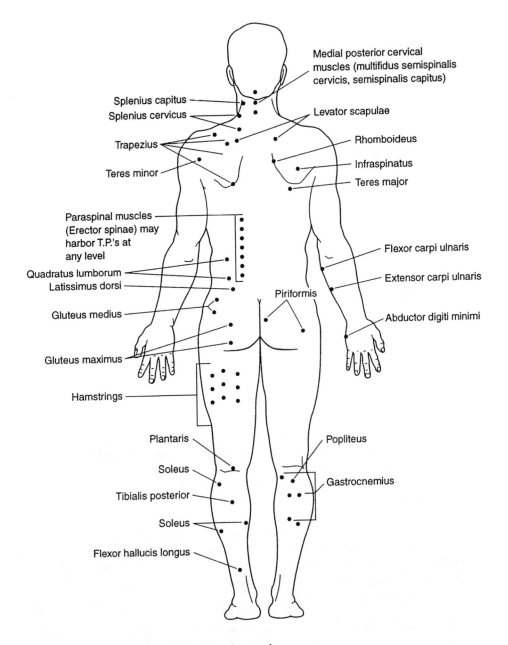

Figure 11.2 Trigger points of the dorsal zone A

Lower Arm, & Hand: Extensor digitorum, extensor indicis, middle and ring finger extensors muscles, and the fourth dorsal interosseus muscles

Lower Torso: Gluteus medius and gluteus minimus muscles

Hip, Thigh, & Knee: Tensor fascia latae, vastus lateralis muscles, and the collateral ligament

Leg, Ankle, & Foot: Peroneus longus, peroneus brevis, peroneus tertius, extensor digitorum longus, extensor digitorum brevis, and the 4th dorsal and plantar interosseus muscles (Figs. 11–5, 11–6, 11–7)

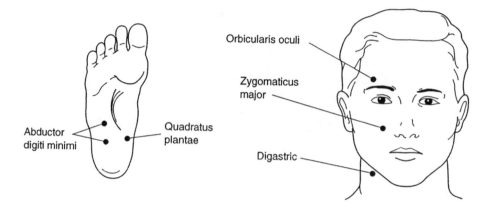

Figure 11.3 Trigger points of the dorsal zone B

MAIN POINTS OF THE VENTRAL ZONE

The main distal acupuncture points of the ventral zone are
St. 43, 40, 39, 38, 37, and 36
L.I. 4, 6, 10, and 11
The main local points are
St. 36–39 for the tibialis anterior muscle
St. 31 and 32 for the rectus femoris and underlying vastus medialis muscle
St. 19–30 for the rectus abdominis muscle
St. 18 and 16–14 for the pectoralis minor and major muscles
St. 13 for the subclavius muscle (between Kid. 27 to St. 13, where most knotted)
St. 12 for the platysma (combined with St. 5 and 6)
St. 9 and 10 for the sternal division of the sternocleidomastoid
St. 5–7 for the masseter and medial and lateral pterygoid muscles
St. 8 for the frontalis muscle
St. 3–4 for the zygomaticus major muscle
St. 1–2 for the orbicularis oculi
L.I. 4 for the 1st dorsal interosseus muscle
L.I. 10 area for the brachioradialis and the extensor carpi radialis longus and brevis muscles
L.I. 14–15 for the deltoid and L.I. 15 anteriorly for the coracobrachialis muscles
L.I. 13 for the biceps brachii and brachialis muscles
L.I. 18 for the sternocleidomastoid
L.I. 19–20 for the orbicularis oris

MAIN MUSCLES OF THE VENTRAL ZONE

Head & Neck: Sternocleidomastoid, masseter, medial and lateral pterygoid, orbicularis oris and oculi, frontalis, and platysma, and scalene muscles

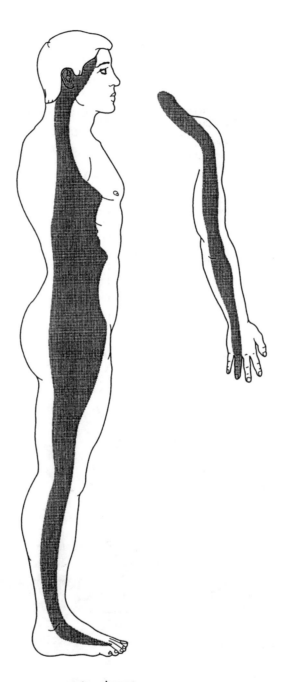

Figure 11.4 Lateral zone acupuncture image

Upper Back, Shoulder, & Upper Arm: Supraspinatus, deltoid, coracobrachialis, biceps brachii, and brachialis muscles

Torso: Pectoralis minor and major, subclavius, sternalis, rectus abdominis, upper external oblique, and pyramidalis muscles

Lower Arm & Hand: Brachioradialis, extensor carpi radialis longus and brevis, supinator (yin associated Lu. 5 area), palmaris longus (yin associated Per. 5

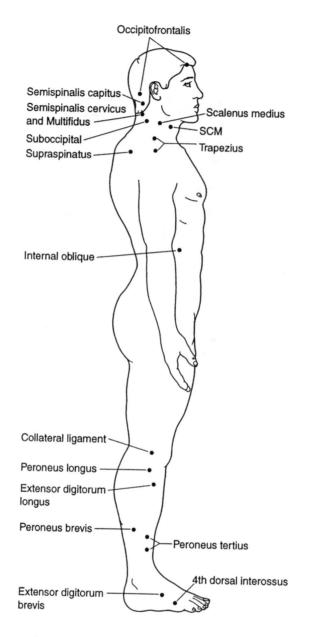

Occipitofrontalis

Semispinalis capitus

Semispinalis cervicus
and Multifidus

Suboccipital

Supraspinatus

Scalenus medius

SCM

Trapezius

Internal oblique

Collateral ligament

Peroneus longus

Extensor digitorum
longus

Peroneus brevis

Peroneus tertius

Extensor digitorum
brevis

4th dorsal interossus

Figure 11.5 Trigger points of the lateral zone A

area), hand and finger flexors (3 arm yin meridians, especially Per. 6, 5, and 4 area), adductor pollicis and opponens pollicis (yin associated Lu. 10 area) and the 1st dorsal interosseus muscles

Lower Torso: Iliopsoas muscle

Hip, Thigh, & Knee: Rectus femoris and vastus intermedius, and three leg yin tendinomuscular and regular meridian associated muscles—sartorius (Sp. 10-Liv. 9), pectineus (Sp. 12-Liv. 12 area), vastus medialis (Sp. 10-Liv. 9 area)—and the adductor longus and brevis (Liv. 10-Sp. 11) muscles

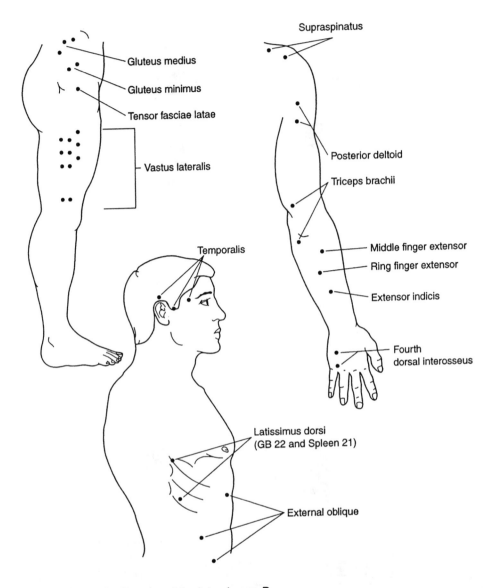

Figure 11.6 Trigger points of the lateral zone B

Leg, Ankle, & Foot: Tibialis anterior, extensor hallucis longus and brevis, 3rd and 2nd dorsal interossei, and three leg yin tendinomuscular and regular meridian associated muscles; adductor hallucis (Kid. 2–4 area); flexor digitorum brevis (inferior to Kid. 2), flexor hallucis brevis (Sp. 3 area), adductor hallucis (Kid. 1-Sp. 3 area), and the 1st dorsal interosseus (Liv.3) muscles (Fig. 11.8)

CONCLUSION

In viewing acupuncture as physical medicine focused on treatment of local and distal reactive points along a myofascial chain or series (meridian), one can

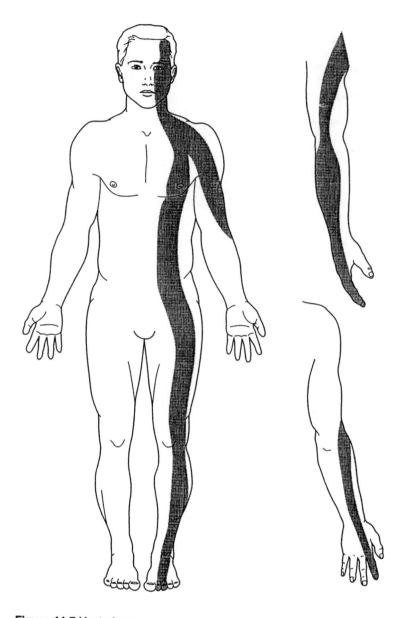

Figure 11.7 Ventral zone acupuncture image

establish a simple protocol for treating the three zones just reviewed, based on the principles of upper/lower, right/left and front/back.

In treating the ventral zone for chronic pain and dysfunction, one would check distal points on the same side of the disorder as well as on the opposite side (right/left), looking for tight tender points in the tibialis anterior of the leg and the brachioradialis of the forearm, for example, for problems of constriction and myofascial pain in the pectoral, rectus abdominus or sternocleidomastoid muscles, as an example. These distal points might well fasciculate just like trigger points do, and their release will already help the local myofascial complaint, but treatment

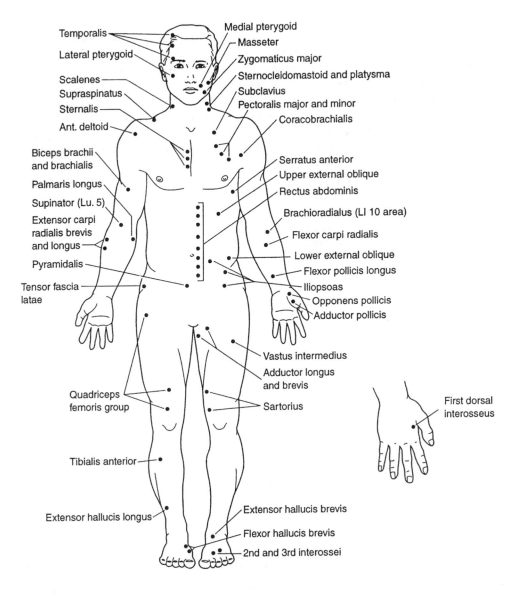

Figure 11.8 Trigger points of the ventral zone

will be rendered far more effective if the local TTPs and trigger points are inactivated as well.

Likewise, for the dorsal zone, distal reactive TTPs could be located and inactivated in the gastrocnemius, plantaris, popliteus and soleus for myofascial complaints affecting the gluteal, piriformis and quadratus lumborum muscles, as well as for problems of the paraspinal muscles, and distal TTPs in the long head of the triceps might be located and inactivated to release myofascial constriction in the infraspinatus and supraspinatus muscles as well as the levator scapulae. This treatment again will be more effective if the local TTPs are also inactivated.

Finally, for the lateral zone, distal points in the peroneal muscles, for example, could be inactivated to release constriction in the tensor fascia lata and lateral obliques, and points in the ring finger extensor might be chosen to release the scalenes and medial deltoid, or even for the temporalis muscle. Distal points should always be checked and treated on both sides wherever reactive (right/left). This treatment of distal points for local problems is again based on the principle of upper/lower. When these two strategies are insufficient, use the principle of front/back, locating and treating reactive pectoralis TTPs directly in front of a stubborn myofascial constriction in the infraspinatus, for example. When shifting from back to front (or even side), use distal reactive TTPs for the new zone being treated. In this way, one is often discovering and releasing an entire complex holding pattern including areas of compensation.

Finally, which is beyond the scope of this chapter, know that the principle of inside/outside (yin/yang) refers to somato-visceral and viscero-somatic interactions whose treatment could be termed, as Japanese acupuncture often does, autonomic nervous system regulation. This is the arena for meridian acupuncture treatment of visceral complaints, fatigue and immune dysfunction.

12

CRAIG–PENS: BASIC THEORY AND CLINICAL APPLICATION

Stephen M. Taylor D.O.

PHILOSOPHY

Craig–PENS is a systematized pain treatment technique involving the stimulation of peripheral nerves, nerve roots, and the autonomic nervous system to dramatically attenuate the transmission, processing and perception of pain by the nervous system. Western researchers have described Acupuncture Analgesia as stress induced analgesia for some time now. This description of AA acknowledges the intimate relationship between the endogenous opioid system and the manipulation/stimulation (i.e., stress) of acupuncture points. However the theories of acupuncture have the underlying goal not necessarily of alleviating pain but of achieving an ideal balance and flow of yin and yang energies in the 12 meridians, and extraordinary meridians. This gap between eastern theories and western neurophysiology has limited the integration of acupuncture into western medicine in the treatment of pain. While acknowledging the contributions and value of TCM and the other acupuncture systems, Craig–PENS focuses not on the meridians but on the structure, function and functional relationships of the human nervous system.

THEORY

Unfortunately what is known about the neurophysiology of pain is still relatively generalized and contains many gaps. For instance we know that many neurotransmitters are involved in pain transmission. These include Substance P, Somatostatin, Oxytocin,[143] Calcitonin-Gene Related Peptide (CGRP), Norepinephrine, Serotonin,[144] Endorphins, Enkephalins,[145,146,147] Dynorphins,[149,150,151] CCK, and Dopamine.[152] It now appears that these neurotransmitters normally maintain a dynamic equilibrium between the transmission of pain and the suppression of pain. When this equilibrium is upset, tissue injury and the inflammatory reactions preceding tissue repair appropriately transmit pain transmitted and the balance shifts towards a predominance of the neurotransmitters involved in the perception of pain. This rise in the pain transmitting neurotransmitters (Substance P, CGRP, etc.) invokes the secretion of pain suppressing neurotransmitters (the endogenous opioid system) which rise in concentration until they suppress the transmission of pain. Chronic pain represents a failure of this system to self-regulate. The precise details and depth of this neurochemical homeostasis are presently unknown. However, we theorize that Craig–PENS involves much more than the simple stimulation of the endogenous opioids and results more importantly in the return of homeostasis in this system. If the neurophysiologic consequences of Craig–PENS or acupuncture ended with the endogenous opioid system there would be no lasting clinical result as opioids have relatively short half lives. Some other system wide effect appears to occur in our clinical outcomes. In practice this is evident by the fact that Craig–Pens frequently induces a dramatic shift in the patients' pain pattern. This shift usually involves variable periods of worsening pain intermixed with periods of pain relief, eventually resulting in a dramatic diminution in the patients overall pain level.

NEUROPHYSIOLOGY

This neurochemical homeostasis occurs within the pain fibers, peripheral nerves, dorsal root ganglia, dorsal horn cells[153], pain tracts, brainstem, midbrain and cortex of the CNS. These structures also have interconnections that result in a fluctuating balance between the transmission of pain and it's suppression.[154] Peripheral nerve endings (nociceptors) sense and transmit pain signals to the dorsal root ganglion. Most pain fibers are small unmyelinated C-fibers which transmit dull, aching or burning sensations of a diffuse nature with slow onset and long duration. Myelinated A-Delta fibers are thicker, and transmit well-localized sharp, stinging pain of short duration. These nerves have their cell bodies within the dorsal root ganglion and axons that terminate in the dorsal horn of the spinal cord. According to Melzack and Wall pain transmission relied upon C fiber stimulation overcoming the tonic inhibition of A fiber driven inhibitory interneurons. That theory has since been challenged and revised many times but remains important. The discovery of multiple neurotransmitters that convey pain (algesic substances) which are frequently colocalized with multiple pain relieving peptides (analgesic substances) has lead to a profusion of research but little clarification.[155,156] In addition nociceptors can become sensitized by repeated stimulation and develop lowered thresholds to further stimulation, though this effect can be inhibited by endogenous opioids.[157] Further modifications in the transmission of pain signals can occur from descending inhibitory pathways activated in the mid brain and brainstem by norepinephrine and serotonin which activate dorsal horn opioid inhibitory neurons.[158] Also important are supraspinal "diffuse noxious inhibitory controls" stimulated segmentally by nociceptors whose effects are augmented by endogenous opioids. Finally the thalamus,[161] arcuate nucleus, trigeminal nucleus, hypothalamus, amygdala, raphe magnus and periaqueductal gray matter (among others) all secrete endogenous opioids and can inhibit pain transmission.[162] Fishman and Carr have described these complicated interactions as "a diffuse interaction of many systems, with predominant mediation by endogenous opioids that modulate the relative contrast between background neuronal activity and nociceptive signals". It is the systematized stimulation of these endogenous opioids[163] through peripheral nerve stimulation[164] that is the fundamental basis of Craig–Pens.[165,166]

CLINICAL APPLICATION

In order to apply the principles of Craig–Pens in the treatment of pain it is important to remember that pain is a subjective experience. That means it is subject to the frailties of the human memory, cultural biases, expectations, secondary gain issues, habit, denial, lack of insight, and ability of the brain to habituate. Therefore it is imperative to be able to take the time to meticulously interview patients and to teach them to assess their pain more objectively.

The following chart contains the most important parameters of the pre-treatment interview. The practitioner who cannot commit to developing the skill necessary to evaluate each treatment in this fashion will falter, even with intimate knowledge of the treatment protocols. By carefully assessing the changes in the time course, location, and quality of the pain, essential information about the effect of the previous treatment is obtained which guides the selection of needle placement, choice of stimulator frequencies and electrical circuit of the current treatment.

Assessing sleep, daily activities, postural tolerances and medication use reveals changes the patient frequently doesn't consciously associate with their pain, which in actuality indicate significant alterations in pain, reflex muscle spasm, and pain behavior. Walking the patient through these questions prior to each treatment also forces the patient to become more conscious of changes and requires their active engagement in the process of each treatment. We sometimes give the patient a copy of the assessment to take home and bring on the next visit as a diary. This serves as a physical reminder for them to attend to changes in their pain, activity, sleep and daily activities.

Needle Configuration

Needles are placed according to the affected spinal nerves' dermatome, myotome, sclerotome or the distribution of the peripheral nerve involved. In a pain syndrome involving pain radiating from a central distribution the central area is usually treated first for 4–5 treatments, depending on the patients response. In some cases the patient may only describe peripheral pain initially, but when the extremity is treated they begin to complain that the pain, has "moved" either because they are now aware of a larger pain area peripherally, or they have developed central pain they were unaware of prior to treatment. In the first case, the distribution of the needles in the affected extremity is broadened to overlap the larger area of pain described by the patient. In the second we move the focus of the treatments more centrally *or* maintain the montage in the periphery and add an additional montage centrally.

Electrical Circuits

The main electrical circuit used is an Arc configuration either in the central cervical or lumbar areas. There are other circuits that may be designed, based on pain patterns. For simplicity 5 leads are used which allows the use of the G6805 as the main generator and it has 5 leads (Fig. 12.1, 12.2, 12.3).

Table 12.1. Craig-PENS pre-treatment assessment

Pain	During tx	4–6 hrs after tx	That evening & night		Next day & night	Following days	Now
Increased							
Decreased							
Same							

Location		Quality				Sleep	
Same area		Same		Sharp		Same	
Different area		Different		Stabbing		Improved	
Larger area		Aching		Cold		Worse	
Smaller area		Burning		Warm		Times awakened	
		Stinging		Cramping		by pain	
		Throbbing					
Daily Activities (housework, work, riding in car, shopping, yard work)	↑ = ↓	*Walking*	↑ = ↓	*Standing*	↑ = ↓	*Sitting*	↑ = ↓
Medications	↑ = ↓	Comments:					

Frequencies

The following algorithm [Fig. 12.4] is designed to lead the practitioner to use the most effective frequencies at each stage of treatment. It must be cautioned that failure to assess the results of each previous treatment will invariably lead to poor results and unnecessary treatments.

Frequencies used are based on the now extensive evidence indicating that low frequencies (2 and 4 hz) stimulate endorphins and enkephalins, and higher frequencies (100–200 hz) stimulate dynorphins.[4,167,168] We have also found that frequently the more long standing pain syndromes and neuropathic pain syndromes tend to respond best at higher frequencies initially. We have found that progressing from 4 hz for 1 treatment, 15/30 hz for 1–2 treatments, and then 100 hz for 1–3 treatments, followed by dropping the frequency back to 2–4 Hz for the remaining treatments is very effective.

In normal practice we find that approximately 75 to 85% of our patients obtain a sustained reduction of 50–100% their pain. This response seems to require a mean of 10–15 treatments at the rate of three treatments a week for the initial 3 weeks, then treating less frequently depending on the duration of relief or rebound pain episodes occurring in response to each treatment. Because the endogenous opioids

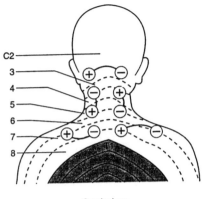

Cervical arc

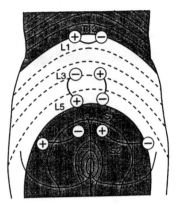

Lumbar arc

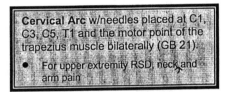

Cervical Arc w/needles placed at C1, C3, C5, T1 and the motor point of the trapezius muscle bilaterally (GB 21).

- For upper extremity RSD, neck and arm pain

Lumbar Arc w/needles placed at T12, L3, L5, S1 and at the motor point for the piriformis muscle (B54).

- For lower extremity RSD, back pain, sciatica, and leg pain

Figure 12.1 Cervical Arc; Lumbar Arc. The arc is a group of five leads run in an electrical series as shown. Whether the series begins with a positive or a negative lead is not important as long as the alternating positive-negative-positive polarity is maintained.

have a half-life of less than 5 minutes the clinical response we see can not reasonably be attributed solely to this system. We propose that some, as yet unknown, "second messenger system" such as one or more of the nerve growth factors is stimulated enough to result in a change in the plasticity of the nociceptive/analgesic system.

Rebound Pain

Pain patients are frequently attracted to Craig–PENS as a type of acupuncture and arrive with the perception that each treatment will make them better and better in a linear progression. In fact this type of response can occur, but frequently there is an initial decrease in the pain lasting from minutes to hours, which is followed by a substantial increase the pain which may last up to 3 days.

We are careful to let patients know from the beginning that we are looking for changes in the hourly to daily pattern of their pain. We feel this rebound state is a result of the effect on the balance between the nociceptive and intrinsic analgesic systems, **and is a positive response to treatment**.

This rebound pain usually has one of two consequences. In the best case scenario this induced flare-up of pain resolves with an overall diminution of pain

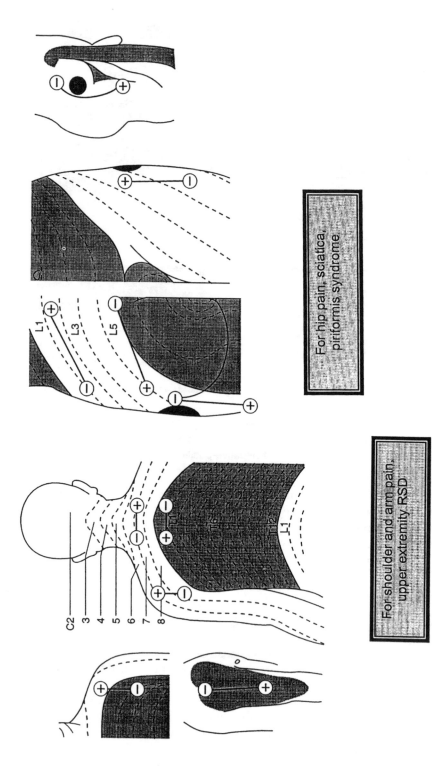

Figure 12.2 Additional treatment protocols—Shoulder and Hip. The arc montages are always used initially with low frequency stimulation (2–4 Hz). Response varies but patients usually find this treatment pleasant. There is usually a minimum of rebound pain and some patients obtain dramatic sustained relief with this montage. More commonly they report a transient sense of relief followed by a better-defined area of discomfort. This clarification of the patients' perception of the key area of pain is quite useful.

For hip pain, sciatica, piriformis syndrome

For shoulder and arm pain, upper extremity RSD

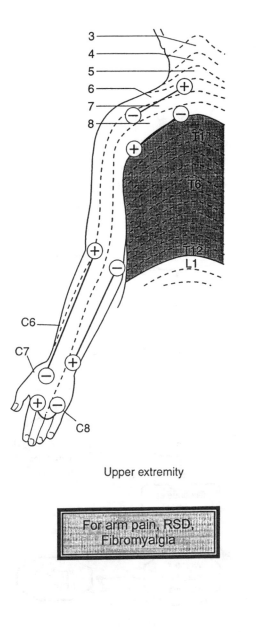

Upper extremity

For arm pain, RSD,
Fibromyalgia

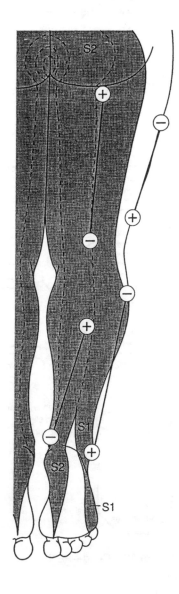

Figure 12.3 Upper Extremity; Lower Extremity

of 20–50%. For this group of patients the question becomes—to which frequency did they respond best. If they seemed to be progressing well at low frequencies, but we then used higher frequencies as part of the algorithm then we may have to adjust the frequency back down for the next treatment. If, on the other hand they have not done well with low frequencies and we are trying higher and higher frequencies to try to get some kind of response, then we stay with the higher

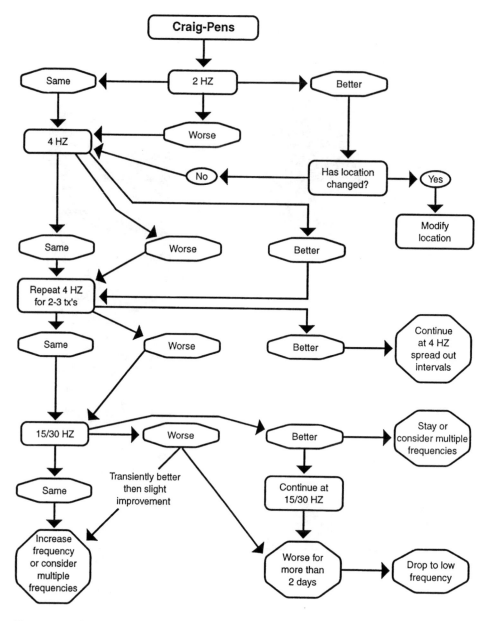

Figure 12.4 Craig—PENS

frequencies. In some patients the flare-up continues until the next treatment, (if that has been 2–3 days we resume treatment at low frequency (2–4 hz)).

TREATMENT ASSESSMENT—THE MAGIC INGREDIENT

It must be cautioned that failure to assess the results of each previous treatment will invariably lead to poor results and unnecessary treatments. In order to apply the principles of Craig–Pens in the treatment of pain it is important to remember that pain is a subjective experience. That means it is subject to the frailties of the human memory, cultural biases, expectations, secondary gain issues, habit, denial, lack of insight, and ability of the brain to habituate. Therefore it is imperative to be able to take the time to meticulously interview patients and to teach them to assess their pain more objectively.

Discussion

Craig–PENS is a powerful tool, but like all tools in medicine it requires practice, patience and discipline. There is no replacement to learning the natural history of each type of pain disorder. To get good results requires a knowledge of the nature of a given pain syndrome and the nature of It's response to Craig–PENS. Chronic pain is so multifaceted that the affective components can obscure the facts. The pre-treatment assessment is the key to being able to assess the nature of the pain even when the nature of the patient tends to get in the way. The initial 2 weeks of treatment seem to be the most difficult in this regard as the patients and their families are looking for tangible results. We begin by explaining that we may make the pain worse before we make it better and reiterate that again and again. We are looking for a change in the nociceptive system while the patient is often looking for immediate relief, this frequently results in tense encounters early on. Our staff is trained to support the patient with education and appropriate concern. Give the treatments a chance to work then change the frequency or needle distribution. Try to always keep the anatomy of the nervous system in mind.

REFERENCES

1. Kleinhenz, J. 1995. Acupuncture Mechanisms, Indications and Effectiveness According to Recent Western Literature. *Am. J. Acupuncture* 23(3): 211–218.
2. Croley, T. E., and M. Carlson. 1991. Histology of the Acupuncture Point. *Am. J. Acupuncture* 19(3): 247–253.
3. Dung, H. C. 1984. Anatomical Features Contributing to the Formation of Acupuncture Points. *Am. J. Acupuncture* 12(2): 139–143.
4. ———— 1984. Clinical Classification of Acupuncture Points. *Am. J. Acupuncture* 12(4): 333–338.
5. ———— 1984. Three Principles of Acupuncture Points. *Am. J. Acupuncture* 12(3): 263–266.
6. ———— 1985. A Simple New Method for the Quantitation of Chronic Pain. *Am. J. Acupuncture* 13(1): 57–62.
7. Bossy, J. 1984. Morphological Data Concerning the Acupuncture Point and Channel Network. *Acupun. Elec.* 9: 79–106.
8. Rosenblatt, S. L. 1982. The Electrodermal Characteristics of Acupuncture Points. *Am. J. Acupuncture* 10(2): 131–137.
9. Zhu et al. 1984. Experimental Meridian Line of Stomach and Its Low Impedance Nature. *Acupun. Elec.* 9: 157–164.
10. DeVernejoul, P., J. C. Darras, and P. Albarede. 1984. Isotopic Approach to the Visualization of Acupuncture Channels. *Innov. Tech. Biol. Med.* 5(4): 465–472.
11. Lazorthes et al. 1990. Acupuncture Meridians and Radiotracers. *Pain* 40: 109–112.
12. Darras, J-C., P. DeVernejoul, and P. Albarede. 1992. Nuclear Medicine and Acupuncture: A Study on the Migration of Radioactive Tracers after Injection at Acupoints. *Am. J. Acupuncture* 20(3): 245–256.
13. Heine, H. 1991. Functional Morphology of the Acupuncture Points of the Du Mai and Ren Mai Vessels. *Akupunktur. Theorie. & Praxis* 19: 215–219.
14. Hyman, S. E., and N. H. Cassem. 1989. In E. Rubinstein, and D. D. Federmann. *Pain.* New York: Scientific American.

15. de Lahunta, A. 1977. *Veterinary Neuroanatomy and Clinical Neurology*. Philadelphia: Saunders.

16. Kendall, D. E. 1989. Part I: A Scientific Model of Acupuncture. *Am. J. Acupuncture* 17(3): 251–268.

17. Klide, A. M., and S. H. Kung. 1977. *Veterinary Acupuncture*. Philadelphia: Univ Pennsylvania Press.

18. Adler, M. W. 1980. Minireview: Opioid peptides. *Life Sci.* 26: 497–510.

19. Simon, E. J., and J. M. Hiller. 1981. In *Basic Neurochemistry*, Siegel et al. Boston: Little Brown.

20. Beaumont, A., and J. Hughes. 1979. Biology of Opioid Peptides. *Ann. Rev. Pharmoacol. Toxicol.* 19: 245–267.

21. Han, J. S., and G. X. Xie. 1984. Dynorphin: Important Mediator for Electroacupuncture Analgesia in the Spinal Cord of the Rabbit. *Pain* 18: 367–376.

22. Yaksh, T. L. 1981. Spinal Opiate Analgesia: Characteristics and Principles of Action. *Pain* 11: 293–346.

23. Wang, Y. J., and S. K. Wang. 1989. Effect of Electroacupuncture on Brain Enkephalins Content at Different Times in Rats. *J. Irad. Chin. Med.* 9(1): 53–56.

24. Latshaw, W. K. 1975. Current Theories of Pain Perception Related to Acupuncture. *J. Am. Anim. Hosp. Assoc.* 11: 449–450.

25. Reichmanis et al. 1979. Laplace Plane Analysis of Impedance on the H Meridian. *Am. J. Chin. Med.* 7(2): 188–193.

26. Reichmanis et al. 1976. DC Skin Conductance Variation at Acupuncture Loci. *Am. J. Chin. Med.* 4(1): 69–72.

27. Levine, D. 1980. Acupuncture in Review: A Mechanistic Perspective. *Am. J. Acupuncture* 8(1): 5–17.

28. Li et al. 1987. Relative Specificity of Points of Acupuncture Analgesia. *J. Trad. Chin. Med.* 7(1): 29–34.

29. Kendall, D. E. 1989. Part II: A Scientific Model for Acupuncture. *Am. J. Acupuncture* 17(4): 343–360.

30. Melzack, R., and P. D. Wall. 1965. Pain Mechanisms: A New Theory. *Science* 150: 971.

31. German Acupuncture Society, Dusseldorf. 1988. Dusseldorf Acupuncture Symposium Report: The Scientific Bases of Acupuncture. *Am. J. Acupuncture* 16(4): 362–365.

32. Macdonald, A. J. R. 1983. Segmental Acupuncture Therapy. *Acup. Electrotherap. Res.* 8(3–4): 267–282.

33. Gideon, L. 1977. Acupuncture: Clinical Trials in the Horse. *J. Am. Vet. Med. Assoc.* 170(2): 220–224.

34. Yang et al. 1979. *The Characteristic Distribution Ratio of Myelinated and Nonmyelinated Afferent Nerve Fibers in Acupuncture Analgesic Point Zusanli*. National Symposium of Acupunture, Moxibustion and Acupuncture Anesthesia, Beijing, China, 414–415.

35. Wang, D. 1979. *The Study of the Clinical Features of Acupuncture Anesthesia (the Analysis of 1,293 Cases of Surgical Operation under Acupuncture Anesthesia)*, National Symposium of Acupuncture, Moxibustion and Acupuncture Anesthesia, Beijing, China, 214–215.

36. Takeshige, C. 1990. Mechanism of Acupuncture Analgesia (AA) Caused by Low Frequency Stimulation of the Acupuncture Point Based on Animal Experiments. Part I:

Acupuncture Afferent and Efferent Pathways and the Nature of AA. *Acupuncture* 1(3): 75–88.

37. Lundeberg et al. 1989. Thomas M. Acupuncture and Sensory Thresholds. *Am. J. Chin. Med.* 17(3–4): 99110.

38. Omura, Y. 1975. Patho-Physiology of Acupuncture Treatment. Effects of Acupuncture on Cardiovascular and Nervous Systems. *Acup. Electrotherap. Res.* 1: 51–140.

39. Bossy, J. 1986. Implication of the Spinal Nucleus of the Trigeminal Nerve in Acupuncture. *Acup. Electrotherap. Res.* 11(3–4): 177–190.

40. Pert, A. 1982. Mechansisms of Opiate Analgesia and Role of Endorphins in Pain Suppression. *Adv. Neurol.* 33: 107–122.

41. Zhou et al. 1981. Effect of Intracerebral Microinjection of Naloxone on Acupuncture and Morphine-Analgesia in the Rabbit. *Sci. Sin.* 24: 1166–1178.

42. Peets, J., and B. Pomeranz. 1985. Acupuncture-Like Transcutaneous Electrical Nerve Stimulation Analgesia is Influenced by Spinal Cord Endorphins but not Serotonin: An Intrathecal Pharmacological Study. In *Advances in Pain Research and Therapy*, 519–525. Edited by Fields et al. New York: Raven Press.

43. Mayer, D. J., and L. R. Watkins. 1984. Multiple Endogenous Opiate and Non-Opiate Analgesia Systems. In *Advances in Pain Research and Therapy*, 253–276. Edited by L. Kruger. New York: Raven Press.

44. Han et al. 1985. Is Cholecystokinin Octapeptide (CCK-8) a Candidate for Endogenous Antiopioid Substrates? *Neuropeptides* 5: 399–402.

45. Zhou et al. 1993. Increased Release of Immunoreactive CCK-8 by Electroacupuncture and Enhancement of Electroacupuncture Analgesia by CCK-8 Antagonist in Rat Spinal Cord. *Neuropeptides* 24: 139–144.

46. Pomeranz, B., and D. Chiu. 1976. Naloxone Blockade of Acupuncture Analgesia: Endorphin Implicated. *Life Sci.* 19: 1757–1762.

47. Zhang et al. 1979. *Endorphins and Acupuncture Analgesia*. National Symposium of Acupuncture, Moxibustion and Acupuncture Anesthesia, Beijing, China, 30–32.

48. Wang, Y. J., and S. K. Wang. 1989. Effects of Phentolamine and Propranolol on the Changes of Pain Threshold and Contents of Mek and Lek in Rat Brain after EA. *J. Trad. Chin. Med.* 9(3): 210–214.

49. Chou et al. 1984. Action of Peptidase Inhibitors on Methionine 5-Enkephalin-Arginine 6-Phenylalanine 7 (YGGFMRF) and Methionine 5-Enkephalin (YGGFM) Metabolism and on Electroacupuncture Antinociception. *J. Pharmacol. Exp. Ther.* 230: 349–352.

50. Pan et al. Electro-Acupuncture Analgesia and Analgesic Action of NAGA. *J. Trad. Chin. Med.* 4(4): 273–278.

51. Cheng, R., and B. Pomerantz. 1980. A Combined Treatment with D-Amino Acids and Electroacupuncture Produces a Greater Anesthesia than Either Treatment Alone: Naloxone Reverses these Effects. *Pain* 8: 231–236.

52. Ehrenpreis, S. 1985. Analgesic Properties of Enkephalinase Inhibitors: Animal and Human Studies. *Prog. Clin. Biol. Res.* 192: 363–370.

53. Peets, J., and B. Pomeranz. 1978. CXBX Mice Deficient in Opiate Receptors Show Poor Electroacupuncture Analgesia. *Nature* 273: 675–676.

54. Han et al. 1982. Enkephalin and B-Endorphin as Mediators of Electro-Acupuncture Analgesia in Rabbits: An Antisera Injection Study. In *Regulatory Peptides: From Molecular Biology to Function*, 369–377. E. Costa and M. Trabucchi. New York: Raven Press.

55. He, L. F. 1987. Review Article: Involvement of Endogenous Opioid Peptides in Acupuncture Analgesia. *Pain* 31(1): 99–121.

56. Pomeranz, B. 1987. Scientific Basis of Acupuncture. In *Acupuncture Textbook and Atlas*, 1–34. Edited by G. Stux, and B. Pomeranz. New York: Springer-Verlag.

57. Liao, S. 1978. Recent Advances in the Understanding of Acupuncture. *Yale J. Biol. Med.* 51: 55–65.

58. Li et al. 1983. The Relationship Between Needling Sensation and Acupuncture Effects, with Special Reference to their Ascending Pathway in the Spinal Cord. *Acup. Electrotherap. Res.* 8:1 05–110.

59. Chen, G. B. 1981. Role of the Nervous System of the Human Body with Regard to Acupuncture Analgesia. *Acup. Electrotherap. Res.* 6(1): 7–17.

60. Chen, X. H., and J. S. Han. 1992. Analgesia Induced by Electroacupuncture of Different Frequencies is Mediated by Different Types of Opioid Receptors: Another Cross-Tolerance Study. *Behavioural Brain. Res.* 47(2): 143–149.

61. Chang, H. T. 1980. Neurophysiological Interpretation of Acupuncture Analgesia. *Endeavor* 4(3): 92–96.

62. Chen et al. 1986. Clinical Studies on Neurophysiological and Biochemical Basis of Acupuncture Analgesia. *Am. J. Chin. Med.* 14(1–2): 86–95.

63. Zhong et al. 1989. Correlation Between Endogenous Opiate-Like Peptides and Serotonin in Laserpuncture Analgesia. *Am. J. Acupuncture* 17(1): 39–43.

64. Han, J. 1979. *The Role of Some Central Neurotransmitters in Acupuncture Analgesia.* National Symposium of Acupuncture, Moxibustion and acupuncture Anesthesia, Beijing, People's Republic of China, 27–30.

65. Han, J. S., and I. Terenius. 1982. Neurochemical Basis of Acupuncture Analgesia. *Ann. Rev. Pharmacol. Toxicol.* 22: 193–220.

66. Sun et al. 1984. Electroacupuncture Alters Catecholamines in Brain Regions of Rats. *Neurochem Res.* 10(2): 251–258.

67. Ge et al. 1989. Comparison of the Effects Between the Conventional and Electrical Acupuncture on Some Cytochemical Components of Median Eminentia and Supraoptic Nucleus. *J. Trad. Chin. Med.* 9(1): 57–62.

68. Yang, M. M. P., and S. H. Kik. 1979. Further Study of the Neurohumoral Factor, Endorphin, in the Mechanism of Acupuncture Analgesia. *Am. J. Chin. Med.* 7(2): 143–148.

69. Pian, M. C. M. 1981. *The Effect of Electroacupuncture on Plasma and Cerebrospinal Fluid Beta-Endorphin Levels in the Rat, Thesis.* Cambridge, MA: Harvard University.

70. Bossut et al. 1983. Plasma Cortisol and Beta-Endorphin in Horses Subjected to Electroacupuncture for Cutaneous Analgesia. *Peptides* 4: 501–507.

71. Masala et al. 1983. Suppression of Electroacupuncture (EA)-Induced Beta-Endorphin and ACTH Release by Hydrocortisone in Man: Absence of Effects on EA-Induced Anesthesia. *Acta. Endocrinologica.* 103: 469–472.

72. Szczudlik, A., and A. Lypka. 1983. Plasma Immunoreactive Beta-Endorphin and Enkephalin Concentration in Healthy Subjects Before and After Electroacupuncture. *Acup. Electrotherap. Res.* 8: 127–137.

73. Peng et al. 1983. The Effects of Acupuncture on Blood Pressure: The Interrelation of Sympathetic Activity and Endogenous Opioid Peptides. *Acup Electrotherap Res* 8: 45–56.

74. Bossut, D. F., and D. J. Mayer. 1991. Electroacupuncture Analgesia in Naive Horses: Effects of Brainstem and Spinal Cord Lesions and Role of Pituitary-Adrenal Axis. *Brain Res* 549: 52–58.

75. Pullan et al. 1983. Endogenous Opiates Modulate Release of Growth Hormone in Response to Electroacupuncture. *Life Sci.* 32(15): 1705–1709.

76. Xie, Q. W. 1982. Endocrinological Basis of Acupuncture. *Am. J. Chin. Med.* 9(4): 298–304.

77. Chao, W. K., and J. W. P. Loh. 1987. The Immunologic Responses of Acupuncture Stimulation (abstract). Acupunct. Electrother. *Res.* 12: 282–283.

78. Chin et al. 1988. Induction of Circulating Interferon in Humans by Acupuncture. *Am. J. Acupuncture* 16(4): 319–322.

79. Takeshige, C. 1987. Mechanism of the Relief of Muscle Pain by Acupuncture (abstract). *Acup. Electrotherap. Res.* 12(3–4): 249–250.

80. Xia et al. 1985. Inhibitory Effect of Analogous Electro-Acupuncture on Experimental Arrhythmia. *Acup. Electrotherap. Res.* 10: 13–34.

81. Xia et al. 1987. Irhibitory Effect of Analogous Electroacupuncture on Sympathetic Cardiovascular Response to Stimulation of Hypothalamic Defense Area in Rabbits. *J. Trad. Chin. Med.* 7(3): 211–214.

82. Sun et al. 1984. The Effect of Electroacupuncture on the Function of Sympatheto-Adrenal Medulla. *J. Trad. Chin. Med.* 4(1): 11–14.

83. Bresler, D. E., and R. J. Kroening. 1976. Three Essential Factors in Effective Acupuncture Therapy. *Am. J. Chin. Med.* 4(1): 81–86.

84. Tsibulyak et al. 1992. Humoral Factors in the Mechanism of Electroacupuncture Analgesia. Scand. *J. Acupunct. Electrotherap.* 7: 2–6.

85. Becker, R. O., and G. Selden. 1985. *The Body Electric.* New York: William Morrow and Co.

86. Nordenstrom, B. E. W. 1987. An Additional Circulatory System. Vascular-Interstitial Closed Electric Circuits (VICC). *J. Biol. Phys.* 15: 43–55.

87. Nordenstrom, B. E. W. 1989. An Electrophysiologic View of Acupuncture: Role of Capacitive and Closed Circuit Currents and Their Clinical Effects in the Treatment of Cancer and Chronic Pain. *Am. J. Acupuncture* 17(2): 105–117.

88. Takase, K. 1983. Revolutionary New Pain Theory and Acupuncture Treatment Procedure Based on New Theory of Acupuncture Mechanism. *Am. J. Acupuncture* 11(4): 305–323.

89. Watkins, L. R., and D. J. Mayer. 1982. Organization of Endogenous Opiate and Nonopiate Pain Control Systems. *Science* 216: 1185–1192.

90. Lee et al. 1982. The Autonomic Effects of Acupuncture and Analgesic Drugs on the Cardiovascular System. *Am. J. Acupuncture* 10(1): 5–28.

91. Clifford et al. 1983. Effects of Dimethylsulfoxide and Acupuncture on the Cardiovascular System of Dogs. *Ann. NY Acad. Sci.* 411: 84–93.

92. Andersson, S. A., and E. Holmgren. 1976. Analgesic Effects of Peripheral Conditioning Stimulation-III: Effect of High Frequency Stimulation; Segmental Mechanisms Interacting with Pain. *Acup. Electrotherap. Res.* 3: 23–36.

93. Ehrenpreis, S. 1987. Endorphins and Acupuncture Analgesia (abstract). *Acup. Electrotherap. Res.* 12: 248.

94. Izatt, E., and M. Fairman. 1977. Staphylococcal Septicemia with Disseminated Intravascular Coagulation Associated with Acupuncture. *Postgrad. Med. J.* 53: 285–286.

95. Kirschenbaum, A. E., and C. Rizzo. 1997. Glenohumeral Pyarthrosis Following Acupuncture Treatment. *Orthopaedics* 20(12): 1184–1186.

96. Lee, R. J., and J. C. McIlwain. 1985. Subacute Bacterial Endocarditis Following Ear Acupuncture. *Int. J. Cardiol.* 7(1): 62–63.

97. Spelman, D. W., A. Weinmann, and W. J. Spicer. 1993. Endocarditis Following Skin Procedures. *J. Infect.* 26(2): 185–189.

98. Gray, R., G. S. Maharajh, and R. Hyland. 1991. Pneumothorax Resulting From Acupuncture. *Can. Assoc Radiol. J.* 42(2): 139–140.

99. Zexin, Z. 1992. The Clinical Application of Corresponding Acupoints. *J. Trad. Chinese Med.* 12(4): 272–274.

100. Chen—Kaoshung, Taiwan—Personal communication.

101. Hong. Yan, Y.Z. 1995. The Crossing Method of Point Selection. *J. Chinese Med.* 49: 17–19.

102. Bernfield, Korngold. 1991. Between Heaven and Earth: A Guide to Chinese Medicine. *Balantine.*

103. Melzak, R., D. M. Stillwell, and E. J. Fox. 1977. Trigger Points and Acupuncture Points for Pain: Correlations and Implications. *Pain* 3: 2–23.

104. Macdonald, A. J. R., K. D. Macrae, B. R. Master, and A. P. Rubin. 1983. Superficial Acupuncture in the Relief of Chronic Low Back Pain: A Placebo Controlled Randomised Trial. *Ann. Royal Coll. Surg. Engl.* 65: 44–46.

105. Helms, J. M. 1995. *Acupuncture Energetics. A Clinical Approach for Physicians*, 89. Berkeley, CA: Medical Acupuncture Publishers.

106. Brattberg, G. 1983. Acupuncture Therapy for Tennis Elbow. *Pain* 16: 285–288.

107. Junnila, S. Y. T. 1982. Acupuncture Superior to Piroxicam in the Treatment of Osteoarthrosis. *Am. J. Acupuncture* 10(4): 341–346.

108. Molsberger, A., and E. Hille. 1994. The Analgesic Effect of Acupuncture in Chronic Tennis Elbow Pain. *Br. J. Rheumatol.* 33: 1162–1165.

109. Man, S. C., and F. D. Baragar. 1974. Preliminary Clinical Study of Acupuncture in Rheumatoid Arthritis. *J. Rheumatol.* 1: 126–129.

110. Christensen, B. V., I. U. Iuhl, H. Vilbek, H. H. Bulow, N. C. Dreijer, and H. F. Rasmussen. 1992. Acupuncture Treatment of Severe Knee Osteoarthrosis. A Long-Term Study. *Acta. Anaesthesiol. Scand.* 36: 519–525.

111. Dengqi, W. 1994. Seventy-Five Cases of Stiff Neck Treated by Acupuncture at Acupoint Ynaglao (SI 6). *J. Trad. Chinese Med.* 14(4): 269–271.

112. Shigang, H., and Z. Yanqiu. 1992. Clinical Observations on the Treatment of 50 Cases of Stiff Neck by Acupuncture. *J. Trad. Chinese Med.* 12(1): 57–58.

113. Chen, A. 1990. Effective Acupuncture Therapy for Sciatica and Low Back Pain: Review of Recent Studies and Prescriptions With Recommendations for Improved Results. *Am. J. Acupuncture* 18(4): 305–323.

114. Gunn, C. C., and W. E. Milbrant. 1978. Early and Subtle Signs in Low Back Sprain. *Spine* 3: 3 p. 267–281.

115. Chapman, C. R., and C. C. Gunn. 1990. *Acupuncture in the Management of Pain.* Edited by Bonica, Vol 2 Philadelphia: John J. Lea and Fediger.

116. Filshie, J. 1997. *Medical Acupuncture: A Western Scientific Approach.* Edinburgh: Churchill Livingstone.

117. Lee, M. H. M., and S. J. Liao. 1990. Acupuncture in Physiatry. In *Krusen's Handbook of Phys Med and Rehabilitation*, Fourth Edition. Edited by F. J. Kottke, and F. Lehmann Philadelphia: W B Saunders.

118. Sivin, N. 1987. Traditional Medicine in Contemporary China. *Science, Medicine, and Technology in East Asia Center for Chinese Studies*. The University of Michigan.

119. Gunn, C. C. 1996. *The Gunn Approach to the Treatment of Chronic Pain—Intramuscular Stimulation (IMS) for Myofascial Pain of Radiculopathic Origin*. Edinburgh: Churchill Livingstone.

120. Cannon, W. B., and A. Rosenblueth. 1949. *The Supersensitivity of Denervated Structures, A Law of Denervation*. New York: The MacMillan Company.

121. Gunn, C. C. 1990. The Mechanical Manifestation of Neuropathic Pain. *Annals of Sports Medicine* 5: 3.

122. Gunn, C. C. 1978. "Prespondylosis" and Some Pain Syndromes Following Denervation Supersensitivity. (1980) *Spine* 5: 2.

123. Culp, W. J., and I. Ochoa. 1982. *Abnormal Nerves and Muscles as Impulse Generators*. New York: Oxford University Press.

123. Lomo, T. 1976. The Role of Activity in the Control of Membrane and Contractile Properties of Skeletal Muscle. In *Motor Innervation of Muscle* Edited by S. Thesleff Academic Press. New York: 289–316.

124. Gunn, C. C. 1989. Neuropathic Pain: A New Theory for Chronic Pain of Intrinsic Origin. *Annals of the Royal College of Physicians and Surgeons of Canada* Vol 22(5): 327–330.

125. Thomas, P. K. 1984. Symptomatology and Differential Diagnosis of Peripheral Neuropathy: Clinical & Differential Diagnosis. In *Peripheral Neuropathy*, Edited by P. J. Dyck, P. K. Thomas, E. H. Lambert, and R. Bunge. Philadelphia: W B Saunders. 1169–1190.

126. Thesleff, S., and L. C. Sellin. 1980. Denervation Supersensitivity. Trends in NeuroSciences August: 122–126.

127. Sharpless, S. K. 1975. Supersensitivity—Like Phenomena in the Central Nervous System. *Federation Proceedings* 34(10): 1990–1997.

128. Klein, L., M. H. Dawson, and K. G. Heiple. 1977. Turnover of Collagen in the Adult Rat after Denervation. *J. Bone Jt. Surgery* 59A: 1065–1067.

129. Wall, P. D., S., Waxman, and A. L., Basbaum, 1974. Ongoing Activity in Peripheral Nerve Injury Discharge. *Exp Neurol* 45: 576–589.

130. Mense, S. Nociception from Skeletal Muscle in Relation to Clinical Muscle Pain. *Pain* 54(1993): 241–289.

131. Han, J. S., and L. Terenius. 1982. Neurochemical Basis of Acupuncture Analgesia. *Annual Review Pharmacology Toxicology* 22: 193–22.

132. Gunn, C. C., F. G. Ditchburn, M. H. King, and G. J. Renwick. 1976. Acupuncture Loci: A Proposal for Their Classification According to Their Relationship to Known Neural Structures. *American Journal of Chinese Medicine* Vol 4(2): 183–195.

133. Lomo, T. 1976. The Role of Activity in the Control of Membrane and contractile Properties of Skeletal Muscle. In *Motor Innervation of Muscle* Edited by S. Thesleff. New York: Academic Press. 289–316.

134. Jaffe, L. F. 1985. Extracellular Current Measurements with a Vibrating Probe. *TINS* December: 517–521.

135. Ross, R., and A. Vogel. 1978. The Platelet—Derived Growth Factor. *Cell* 14: 203–210.

136. Gunn, C. C., and W. E. Milbrandt. 1980. Dry Needling of Muscle Motor Points for Chronic Low Back Pain. A Randomized Clinical Trial with Long-Term Follow-Up. *Spine* 5: 3.

137. Seem, Mark D. 1993. *A New American Acupuncture: Acupuncture Osteopathy: The Myofascial Release of the Bodymind's Holding Patterns.* Boulder, CO: Blue Poppy Press.

138. Travell, Janet, and David Simmons. 1983. *Myofascial Pain and Dysfunction: The Trigger Point Manual.* Vol. I, 4. Baltimore: Williams and Wilkens.

139. Gunn, C. Chan. 1996. *The Gunn Approach to the Treatment of Chronic Pain.* New York: Churchill Livingston.

139. Jaffe, L. F. 1985. Extracellular Current Measurements with a Vibrating Probe. TINS December: 517–521.

140. Hong, Dr. Chang-Zern. 1994. Considerations and Recommendations Regarding Myofascial Trigger Point Injection. *Journal of Musculoskeletal Pain* 2(1): 29–59. The Haworth Press, Inc.

141. Headley, B. J. July/August 1990. EMG and Myofascial Pain. *Clinical Management* 10: 43–46.

142. Ni, Dr. Yitian, and Richard L. Rosenbound. 1996. *Navigating the Channels of Traditional Chinese Medicine.* San Diego: Oriental Medicine Center.

143. Daddona, M. M., and J. Haldar. 1994. Opioid Modulation of Oxytocin Release from Spinal Cord Synaptosomes. *Neuroreport.* 5(14): 1833–5.

144. Kondo, Y., et al. 1993. Regional Changes in Neuropeptide Levels after 5,7-Dihydroxy-tryptamine-induced Serotonin Depletion in the Rat Brain. *J. Neural Transmission*—General Section, 92(2–3): 151–7.

145. Rosen, H., and Z. Bar-Shavit. 1994. Dual Role of Osteoblastic Proenkephalin Derived Peptides in Skeletal Tissues. [Review]. *J. Cellular Biochemistry.* 55(3): 334–9.

146. Schulteis, G., and J. L. Martinez, Jr. 1992. Peripheral Modulation of Learning and Memory: Enkephalins as a Model System. [Review]. *Psychopharmacology,* 109(3): 347–64.

147. Nabeshima, T., et al. 1992. Page Number: 81 Stress-Induced Changes in Brain Met-Enkephalin, Leu-Enkephalin and Dynorphin Concentrations. *Life Sci.* 51(3): 211–7.

148. Ceccatelli, S., et al. 1992. Presence of a Dynorphin-Like Peptide in a Restricted Subpopulation of Catecholaminergic Neurons in Rat Nucleus Tractus Solitarii. *Brain Research.* 589(2): 225–30.

149. Griffond, B., et al. 1994. Evidence for the Expression of Dynorphin Gene in the Prolactin-Immunoreactive Neurons of the Rat Lateral Hypothalamus. *Neuroscience Letters.* 165(1–2): 89–92.

150. Hardebo, J. E., N. Suzuki, and C. Owman. 1994. Dynorphin B is Present in Sensory and Parasympathetic Nerves Innervating Pial Arteries. *J. Autonomic Nervous System.* 47(3): 171–6.

151. Hassan, A. H., et al. 1992. Dynorphin, A Preferential Ligand for Kappa-Opioid Receptors, is Present in Nerve Fibers and Immune Cells within Inflamed Tissue of the Rat. *Neuroscience Letters.* 140(1): 85–8.

152. Kemel, M. L., et al. 1992. Control of Dopamine Release by Acetylcholine and Dynorphin in the Striosomal and Matrix Compartments of the Cat Caudate Nucleus Expression of Nitric Oxide Synthase in Enkephalin and Dynorphin Systems of the Rat Hypothalamus. *Neurochemistry International.* 20 Suppl(8): 111S–114S.

153. Lima, D., A. Avelino, and A. Coimbra. 1993. Morphological Characterization of Marginal (lamina I) Neurons Immunoreactive for Substance P, Enkephalin, Dynorphin and Gamma-Aminobutyric Acid in the Rat Spinal Cord. *J. Chemical Neuroanatomy.* 6(1): 43–52.

154. Fishman, S. M., and D. B. Carr. 1992. Basic Mechanisms of Pain. *Hospital Practice.* (OCT 15 1992): 63–76

155. Zieglgansberger, W. and T. R. Tolle. 1993. The Pharmacology of Pain Signalling. [Review]. *Current Opinion in Neurobiology.* 3(4): 611–8.

156. Stinus, L., M. Cador, and M. Le Moal. 1992. Interaction Between Endogenous Opioids and Dopamine within the Nucleus Accumbens. [Review]. *Annals of the New York Academy of Sciences.* 654: 254–73.

157. Stein, C., et al. 1993. Local Analgesic Effect of Endogenous Opioid Peptides [see comments]. *Lancet.* 342(8867): 321–4.

158. Lichtman, A. H., and M. S. Fanselow. 1991. Opioid and Nonopioid Conditional Analgesia: The Role of Spinal Opioid, Noradrenergic and Serotonergic Systems. p. 97 *Behavioral Neuroscience.* 105(5): 687–98.

159. Rosenfeld, J. P. 1994. Interacting Brain Stem Components of Opiate-Activated, Descending, Pain-Inhibitory Systems. [Review]. *Neuroscience & Biobehavioral Reviews.* 18(3): 403–9.

160. Valverde, O., et al. 1994. Participation of Opioid and Mechanisms on the Antinociceptive Effect Induced by Tricyclic Antidepressants in Two Behavioural Pain Tests in Mice. *Progress in Neuro-Psychopharmacology & Biological Psychiatry.* 18(6): 1073–92.

161. Guoxi, T. 1991. The Action of the Visceronociceptive Neurons in the Posterior Group of Thalamic Nuclei: Possible Mechanism of Acupuncture Analgesia on Visceral Pain. *Kitasato Archives of Experimental Medicine.* 64(1): 43–55.

162. Miaskowski, C., and J. D. Levine. 1992. Antinociception Produced by Receptor Selective Opioids: Modulation of Spinal Antinociceptive Effects by Supraspinal Opioids. *Brain Research.* 595(1): 32–8.

163. Kayser, V., and G. Guilbaud. 1991. Physiological Relevance and Time Course of a Tonic Endogenous Opioid Modulation of Nociceptive Messages, Based on the Effects of Naloxone in a Rat Model of Localized Hyperalgesic Inflammation. *Brain Research.* 567(2): 197–203.

164. Han, J. S., and R. L. Zhang. 1993. Suppression of Morphine Abstinence Syndrome by Body Electroacupuncture of Different Frequencies in Rats. *Durg & Alcohol Dependence.* 31(2): 169–75.

165. Nam, T. S., et al. 1992. Effect of Peripheral Nerve Stimulation on the Dorsal Horn Cell Activity in Cats with Cutaneous Inflammation. *Yonsei Medical J.* 33(2): 109–20.

166. Chen, X. H., and J. S. Han. 1992. Analgesia Induced by Electroacupuncture of Different Frequencies is Mediated by Different Types of Opioid Receptors: Another Cross-Tolerance Study. *Behavioural Brain Research.* 47(2): 143–9.

167. Cheng, R. R. S., and B. Pomeranz. 1979. Electroacupucture Analgesia Could be Mediated by at Least Two Pain Relieving Mechanisms: Endorphin and Non-Endorphin systems. *Life Sci.* 25: 1957–1962.

168. He, X., et al., 1993. The Extensiveness and Specificity of Analgesia of Electroacupuncture (EA) at Different Points on the Nociceptive Responses of Neuron in Spinal Dorsal Horn. *Chen Tzu Yen Chiu Acupuncture Research.* 18(4): 271–5.

INDEX